JAPAN'S SECURITY RENAISSANCE

Contemporary Asia in the World

CONTEMPORARY ASIA IN THE WORLD
David C. Kang and Victor D. Cha, Editors

This series aims to address a gap in the public-policy and scholarly discussion of Asia. It seeks to promote books and studies that are on the cutting edge of their disciplines or promote multidisciplinary or interdisciplinary research but are also accessible to a wider readership. The editors seek to showcase the best scholarly and public-policy arguments on Asia from any field, including politics, history, economics, and cultural studies.

JAPAN'S SECURITY RENAISSANCE

New Policies and Politics for the Twenty-First Century

Andrew L. Oros

Columbia University Press
New York

Columbia University Press
Publishers Since 1893
New York   Chichester, West Sussex
cup.columbia.edu
Copyright © 2017 Columbia University Press
All rights reserved
Library of Congress Cataloging-in-Publication Data
Names: Oros, Andrew, author.
Title: Japan's security renaissance : new policies and politics
for the twenty-first century / Andrew L. Oros.
Description: New York : Columbia University Press, 2017. | Series: Contemporary
Asia in the world | Includes bibliographical references and index.
Identifiers: LCCN 2016014024 (print) | LCCN 2016031340 (ebook) | ISBN 9780231172608
(cloth : alk. paper) | ISBN 9780231172615 (pbk.) | ISBN 9780231542593 (electronic)
Subjects: LCSH: National security—Japan. | Japan—Strategic aspects. | Japan—
Politics and government—1989– | Japan—Foreign relations—1989–
Classification: LCC UA845 .O74 2017 (print) | LCC UA845 (ebook) | DDC 355/.033552—dc23
LC record available at https://lccn.loc.gov/2016014024
∞
Columbia University Press books are printed on permanent and durable acid-free paper.
Printed in the United States of America

COVER DESIGN: Milenda Nan Ok Lee
COVER PHOTO: Junko Kimura © Getty images

To the next generation, including Jared and Donna Belen

Contents

Figures and Tables

Preface

This book is about Japan's security, but it began in China. This is strangely appropriate as China's choices about its security policies have greatly influenced Japan's. In order to better understand this interaction, in 2010 I spent four months at Peking University researching China's views of Japan. There I was able to witness firsthand the huge swing in Japan-China relations that was under way as China's economic size surpassed Japan's and, in September of that year, the first major escalation of the territorial dispute between Japan and China took place over an incident caused by a confrontation between a Chinese fishing trawler captain and the Japan Coast Guard in waters claimed by both countries. Seeing how China's state-controlled media shifted the conversation and tone away from celebrating warm relations between Japan and China in advance of a large binational friendship conference held in Beijing in August to vilifying Japanese as unrepentant militarists just weeks later drove home to me the challenges Japan's diplomats and military planners must manage.

I traveled from Beijing to Tokyo in October 2010 and witnessed the resolution of the Fishing Trawler Incident (as it has come to be called) through the eyes of the Japanese media, which offered a much wider range of views about the origins of and the paths to resolution of the Japan-China crisis that unfolded over the course of about a month.

The Japanese media also offered countless stories and opinion pieces about the broader challenges posed by China's economic and military rise. Since that time, China's economy and its military spending have roughly *doubled*, and several more crisis incidents related to the Senkaku Islands dispute have occurred, prompting a number of changes to Japan's defense posture.

China is far from the only issue on the minds of Japanese security planners, political leaders, and the general public, however. March 11, 2011, became a date seared into Japanese collective memory. A massive earthquake off the east coast of Japan's main island caused a tsunami that washed miles inland, killing around twenty thousand people, making hundreds of thousands homeless, and leading to the meltdown of two nuclear power reactors situated along the coast near the town of Fukushima, a few hours north of Tokyo. That there was not a massive explosion or greater spread of radiation beyond the limited amount that did escape is a testament to Japanese courage and planning, whatever the mistakes and lapses that have been revealed in retrospect.

I spent the summer of 2011 conducting research for this book in offices with half the lights shut off to conserve energy and full of workers in short sleeves and without neckties to cope with higher air-conditioning settings in a shared effort to address Japan's deep dependence on energy imports with its fifty-three nuclear power reactors either disabled or shut down as a precaution until safety inspections could be conducted. The first of these reactors restarted only four years later, and many others probably never will. This energy dependence—long an aspect of Japan's broader security planning—thus became a second major crisis to unfold that year.

Japan's resilience in the face of the March 11, 2011, triple disasters of the massive earthquake, tsunami, and meltdown of two reactors at the Fukushima Daiichi nuclear plant has been noted by many, including Japan's military security planners and those who craft military doctrine elsewhere in the region and beyond. The crisis helped two longtime allies—Japan and the United States—heal some recent wounds inflicted over Japan's rocky political transition from long-standing rule by the conservative Liberal Democratic Party to the progressive Democratic Party, a change of power that had taken place for only nine months in the nearly sixty years the US-Japan Security Treaty had been in effect.

Since my return to Washington, DC, in 2011, I have traveled back to Japan a dozen times and spoken to security planners, politicians, and friends around the dinner table about many other challenges that Japan faces—in military security and in a troubling range of other areas, from its economic sluggishness to its low birthrate. What I heard was a mix of openness to new approaches—inspired, I believe, by both difficult circumstances and hope about new possibilities in a period of political change—and a deep nostalgia for the past. Discussion of Japan's history—and divisive debates over it—raged in the Japanese media and on the streets in demonstrations large and small; these debates and demonstrations continue.

Over the course of writing this book, debates concerning historical narratives and remembrance were raging also in the places I live, Maryland and Washington, DC. Related to the subject of this book, Korean-Americans and other supporters in nearby Virginia had successfully advocated for placing a statue commemorating the "comfort women" forced to service the Japanese military during World War II, and Japan's prime minister Shinzō Abe made a historic state visit to Washington, DC, where he became the first Japanese prime minister to address a joint session of Congress, during which he expressed "repentance" for the pain and suffering inflicted on Americans and others by Japan during World War II.

But these were not the only debates over history and remembrance I was encountering on a daily basis while writing this book. The year that I was on sabbatical leave for completing this book, 2014, was also the two-hundredth anniversary of the conclusion of the War of 1812, that pivotal war for maintaining American independence that most Americans have little knowledge of. Those seeking to commemorate this important milestone in American history struggled to connect with local populations where decisive battles were fought—and even more so with the general public. In the midst of this, I attended a reception at the British embassy in Washington, DC. In his toast to the new year, the affable British ambassador joked that he especially welcomed the arrival of 2015 because it meant the end of a year of apologies he had been making across the United States in his public remarks in 2014, two hundred years after the British had burned down the Capitol, the White House, and most of the rest of Washington, DC, in one of the republic's darkest moments. He even included a slide in his PowerPoint snapshots of the past year of a painting depicting the burning of the White House. "Sorry about that," he quipped, to general laughter in the audience. The United States and Britain have come a long way from those dark days to create a "special relationship" across the Atlantic, just as the United States and Japan have in creating their "most important bilateral relationship, bar none," across the Pacific in the years since Japan's defeat in World War II. And yet it is hard to imagine a gathering where "sorry about that" would be met with laughter in reference to Japanese wartime atrocities. This contrast evokes an important theme running through this book: the strong influence of the past on Japan's security present and future.

There was another commemoration of a war going on at the time I was writing this book: the one hundred fiftieth anniversary of the end of the American Civil War. This was the most devastating war in American history, in terms of both loss of life (more than in all other American wars before and after, *combined*) and persistent, divisive memories. One hundred fifty years later, major US newspapers publish editorials about how school textbooks should present the narrative of that war, which statues should be allowed to commemorate the legacy of the conflict, and what context should be provided in nearby historic signs. Twenty-four-hour news channels covered the lowering "for the last time" (perhaps) of the controversial Confederate battle flag from the South Carolina state capital building in 2015.

It has been fascinating for me to experience these American debates over a war that happened before my great-grandfather had immigrated to this country and to experience the heartfelt passions over the issues in local areas in which I now live but was not raised. But at the same time, these have become my battles, too. I applauded the US Supreme Court ruling in 2015 that allowed US state governors to reject issuance of special car license plates that included the Confederate flag and celebrated with friends the "victory" in South Carolina the day the flag came down.

In Japan, too, I have witnessed such passions in friends and acquaintances as well as total strangers related to Japan's history and postwar security identity. I watched with friends at the Tokyo Foundation headquarters the historic press conference where Prime Minister Abe, on July 1, 2014, released his cabinet statement that reinterpreted Article Nine of Japan's postwar constitution, paving the way for Japan to participate in collective self-defense activities with other friendly states. Afterward I walked around the neighborhood of the prime minister's residence and saw thousands of protestors holding handmade signs rejecting the cabinet decision and calling for "preserving Article Nine" and for "no more wars." I have interviewed members of Japan's parliament who show great emotion in response to one historical narrative over another or to a minor policy decision that nonetheless resonates deeply with core issues of Japan's postwar identity.

I am indebted to scholars in Japan, the United States, and elsewhere who focus their research on these issues despite the challenges of objectively reporting on matters so emotional for so many, sometimes at considerable risk to their academic careers and even their physical safety. My work focuses on the politics around security issues and on policy outcomes as they relate to Japan's evolving regional and global security environment—but it is impossible to understand the currents of this political storm without drawing on scholarship of those who have explained how history issues have unfolded in postwar Japan and in the countries affected by Japan's militarist and imperialist periods.

I am truly humbled by the number of people and institutions that helped me in the creation of this book. My understanding of Japanese security policy has been deeply enriched by their willingness to share their views, provide venues for discussion, and introduce me to others with similar interests. I cannot possibly name everyone who has assisted in this project, but I would like to single out some individuals and institutions for special thanks.

Gerald Curtis swooped in just as I was completing my previous book to encourage me not to rest on my laurels and, importantly, to invite me to participate in a collaborative project on China-Japan-US relations together with Professor Ryosei Kokubun and Professor Wang Jisi. So began my deepened understanding of the regional security environment Japan faces in the twenty-first century. In the years that followed, Gerry contributed important encouragement and feedback. Professor Kokubun did as well and, in addition, provided an institutional home at Keio University for part of a sabbatical leave, as did Professor Wang at

Peking University. I would also like to thank Professor Zhu Feng and Professor Yoshihide Soeya for especially warm welcomes in those locations. Rounding off my institutional homes over the course of this project, Japan's National Institute for Defense Studies granted a research fellowship in the summer of 2009, and the East-West Center in Washington, DC, once again offered a space for me to write up my research findings in 2014. These homes away from home gave me access to both formal and informal feedback from researchers from those countries and others that enriched the quality of this book. I would like to collectively thank the many helpful staff and researchers at these institutions. Thank-you in addition to David Bradley of the Atlantic Media Company for providing quiet office space to complete the writing of the book.

Washington, DC, affords an exceedingly rich environment for the study of Japanese security policy, with its countless American experts on Japan and frequent visitors from Japan's policy and scholarly communities. I have benefited greatly from participation in public and private meetings at the Brookings Institution, the Carnegie Endowment for International Peace, the Center for a New American Security, the Center for Strategic and International Studies, and the Stimson Center. Despite the frenetic pace these specialists keep, many have made time to talk with me about my ideas and to share relevant information. In particular, a small group of experts generously agreed to meet with me monthly over lunch at the East-West Center to discuss five draft chapters of the book. They pushed me to address topics I would not have considered, corrected numerous errors, and offered information and feedback that have led to a much richer narrative. This group includes Kuniko Ashizawa, Suzanne Basalla, Bill Breer, Richard Bush, Emma Chanlett-Avery, Rust Deming, Ellen Frost, Glen Fukushima, Ben Goldberg, Michael Green, Tobias Harris, Komei Isozaki, Kentaro Kaihara, Kazuyo Kato, Weston Konishi, Fumiaki Kubo, Satu Limaye, Mark Manyin, Satoru Mori, Kongdan (Katy) Oh, Ian Rinehart, Grace Ruch, Ben Self, Junko Tanaka, Yuki Tatsumi, and Damien Tomkins. In addition, I would like to thank Kent Calder, Mike Mochizuki, Jim Schoff, Sheila Smith, and Nicholas Szechenyi. On the Japanese side, I offer a collective thank-you to all the rotating staff and visitors who made time to meet with me—a group that included many of Japan's top security policy officials and numerous members of the Diet.

I include a final thank-you to several individuals who provided feedback at the last stages of this book's completion, when Japan's security policies and politics seemed to be evolving daily: Emma Chanlett-Avery, Steve Clemons, Zack Cooper, Ellen Frost, Brad Glosserman, Jeffrey Hornung, Eric Langenbacher, Katy Oh, and Hiroshi Yamazoe. Naturally all remaining errors of fact are on me!

Research for the book was funded in part by a Japan Foundation Abe fellowship and Washington College faculty enhancement and sabbatical leave grants. The Mike and Maureen Mansfield Foundation's US-Japan Network for the Future program also offered valuable support over the course of this project. Research assistance at the East-West Center in Washington, DC, and at Washington College was provided by Ji Eun Choi, Alex Forster, Naoko Funatsu, Olivia Hughes, and Bradley Janocha. Kuniko Ashizawa, in addition, provided valuable research assistance and suggestions during the project's final stages.

Lastly, but first in my heart, thank-you to my husband and family for their understanding during all my time away from occasions large and small.

Note on Asian Family and Place-Names

Seasoned Asia hands are accustomed to the irregular order of Asian family and given names seen in English and formal versus informal designations of countries in the region. In an effort to make this book readily accessible to nonspecialists, I have chosen to follow typical English-language conventions. Thus, I present Japanese personal names in standard Western order (given name followed by family name—e.g., Shinzō Abe), a long-established practice among Japanese authors when writing in English. China and Korea do not have this custom, and so I follow the name order used in those places: family name, given name—for example, Xi Jinping. I have chosen to include macrons in Japanese names and terms for those seeking original sources while omitting them in certain place-names well established in English without them (e.g., Tokyo rather than Tōkyō). Also, I employ the common colloquial references to countries in the region: China for the People's Republic of China and Taiwan for the Republic of China; South Korea rather than Republic of Korea and North Korea rather than People's Democratic Republic of Korea. For other place-names in Asia, I follow the Japanese usage, given the focus of this book—thus, Myanmar, Senkaku Islands, Sea of Japan, Takeshima Island, and Northern Territories for these places that are referred to differently in other Asian languages. Finally, I refer to the two houses of the bicameral Japanese parliament, the Diet, by their common referents of Lower House and Upper House rather than the more formal House of Representatives and House of Councillors.

Abbreviations and Acronyms

ACM	Alliance Coordination Mechanism
ACSA	acquisition and cross-servicing agreement
ADMM+	ASEAN Defense Minister's Meeting–Plus
ARF	ASEAN Regional Forum
ASEAN	Association of Southeast Asian Nations
ASW	anti-submarine warfare
CLB	Cabinet Legislative Bureau
CSD	collective self-defense
DDH	destroyer-helicopter ships
DPJ	Democratic Party of Japan
DPRI	Defense Policy Review Initiative
EAS	East Asian Summit
EEZ	exclusive economic zone
EMP	electromagnetic pulse
GDP	gross domestic product
HADR	humanitarian assistance and disaster relief
ISR	intelligence, surveillance, and reconnaissance
JASDF	Japan Air Self-Defense Force
JCG	Japan Coast Guard
JCP	Japan Communist Party
JGSDF	Japan Ground Self-Defense Force

JICA	Japan International Cooperation Agency
JIP	Japan Innovation Party
JMSDF	Japan Maritime Self-Defense Force
JRP	Japan Restoration Party
JSDF	Japan Self-Defense Forces
JSP	Japan Socialist Party
LDP	Liberal Democratic Party
METI	Ministry of Economy, Trade, and Industry
MOD	Ministry of Defense
MOFA	Ministry of Foreign Affairs
MTDP	Midterm Defense Plan
NDPG	National Defense Program Guidelines
NDPO	National Defense Program Outline
NHK	Nippon Hoso Kyokai (Japan Broadcasting Corporation)
NSC	National Security Council
NSS	National Security Secretariat
ODA	overseas development assistance
PPP	purchasing power parity
PR	proportional representation
SCAP	Supreme Commander for the Allied Powers
SDP	Social Democratic Party
SDS	specially designated secrets
SIASJ	situations in areas surrounding Japan
SMD	single-member districts
TPP	Trans-Pacific Partnership
UNPKO	United Nations Peacekeeping operations
YP	Your Party

JAPAN'S SECURITY RENAISSANCE

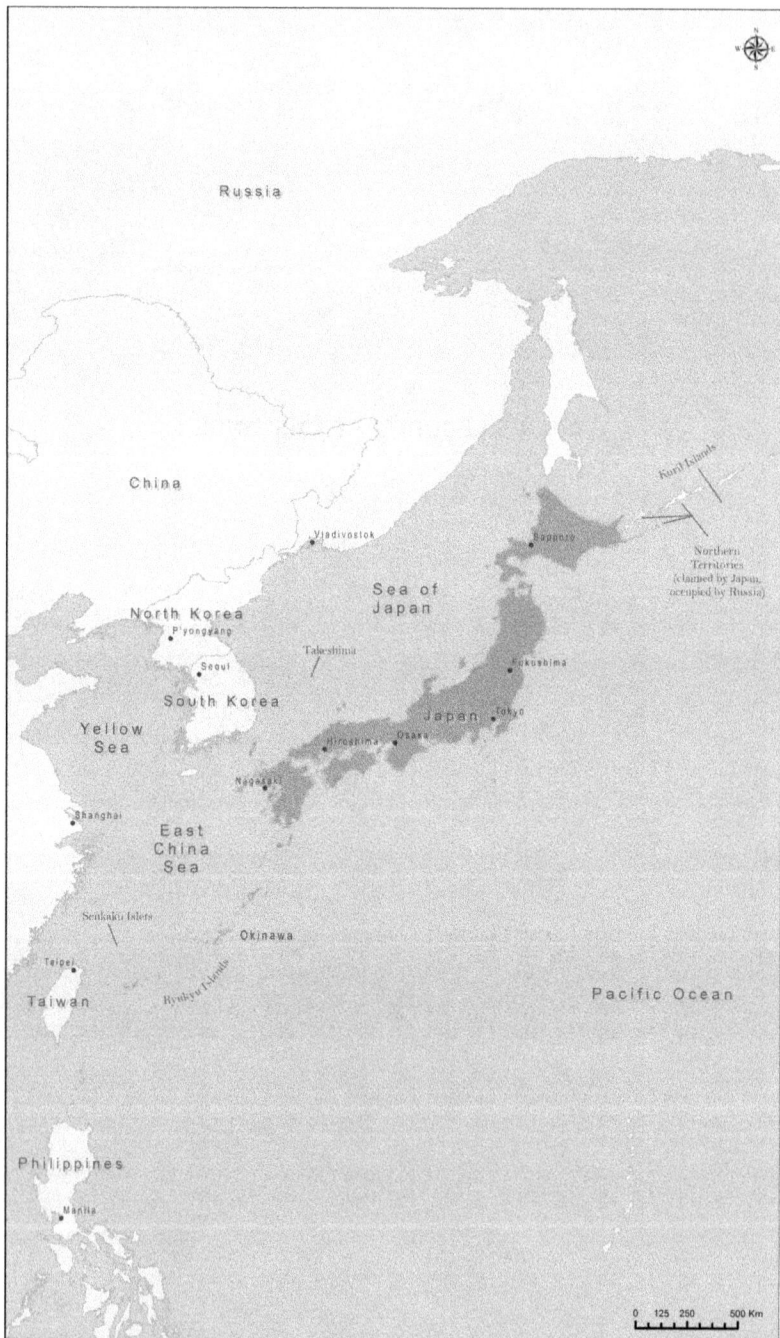

Map of Japan and Its Region

CHAPTER ONE

Japan's Twenty-First-Century Security Renaissance

In the area of military security, "Japan is back." The Japan Self-Defense Forces (JSDF), as Japan's postwar military is called, possesses among the most advanced military hardware and technology in the world and has started providing it to others; jointly patrols commercial sea lanes with the United States and other countries; leads anti-piracy operations as far away as the Gulf of Aden (where the bulk of Japan's energy imports transit); and its uniformed officers can be seen in major capitals around the world coordinating global defense strategies or in conflict hotspots participating in United Nations peacekeeping operations (UNPKO). Japan has even established its first fledgling overseas military base, in Djibouti (in 2009), as a hub for JSDF operations in that area.

Japanese civilian officials, especially those working in the new Ministry of Defense (MOD), established in 2007, and the National Security Council (NSC), established 2013, coordinate military strategy across government and engage the Japanese citizenry in increasingly pragmatic discussions of the complex challenges Japan faces to ensure its security well into the twenty-first century. Japanese political leaders from both left and right have supported Japan's development of greater military capabilities and more efficient coordinating institutions and strategies for what they both describe as an increasingly unpredictable and hostile security environment—a marked shift from most of the previous seventy years of domestic debates over Japan's proper security path.

For decades Japan eschewed the potential leadership role in regional and global security its power resources would allow in favor of a focus on economic and "soft-power" diplomacy and a deepening security alliance with the United States. Since the end of the Cold War, Japan's regional and global security contributions have been growing and its military capabilities and security doctrine updated for a quickly changing regional and global security environment, illustrating a gradual awakening to new security challenges that has culminated in the "security renaissance" of the past decade.

Japan's growing regional and global naval, air, and reconnaissance capabilities and activities have been welcomed and encouraged by some, while others have sought to revive questions about whether Japan has sufficiently atoned for and corrected flaws in its government and society that led to disastrous consequences for Japan's neighbors, the United States, and many others (including many Japanese) in a war that ended with the world's first and only wartime use of atomic weapons, in August 1945, and tens of millions of military and civilian deaths. In Japan as well, some welcome and encourage Japan's leaning to greater military capabilities and confidence while others express concern or actively oppose these developments.

This new level of pragmatism about security among both elites and the general public from the political left and right illustrates a security renaissance taking place in Japan during the past decade as Japan adjusts to new power realities in its region. This shift has proceeded through a first-ever postwar transition from the long-ruling party of the right (the Liberal Democratic Party, LDP) to the main party of the left (the Democratic Party of Japan, DPJ)[1] and back again. Japan's security renaissance is evident in broad discussions of contending approaches to security and in a new openness to acting on different ideas about how Japan should best provide for its security. This renaissance is not the result of a small group of elites but has emerged from an interaction between actors across the political spectrum and dynamic forces in civil society, empowered by new forms of activism and media. It represents an innovative melding of old and new ideas aimed at adapting Japan's security practices to a changing domestic and international environment. In this new melding, three historical legacies of the past—contested memories of the Pacific War and imperial Japan, postwar antimilitarist security practices, and the unequal alliance relationship with the United States—play an outsized role in how Japan's contemporary policy decisions are debated and implemented.

The European Renaissance that began in the late fourteenth century provides an imperfect but useful metaphor for describing the environment in which new security policies and practices have formed in the past decade in Japan as it has moved beyond the gradual awakening that preceded the renaissance. All historical analogies have limitations, but four aspects of Europe's Renaissance parallel the changes apparent in Japan of the past decade, in terms of both how security policy is discussed in contemporary Japan and policy outcomes.

A first parallel is a recasting of what is taboo in public discourse. The Renaissance marked a turning point in scientific inquiry due to a willingness to utilize previously known but discouraged theories, such as the heliocentric view of the solar system. The transformative idea of the Earth's not being at the center of the universe was *not* new to the time, but this theory was taboo until the period now known retrospectively as the Renaissance. Japan today is experiencing its own renaissance in its thinking and approaches to security. Security policies there are more often argued on their merits rather than judged by how they comport with past practice and ideology—though, to be sure, plenty of "old-school" thinking about security remains visible in public protests and discourse. The legacies of the past continue to play a role—as they did in Europe's Renaissance—but preceding frames are now also used to fuel alternative perspectives on Japan's security future. The postwar antimilitarist history of activist fervor toward Article Nine of Japan's postwar constitution is still apparent in security debates,[2] but social commentary across the political spectrum also actively engages with less-rigid points of view in today's Japan: even entertainment magazines, from the school-girl-focused *Seventeen* to male-focused *Weekly Playboy*, engaged their readerships in 2015 with discussion of changing the postwar constitution and adopting new security legislation to allow the JSDF to work collectively with other states. Titles such as "Let's Think About the Seventy Years of the Postwar Period at the Age of Seventeen" and "Chanting Pacifism Will Not Make Japan Immune from the Islamic State's Threats" are but two of hundreds of article titles that blanketed Japanese weeklies and monthlies in the lead up to the passage of important new security legislation in September 2015.[3] Japanese bookstores are filled with quickly published and marketed books that argue, on the one hand, that *Our Security Rests on Article Nine* to, on the other, how *"Defense Tone Deafness" Will Destroy Our Nation*—and many positions in the middle.[4] Japanese elites and public alike are reconsidering past positions on security-related issues in the face of Japan's new security environment, which has enabled those who have long sought for Japan to play a more active security role to enact changes long imagined but previously unattainable.

In a second parallel, the European Renaissance was both the result of and itself led to a period of great change in the world outside its Italian birthplace. Constantinople fell in 1453 and the New World was "discovered" in 1492. Japan's political and intellectual discourse on security issues today similarly has been greatly influenced by momentous events of the past few decades, in particular the end of the Cold War with the Soviet Union and the dramatic rise of China's economic and military might. The most striking driver of this transformation of Asia is China's reemergence as a shaper of the Asian security environment, a role it played previously over many centuries, before Japan became the leading power in East Asia after its surprising victory over China in the first Sino-Japanese war of 1894–1895 marked Japan as a rising world power. China has become a dominant regional actor and continues to grow economically, militarily, and in international influence. China's GDP and military spending were roughly twice as large at the start of the second Abe administration in December 2012 as at the beginning of his first term in September 2006. Taking a somewhat longer view, with the dissolution of the Soviet Union in 1991, Japan became the world's second-largest military spender and was spending three times more than China on national defense; twenty-five years later, China now ranks number two and is spending at least three times more than Japan on its military.[5] This is an astonishing reversal, even more so that it occurred via peaceful change—not as a result of interstate war—and that Japan greatly assisted China in its economic rise via extensive economic development assistance, trade, and foreign direct investment by Japanese firms.

Important regional change is not limited to China, however. South Korea—one of the poorest countries in the world at the time that US and other soldiers fought in the Korean War from 1950 to 1953—is now the eleventh-largest economy in the world, a member of the Organisation for Economic Co-operation and Development, and competes head-to-head with Japan in many industries. South Korea–Japan relations have become acutely strained as history and territorial issues have been politicized in both states and concerns about South Korea's growing closeness to China have arisen among Japanese defense planners. In Southeast Asia as well, an economic boom in many states in that region has fueled a rise in military spending and capabilities. Asian states spent more on their militaries than European states for the first time in 2012, $287.4 billion versus $259 billion.[6] (Note that the United States alone spent $685 billion that year.) Regional economic growth has also led to a stronger voice for the ASEAN regional grouping of the ten largest Southeast Asian nations, a bloc that in 2014 bought nearly as many exports from Japan as from the United States.[7] Japan's growing defense capabilities and international security practices themselves are contributors to a dramatic shift in the regional security environment. Japanese security practices are being reconfigured in response to the transformation of Asia, and Japan itself is contributing to Asia's dynamic security ecosystem and furthering Asia's transformation in the process.

In a third parallel, the Renaissance was also a cultural movement that profoundly affected European social and intellectual life not just by looking forward through an embrace of new ideas but also by gazing back with nostalgia to classical antiquity and what had been lost during the so-called Dark Ages. Many groups in Japan today look back to different aspects of Japan's past with nostalgia, combining their views of the past with visions of Japan's future rooted in new thinking about the world around them. Some on the far right romanticize Japan's imperialist past, leading to condemnation for activities such as making offerings and paying respects at the former locus of Japan's wartime state religion, Tokyo's Yasukuni Shrine, or building an elaborate museum adjacent to the shrine that presents their revisionist worldview to future generations. Many others look back to a more recent past of relative stability under a security doctrine based on strict constitutional prohibitions on weapons production and on military activities outside

Japan. As with most nostalgia, however, remembrances of the past do not always comport with historic realities: Japan's wartime conduct was not as benign as many on the far right purport, and even Japan's strongly antimilitarist past was not as antimilitarist as often portrayed.[8] Nevertheless, it remains true that no member of Japan's postwar military forces has been killed in combat—ever. Many Japanese are not eager to leave that aspect of their more recent history behind and will take to the streets to protest significant moves in that direction.[9]

In a fourth parallel, Europe's Renaissance was empowered by the ability to share new ideas cheaply and widely beyond elite circles thanks to the innovation of movable-type printing presses and the wider availability of paper. Japan has long been one of the largest publishing markets in the world (including several of the world's largest circulation newspapers), but the proliferation of blogs, websites, chat rooms, and social media such as Twitter and Facebook have allowed ideas outside the mainstream to be more widely shared and, importantly, engaged with—altering the nature of discourse over security issues in Japan in the past decade. Prime Minister Shinzō Abe himself has been widely credited with an adept "net strategy" to garner support for his positions on security-related issues. Concomitantly, however, he is also subject to pressures from this new media to pursue a wide range of alternative policy options.[10] It is remarkable in this context to note that in 1997, when the previous US-Japan Guidelines for Defense Cooperation were adopted, Google did not even exist as a company—much less a verb—illustrating the very different media environment in which security policy decision making was made in even recent years.

Japan today, of course, is not fourteenth-century Italy. Many more things are different than similar—but the metaphor of the Renaissance aptly conveys that change in both discussion and action on security issues in Japan in the past decade is not simply a matter of political realignment, a purported shift to the right in Japanese politics, or the "salami slicing" away of Japan's postwar constraints that has been evident for decades. The metaphor also helps to clarify that Japan's new security choices are firmly rooted in past practices, perhaps too firmly in the views of some. In this sense, Japan's security renaissance is not evidence of a break from the past, contrary to what many have argued and continue to argue, just as the Renaissance in Europe was born of preceding tectonic shifts. Japanese security practices have developed in innovative ways but still have well-known and recognized antecedents.

The Timing and Implications of Japan's Security Renaissance

Issues related to Japan's military have long been controversial at home and abroad, and theories of a "Japan rising" also have been heard for decades.[11] As with the European Renaissance, the precise start of Japan's security renaissance is difficult to pinpoint. Indicators would include several important security policy decisions taken from 2010 to 2016 as well as the elite and public responses (or lack thereof) to these decisions. The repositioning of Japan's military forces to counter newly perceived military threats set out in the 2010 and the 2013 National Defense Program Guidelines (NDPGs) also strongly illustrates this renaissance. No doubt, however, there were important precursors. Some, therefore, would date the start of what could be called Japan's security awakening much earlier than in this book. And, indeed, as explained in chapter 2, developments in Japan's security policy in the 1990s and the following decade in particular laid a foundation for the steps taken more recently. These earlier security developments, however—the Gradual Awakening—are insufficient to be termed a security renaissance. The past decade—from 2006 to 2016—is different for four reasons.

First, the alternation of political power from the LDP to the DPJ and back forced the primary political opposition to soberly confront Japan's real security challenges and to endorse policies long associated with only the political right. The DPJ leadership from 2009 to 2012 advocated quite similar next steps in Japan's security evolution to what the LDP had articulated previously and that at the time (from 2006 to 2009) the DPJ often opposed—in particular the development of further capabilities of the JSDF, the strengthening of the US-Japan alliance, and the creation of security partnerships beyond the US-Japan alliance regionally and even globally in terms of new defense production arrangements. These three factors are stressed in Japan's first proclaimed national security strategy in 2013 but mirror policies put in place under the DPJ in the 2010 NDPG.

A second distinctive aspect of Japan's security renaissance is the reformulation of military doctrine, capabilities, and positioning for newly perceived threats that have come about in a transformed, multipolar Asia where Japan is experiencing relative decline. Adaptation to a changed region began in the 1990s, such as in response to the North Korea threat in particular, and related to widespread public concerns about inadequate crisis-management capabilities in the Japanese government. Policy reactions to a changing region are thus not a new phenomenon. Previous work has argued convincingly that such reactiveness has been a hallmark of Japan's foreign policy decision making since the emergence of Japan as a great power in the late nineteenth century. Rather, the security renaissance that is the focus of this book is in response to a transformed Asia where Japan is not a rising power or regional hegemon but rather a state experiencing relative decline and an uncertain domestic and regional future.

Third, there has been a transformation of elite attitudes among party leaders and senior bureaucrats about Japan's security needs. In particular, there has been a shift in the LDP to what were once considered antimainstream positions, a growing acceptance of new security approaches by the Kōmei Party (the LDP's coalition partner),[12] and a move in the DPJ away from the strong influence of the former socialists and their ideological sympathizers. Elite bureaucrats offered continuity during this time of frequent transitions in electoral politics (seven different prime ministers from 2007 to 2012!), and therefore their views are also pivotal in the unfolding of Japan's security renaissance.

A fourth area of distinctiveness of Japan's security renaissance relates to broader public attitudes concerning national security in contemporary Japan. Here a stark transformation is *not* evident, but in many cases we see acquiescence to policy shifts that one could counterfactually imagine would have become larger political issues at an earlier time. There was strong public opposition to some policies enacted in recent years—such as against the JSDF's fighting together with other militaries overseas and the 2014 decision to implement a state secrets law—but general acquiescence to other significant changes despite a lack of support shown in public opinion polls (such as to relaxing arms export restrictions or to using ODA for military-related purposes). Public opposition to changing Article Nine of the postwar constitution also remains high, yet such a change is listed as a policy objective in the political manifesto of Japan's most supported party, the LDP, and is a well-known personal ambition of the popular Prime Minister Abe.

Thus, Japan's security policies and attitudes today do not reflect a wholesale change or the dramatic break from the past that some have suggested. And yet the shifts occurring are important and distinctive. To dismiss their importance would be a mistake, even if they have not risen to a level that strident proponents of the US-Japan alliance or of a more militarily assertive Japan would like.

Japan's security renaissance has important implications for Japan's allies and competitors in Asia as well as globally. Japan's national security strategy objectives of enhancing military capabilities and creating stronger security linkages with some of Japan's neighbors dovetails with the US goal of creating broader linkages among US allies and other friendly states in the region as part of the effort of the administration of President Barack Obama to "rebalance" its global military presence with a greater focus on East Asia. New US-Japan Guidelines for Defense Cooperation adopted in April 2015 recommit Japan to providing vital bases for the United States to continue to project its military power in the region far into the twenty-first century and craft a larger Japanese role in joint operations with the United States and other military forces.

Other states in the region seeking to adjust to a new regional distribution of power and new security threats—such as Australia, the Philippines, Vietnam, and others—also stand to benefit from Japan's growing security resources and expertise as well as its more active participation in regional security institutions. Japan has already created a special security partnership with Australia, entered into a classified-intelligence-sharing agreement with India, and furnished equipment to boost the coastal defenses of Indonesia, the Philippines, and Vietnam.

For longtime regional rival China, Japan's growing capabilities and participation in regional and global security activities complicate its security planning and aspirations—and have been actively opposed and undermined. Japan's former colonial possession South Korea occupies a middle ground, with potential strategic benefits from expanded security cooperation with a fellow US ally but continued reservations about assenting to increased Japanese military capabilities and participation in regional and global security.

What will Japan's security future be when China's economy is triple the size of Japan's or larger, after another decade of demographic pressures increase the proportion of those past retirement age in Japan even more than its current historic high, or if one of many possible cataclysmic security contingencies in the region takes place? An understanding of how Japan's security renaissance has reshaped thinking about military security in Japan in the past decade (as well as how it has *not*), of the new institutions and practices that have been created, and of the altered domestic political landscape in Japan will enable better predictions of how Japan will adapt to the next decades of change in the international environment—both widely predicted change such as the continued economic growth of East Asian states as well as unpredictable X factors such as an outbreak of open military conflict, prolonged economic recession, or other unlikely but possible sources of future change.

Japan's security renaissance is not about Japan becoming more "normal." All change in Japan's security policy should not be viewed through a lens of more or less normal. As I have argued in earlier work, the past half century of security and prosperity that Japan has enjoyed *is* normal for Japan—illustrated by three generations of overwhelming continuity in security practices.[13] To be sure, some political actors inside and outside Japan use a terminology rooted in normalization to argue for their policy preferences,[14] but the majority of Japanese choose whether to support changes in Japan's security policy and practices based not on whether they want Japan to become normal but rather on whether they believe that change will make Japan more prosperous and secure. Nevertheless, the discourse on Japan's need to "normalize" its security practices is so pervasive and so politicized, it cannot be ignored—and thus will be considered in the pages that follow in light of numerous policy choices that Japan has faced and addressed in the past decades.[15]

Adapting Security Approaches to Protect Japan

To understand Japan's efforts to provide for its security, one must first consider what sorts of threats modern Japan has faced—ranging from reckless and aggressive behavior of Japan's close neighbors and imperialist "great powers" oceans away to the threats of resource scarcity and more contemporary threats posed by nuclear weapons, cyber attack, and terrorist attacks from nonstate actors. At the very start of such inquiry, however, one must consider what exactly Japanese defense planners have sought to protect: Japanese territory, Japanese lives, and Japanese livelihood.

The Japanese islands span a great distance along the eastern edge of the Asian continent, flanking Russia's sea access to the north then past the Korean Peninsula to China's northern access to the Pacific in the south (see map). Although small in relation to continental great powers, Japan's land area is slightly larger than Germany, and its location poses both geostrategic importance and logistical challenges. Japan's territory is composed of four main islands (Hokkaido, Honshu, Shikoku, and Kyushu) and over sixty-eight hundred smaller islands, totaling more than twenty-one thousand miles of coastline. Most of the smaller islands are uninhabited (such as the five disputed Senkaku islets), but the main island of the Okinawan chain is home to over one million Japanese and the vast majority of US military forces stationed in Japan; moreover, several of the smaller islands help to greatly expand Japan's maritime space and provide strategic benefits even if sparsely populated. Japan's maritime territory and EEZ cover almost 2.8 million square miles, making it the sixth-largest state in the world in terms of maritime area.[16]

Roughly 127 million Japanese live on these resource-poor islands and rely on trade from abroad for sufficient food, energy, and other materials to provide for daily needs and industrial production.[17] Japan's population and industrial production have grown substantially in its modern history, leading to even greater needs for imports; but this dependence has been an important facet of Japan's security planning since the nineteenth century and one addressed via different strategies over time. In the mid-nineteenth century, when Japan was forced to suspend its self-imposed isolation by the Western powers (beginning with Commodore Matthew Perry's arrival in what is now Tokyo Bay in 1853), Japan experienced a direct threat from Western imperialism, which had already compromised the sovereignty of several states in Asia (in particular, China) and threatened a number of others. Japan's military response to this perceived threat—including the first Sino-Japanese War of 1894–1895, which led to Japan's colonization of Taiwan, and the defeat of

Russia's Pacific forces in the Russo-Japanese War of 1904–1905, paving the way for Japanese colonization of the Korean Peninsula—drew Japan into the global international order and ultimately into a world war. As tensions rose in response to Japan's creeping expansion into the Asian continent—including the establishment of the puppet state of Manchukuo in 1932—Japan sought to address its resource and maritime dependency by expanding further and ultimately advancing across East Asia, leading to a global response that brought its crushing defeat and the formal collapse of the machinery of imperial Japan.[18]

In the period 1945 to 2006, Japan steadily rose from its status as a defeated "enemy state" of the United Nations to one of its strongest supporters, and from economic devastation to becoming the second-largest economy in the world. This economic and political recovery was widely described as a miracle. The path of this recovery created a new set of historical legacies that those seeking a more proactive security role for Japan were limited by and that required concerted political effort to overcome. These new, postwar legacies are seen in the introduction to Japan's first formal national security strategy, issued in December 2013, which makes multiple references to Japan's postwar commitment to peaceful approaches to international relations and its commitment to the US-Japan alliance.[19]

Despite strong opposition to Japan's rebuilding military capabilities after its defeat—both from countries that suffered from Japan's wartime and prewar conduct and from many Japanese—Japan did build substantial military capabilities over the course of the long postwar period, from the creation of the JSDF in 1954 to its first overseas deployment in a postcombat minesweeping operation in 1991 and the 2015 legislation allowing the deployment of the JSDF in collective self-defense (CSD) operations overseas under limited conditions. To some Japanese, including the current prime minister Abe and his intellectual supporters, this growth in military capabilities symbolized a move away from what they saw as a sort of dark ages in which Japan lacked status as a military great power and respect for its accomplishments. This more activist view was eclipsed by a much larger group in postwar Japan advocating the country focus its resources on economic development and only a limited rearmament and those who embraced a new postwar identity of Japan as a peace state.[20]

What has sparked recent changes in Japan's approach to its security that have catapulted once antimainstream views into the policy mainstream? They were generated by an interactive dynamic of domestic political realignment with a shifting international environment, in conjunction with changed preferences more broadly in Japanese society and new political institutions as well—a "perfect storm" that has enabled the security renaissance of the past decade. This interactive dynamic intensified at the end of the Cold War, which coincided with the collapse of Japan's so-called bubble economy and the death of the Shōwa emperor. In the 1990s, important political institutions evolved—such as the new electoral system first utilized in 1996—leading to further change in political outcomes evident more recently.[21]

This book focuses on the period 2006 to 2016, bookended by the two administrations of Shinzō Abe, where the principal drivers of the international-domestic interactive dynamic are the growing suspicions over China's economic and military rise, continued concern with an escalated North Korean military threat, reaction to the so-called Lehman shocks (as the Japanese refer to the global financial crisis of 2008) combined with a more generalized fear of US economic and military decline, and Japan's continued economic stagnation in the context of a region that experienced substantial economic growth in this period. These forces, and other domestically based factors, led to dramatic political party turnover—and also to a series of new Japanese security policies, practices, institutions, and capabilities, which are described this book.

In September 2006 Japan's charismatic and popular prime minister, Jun'ichirō Koizumi, handed over the political reins to his chosen successor, Shinzō Abe. The transition did not maintain the momentum for reform these leaders and many observers expected, however. Instead, Japanese domestic politics entered a period of great instability that saw Abe's term as prime minister end in just a single year and the two succeeding prime ministers from his party suffer the same fate. As a result of this political turmoil in the ruling party, the opposition DPJ took power in August 2009, the first time a single opposition party had won more votes than the LDP in a national election in postwar Japan.[22] The DPJ leadership would prove no more stable, however. Under the DPJ,

Japan again saw three prime ministers in three years, followed by the return of the LDP to power in December 2012.

Despite these frequent political oscillations, over the terms of seven prime ministers from 2006 to 2016—ranging the political left and right—Japan has recrafted its national security strategy, redeployed and developed new military assets, and reemerged as a regional and global security actor by adapting many long-standing security practices into a new guiding doctrine that commits Japan to make "proactive contributions to peace" regionally and globally.[23] Since 2006, Japan has reversed a decade of declining defense spending, developed substantial new military capabilities, adopted its first-ever formal national security strategy, and created new institutions to manage these new goals and resources, including the MOD, upgraded from the former Defense Agency, and the NSC.

Japan's new proactive contributions to peace include transfer of defense-related equipment to like-minded states in the region, enhanced security cooperation with the United States regionally and globally, and participation in international security regimes to combat piracy regionally and as far away as the Gulf of Aden and to contribute to UNPKO regionally and as far away as South Sudan. In November 2013, Japan's navy, the JMSDF, engaged in its largest deployment overseas to date, sending over one thousand sailors on several advanced naval vessels to contribute to relief efforts in the Philippines after the devastating typhoon Haiyan struck. This action was all the more striking in that the last time Japan's naval forces landed en masse on a Philippine island, it was to invade. This turnabout was featured widely in the global media as so-called history issues continue to influence Japan's security practices for better and for worse.

Japan's security renaissance is strongly influenced by three sets of history issues, however, not just one. The issue most frequently evoked is the contending memories of World War II and the years leading up to it. Some in Japan adamantly believe Japan's wartime misconduct has been overstated and that Japan's true mission to liberate other Asians from Western colonialism is wrongly downplayed. This historical legacy has been especially evident under the administrations of Shinzō Abe (2006–2007, 2012–present) but has long been a defining aspect of Japan's postwar political debates domestically and with its neighbors and others abroad. In contrast, a seventy-year accumulation of security policies and practices rooted in Japan's postwar antimilitarist approach to security policy forms a second strong and influential historical legacy that profoundly shapes Japan's current security practices. The strong popular opposition in Japan to reinterpreting Article Nine of Japan's postwar constitution to allow the JSDF to work more closely with foreign militaries apparent in mass demonstrations by concerned Japanese citizens in Tokyo and elsewhere in 2014 and 2015 is one of many examples of the effect of this second historical legacy. A third lasting and complex historical legacy is the deeply intertwined political and security relationship Japan has developed with its former adversary, and now closest ally, the United States. Consistent calls for greater equality in the security relations between the two states—by politicians from the left and the right—and strong opposition in the southern island of Okinawa to new US military facilities are examples of the effects of this third historical legacy.

These three legacies generate strong emotions among political actors within and outside Japan and have created extensive norms and institutions restricting Japan's security practices that require sustained effort and political capital to confront and to adapt, despite being rooted in distant historical events. How Japan's leaders and society navigate these historical legacies will shape the next steps in Japan's security renaissance.

International-Domestic Interaction and Japan's Evolving Security Identity

It is apparent to informed observers of Japan that there has been a shifted internal balance of political power in Japan in the past decade that has strengthened the hand of those who would like to push the country in a more "realist" or "normal" direction.[24] This shift has been reported widely outside Japan in the context of concerns over the purportedly nationalistic tendencies of Prime Minister Abe. This is an important story but one that also deserves more nuanced consideration of the apparent shift rightward—particularly as it relates to concerns over rising nationalism in contemporary Japan. Right-left descriptors can obfuscate more than enlighten Japan's shift in its security posture; the idea of rising nationalism should also be considered in cross-national and historical contexts—as discussed in chapter 5.

It is also commonly observed that the conservative actors pushing Japan to more proactive security practices are greatly facilitated in their efforts by an increasingly threatening international environment, in particular North Korea's missile and nuclear weapons testing and China's dramatic economic and military rise. The scale and speed of such developments, however, are not well understood by many; nor has there been sufficient attention to explaining how important political actors within Japan perceive the changes in Japan's regional environment. Chapter 3 of this study elaborates on important changes in Japan's regional and global security environment and links this transformation of Asia to changes in Japanese domestic politics and its security policies and practices.

Another factor that has not been carefully examined to date is how these two trends—Japan's decline in relative power in the region combined with an increasing perception of security threats and its domestic political reordering—interact to create a new domestic political landscape and new conceptions of how to provide for a secure Japan in this changed international order.[25] It is this *interaction* that has led to the security renaissance illustrated by the flourishing discourse on Japan's security and the development of a number of important new security institutions and practices in the past decade. Japan's security renaissance is not simply the result of how changes in the relative balance of power—domestically or internationally—led to changes in state action; rather, Japan's security renaissance illustrates how changing *perceptions* of the international security environment privilege some domestic political actors over others and lead to new conceptions of appropriate security practices and to new security policy options and choices.

Overt and new security threats to Japan are widely discussed in Japan's vibrant civil society and diverse media environment, with social media platforms assuming a growing role. The implications and appropriate policy responses are subjects of active and often heated debates.

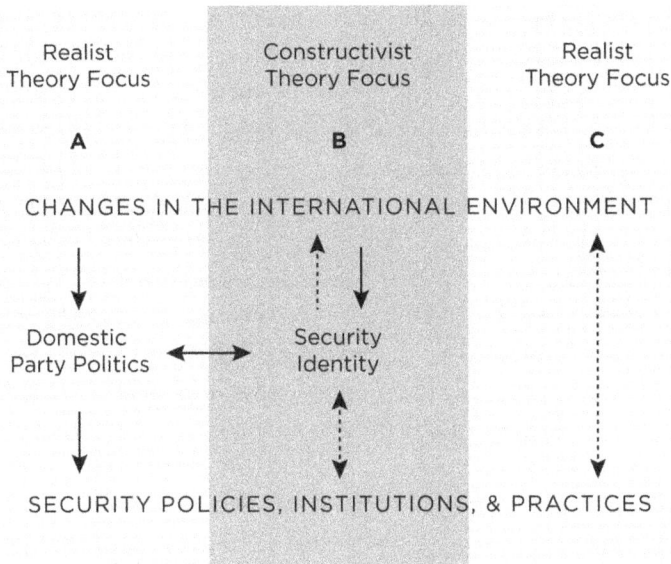

Realist   Constructivist   Realist
Theory Focus   Theory Focus   Theory Focus

A   B   C

CHANGES IN THE INTERNATIONAL ENVIRONMENT

Domestic   Security
Party Politics   Identity

SECURITY POLICIES, INSTITUTIONS, & PRACTICES

FIGURE 1.1 Explaining Japan's security renaissance.

This book focuses on two aspects of how these debates have led to new security practices in Japan and will lead to further change in the future (see figure 1.1).

First, this book develops an argument common to what scholars term realist international relations theory, as seen in column A of the figure: changes in the international environment lead to changes in domestic party politics, which seeks to respond to and capitalize on such change to advance the party agenda, leading in turn to changes in security policies, institutions, and practices.[26] A common narrative of Japanese security policy evolution vis-à-vis North Korea in the 1990s shows this pattern: North Korean development of more accurate and longer-range missiles and the country's audacious test of such a missile by flying one over mainland Japan led to a change in Japan's domestic political debate over acquiring missile defense and surveillance satellite capabilities, empowering those actors who had long argued for such capabilities, tipping the political balance in their favor, and leading to Japan's acquisition of such capabilities.[27]

This explanation for security policy change is incomplete, however—and by itself leads to inaccurate predictions of policies pursued. What is necessary for accurate prediction is an explanation of when and how changes in Japan's international environment are perceived as important. This second step requires consideration of the concept of Japan's security identity, the collectively held principles that have attracted broad political support regarding the appropriate role of state action in the security arena and that are institutionalized in the policy-making process.[28] Heated debates in Japan's freer, postwar civil society and domestic party politics led to an institutionalization of Japan's postwar security identity beginning in the mid-1950s—after the seven-year Allied occupation of Japan had ended—and continuing in the ensuing years. Today this security identity helps to shape policy responses to perceived shifts in Japan's international environment. Moreover, changes in the international environment contribute directly to pressure to alter Japan's security identity and to develop new guiding principles for policy action, as illustrated by the solid arrow in column B of figure 1.1.

It is also possible to consider the effects of the dotted arrows in the figure, but they are not the focus of this study. For example, how Japan's existing security identity leads to a certain type of understanding of changes in the international system and how shifts in Japan's security practices can lead to new conceptions of Japan's security identity are the focus of a more constructivist line of inquiry.[29] Moreover, column C of figure 1.1 illustrates another common realist concern over how changes in state security practices can lead to responses by other states in the system and, consequently, to systemic changes in the international environment. This causal direction is at the root of what scholars call a security dilemma and is arguably evident in East Asia today, where China's military buildup (which, it argues, is necessary to better protect China than in past eras when China's weakness was exploited) causes a reaction by other states such as Japan, which in turn causes a new reaction by a state such as China seeking to counter new Japanese capabilities.[30] The argument of this book acknowledges the validity and contributions of these lines of argument but focuses on the relationships represented by the solid arrows in columns A and B of the figure.

The International Component: Adapting to a
New Regional and Global Environment

Japan's new security posture is the result, in part, of its declining relative power in the region and globally and of a new security environment that is being shaped by China's reemergence as a regional power and global actor as well as the further diffusion of power due to the economic and political rise of other states in the region and, more broadly, away from states to other forces like nonstate actors, international institutions, and multinational corporations.[31] The policies articulated in Japan's formal defense planning documents—such as its NDPG and national security strategy—are not just a reaction to the dramatic change in the past twenty years, however, but also an attempt to make Japan secure for the next twenty years.[32] For example, Japanese public concern is not only about the territorial dispute with China over the Senkaku Islands today but also about what the standoff will look like ten years from now—when China's economy and military power are expected to be twice their size as of 2016. Underlying this and many other security issues is the question of whether current approaches are sustainable. Moreover, it is not merely about the evolving military situation but also about China and other states as competitors more broadly—including in the realms of soft power and economic competition.[33]

Apart from Japan's declining relative economic and military power in the region (discussed in chapter 3), new security threats have emerged in the period of focus of this book, and others greatly intensified from previous periods. Japan has had territorial disputes with its close neighbors since the conclusion of World War II, but only the dispute with the Soviet Union was the subject of heated political debate and risk of military escalation in previous decades. In the past decade, Japan's territorial disputes with South Korea and especially China have intensified to the verge of active military conflict. While the Soviet Union theoretically posed an existential threat to Japan through its nuclear weapons targeting, as well as a conventional military threat of invasion that Japan's military forces were organized to repel, the direct military threat that China poses to Japanese territory in the past decade is at a level of salience not seen since the widespread fear of a US military invasion of Japan in 1944.[34]

North Korea also poses an increased security threat to Japan in the period under examination in this book. The North Korean threat to Japan objectively spiked with Nodong missile tests conducted in 1993, and Japanese public concern over the North Korea military threat was aroused in 1998 with the Taepodong missile test that overflew the Japanese main island of Honshu. North Korean military capabilities have continued to increase since that time via countless additional missile tests and five tests of rudimentary nuclear weapons. North Korea has also sent unmarked ships into Japanese territorial waters and landed such ships surreptitiously on the Japanese main islands. In defense planning documents issued since 2006, North Korea continued to be identified as a primary security threat to Japan and a main driver of Japan's enhanced defense capabilities such as in the areas of missile defense and intelligence, surveillance, and reconnaissance (ISR).

Other long-standing traditional Japanese security concerns have been exacerbated by the growing military capabilities of states in the region. Japan is positioned on the edge of potential war between Taiwan and China and between North and South Korea. In both cases, US forces based in Japan would almost certainly become involved in these conflicts, which very likely would draw Japan in as well. The new US-Japan Guidelines for Defense Cooperation, signed in April 2015, set out a more explicit role for the JSDF in such instances, working together with the militaries of other states. New security legislation passed in the Diet in September 2015 puts into place a new legal framework to allow the JSDF to be utilized for such CSD operations in a limited manner.

Beyond state-based changes in economic and military power, Japan's security renaissance has emerged also in response to a broader transformation in the nature of providing military security in the twenty-first century. Japan's past practices were not designed only for a different regional and global distribution of power but also for different types of military conflicts, threats, and technology. As a result, Japan must shift both its physical capabilities and its security doctrine and practices to counter new, twenty-first-century security threats. Defense planning documents of the past decade delineate in detail these new threats that Japan perceives, including cyber- and outer-space-based threats, and new kinds of conventional threats from the greater technological capabilities of some perceived adversaries.

One important new conceptualization of possible military conflict that has shaped recent Japanese defense doctrine is the idea of gray-zone conflict, meaning a low-level physical attack that does not amount to an outright invasion or declaration of war. Japan's 2010 NDPG expressed concern about this new type of conflict in relation to possible Chinese action in connection with the Senkaku Islands dispute. Since that time, the world has seen an example of such a gray-zone conflict in the case of Russia's support of paramilitary forces in eastern Ukraine—exactly the type of state-supported military activity that other states have judged to not rise to the level of outright invasion but nonetheless has had devastating consequences for Ukraine. That Japanese defense planners anticipated such a situation before the Ukraine crisis and that Japanese news media and civil society discourse engaged in serious discussion of this new potential threat to Japan is another example of the security renaissance that has taken place in Japan in the past decade—a level of realistic and practical discussion of Japan's defense needs unimaginable in previous decades.

The Domestic Component: A Shift in Political Discourse on Security Policy

Domestic political actors in Japan have struggled to adjust to Japan's declining relative power and growing economic insecurity, leading to broad changes in domestic political discourse. This change in discourse has facilitated a shift from mere *thinking* about new approaches to security to cautious *implementation* of new approaches by political actors from the left and the right. This change is visible across the political spectrum from a move to more centrist security policies in the primary political party of the left, the DPJ, a move more to the right of center by the ruling coalition partner, the Kōmei Party, and a significant move to the right by the majority LDP. In addition, new political parties to the right of the LDP have formed for the first time since the creation of the LDP in 1955, creating further pressure for policy action on the LDP.

Japan's long-ruling LDP, the conservative party of Prime Minister Abe, historically was made up of multiple factions that spanned the political center to the right of center, with some individuals also expressing views of the far right.[35] This range within one party grew from the founding strands of the party in 1955 as the union of the Liberal and Democratic parties and was maintained in the subsequent fifty years owing to a multitude of factors that would include Japan's electoral system of a single, nontransferable vote in multimember districts in the lower house until 1994 and an overriding objective among party leaders to maintain political dominance regardless of the ideological consequences.[36] A major shift in the LDP to the right of center has contributed to Japan's security renaissance, though it is far from the only political factor. The return of the LDP to power as a result of the December 2012 national elections completed the shift in the LDP from the dominance of the Yoshida school, which had codified Japan's extensive antimilitarist security policies and institutions, to the more conservative internationalist school of former prime ministers Nobusuke Kishi, Yasuhiro Nakasone, Koizumi, and Abe.[37]

This is not to say that the new conservative realists (formerly the antimainstream faction) have achieved their long-standing goal of remilitarizing Japan or face unimpeded political terrain ahead. In fact, Abe has faced considerable headwinds as he has sought to use his 2012, 2013, and 2014 election mandates to streamline and strengthen national security policy, practices, and institutions—just as conservative prime ministers had before him. Nevertheless, the tables have clearly turned in the LDP, with many former mainstreamers having now retired (including such leading figures as Kōichi Katō and Hiromu Nonaka) and the few remaining moderates struggling to influence Japan's future security policy direction (such as Sadakazu Tanigaki in the third Abe cabinet).[38]

This role reversal in the LDP is not just about Abe. It represents a shift in the LDP writ large. For example, all five challengers to Abe in the September 2012 contest for the presidency of the LDP supported reinterpreting constitutional provisions connected with the practice of exercising the right of CSD—once considered an antimainstream position. In September 2015, Abe ran unopposed for reelection as president of the LDP despite fierce public opposition to his signature goal of constitutional revision. Very few LDP Diet members publicly opposed the 2015 security legislation to implement the exercise of CSD in limited scenarios—illustrating that the previous factional split over security issues is no longer plainly visible.

Importantly, this shift in attitudes on security policy is not restricted to the LDP. Significant security policy innovation toward greater military capabilities and international security contributions is evident in the DPJ as well. The 2010 NDPG arguably marked a more significant departure from past practice than the subsequent guidelines released by Abe in 2013.[39] Moreover, the first major escalation of the territorial dispute with China over the Senkaku Islands took place under DPJ prime minister Naoto Kan, and the even more escalatory "nationalization" of the islands was implemented under DPJ prime minister Yoshihiko Noda.[40] In addition to the new NDPG, a number of other significant foreign policy shifts often attributed to the recent Abe administration also have their origins before 2012—for instance, enhanced security cooperation with India and Australia and expanded economic and security interests in Southeast Asia. It is even worth considering that without Abe in power, Japanese security policy may have become *more* internationalized and proactive, because it may not have generated as much controversy without Abe's at times inflammatory rhetoric and those of his controversial supporters. This hypothesis is considered further in chapter 4, where I examine DPJ policy innovation and the blueprint for future years that it was unable to implement due to losing the majority of seats in the Diet in the December 2012 Lower House election.

Another new structural factor in Japanese domestic politics is the rise of political parties on the right of the political spectrum—the Japan Restoration Party (JRP) and its successors, Your Party (YP), and others. Former Tokyo governor Shintarō Ishihara was once part of the LDP, and his conservative views were somewhat balanced within the party. After leaving the LDP, Ishihara's new party, the JRP, regularly criticized the LDP for not espousing policies far enough to the right. Its successor, the Japan Innovation Party (JIP), continued the criticism of the LDP from a position on the right (though not always further right in terms of security policy), challenging LDP party dominance in ways not seen previously in postwar Japan. This situation should be familiar to observers of US domestic politics, where the standard-bearers of the US Republican Party face regular haranguing from Tea Party–backed candidates, who are further on the right—though in the United States this dynamic is taking place *within* the Republican Party, which is no longer the case with the LDP in Japan (though certainly intraparty disagreements continue in the LDP was well).

The rise of new media and social media has also shaped Japan's security renaissance by empowering the political extremes, forcing politicians to address organized constituencies outside the previous filters of the mainstream media. This factor can be seen globally in political-party splintering and increasing disunity—and not just in advanced industrial democracies but in authoritarian states such as China, where even the more constrained social media demands government responsiveness and often fuels nationalist sentiment. One recent example in Japan is the hate posts to the website of the US embassy in Tokyo after the embassy expressed "disappointment" about Abe's controversial visit to Yasukuni Shrine in December 2013. Despite Abe's efforts to deepen Japan's alliance with the United States, critics who perceive too much compromise to a US-led agenda now have greater public opportunities to express their disagreement and to force a prime minister to respond. Prime Minister Abe himself has described his use of social media to directly connect with the public, in part in response to his critics.[41]

The strong international reaction against both the policies and the personality of Abe, a reaction that resonates with some in Japan as well, illustrates the many continuing constraints on Japanese security policy action—some of them rooted in history and identity, others at the practical level of limited resources, capabilities, and expertise. Consideration of these history issues concludes this chapter and serves to frame the chapters that follow.

The Weight of History:
Three Legacies of the Past Shaping
Japan's Security Future

We will engrave in our hearts the past. . . .

—PRIME MINISTER SHINZŌ ABE, CABINET STATEMENT ON THE SEVENTIETH
ANNIVERSARY OF THE END OF WORLD WAR II, AUGUST 14, 2015

Although Japan's security renaissance marks a renewal of thinking and approaches, it does not represent the break with the past that Japan has experienced twice in its modern history: with its defeat in World War II and, prior to that, the forced opening to the West under threat of force in the late nineteenth century.[42] Old ideas and memories continue to influence Japan's thinking about its security—among elites and across society. Three legacies of the past—or what some describe as sets of contested memories—in particular strongly influence Japan's security renaissance in ways that are not entirely predictable. The most apparent of the three legacies are the contested memories of Japan's colonialist period through the conclusion of World War II. This legacy is commonly referred to as *the* history issue (*rekishi mondai*), but two other legacies of the more recent past also substantially influence how Japanese recraft their security policies and practices for the twenty-first century: the legacy of seventy years of antimilitarist constraints on Japan's defense establishment and the complex legacy of the unequal postwar security alliance with the United States. How Japan's leaders, and its political system and society at large, engage with, recraft, and address these *three* historical legacies will play a major role in the future direction of Japan's security renaissance. In the past decade, each of these legacies has strongly shaped Japan's new security policies and precluded other possible policies and practices from emerging.

Legacy One: Contested Memories of the Pacific War and Japanese Colonialism

> During a certain period in the not too distant past, Japan, following a mistaken national policy, advanced along the road to war, only to ensnare the Japanese people in a fateful crisis, and, through its colonial rule and aggression, caused tremendous damage and suffering to the people of many countries, particularly to those of Asian nations.
>
> —PRIME MINISTER TOMIICHI MURAYAMA, AUGUST 15, 1995

Japan's efforts to adapt its security politics and practices to new concerns inevitably evoke strong responses both within Japan and abroad related to Japan's past military conduct in the region. This has been the case throughout the postwar period but has become especially apparent in the past decade as Japan's security roles in the region have greatly expanded and as some Japanese political figures have become more emboldened to confront contested historical memories head-on.

The Japanese government has officially apologized for its colonial-era and wartime aggression on numerous occasions in the postwar period. A landmark public apology was delivered in 1995 by Prime Minister Tomiichi Murayama on the occasion of the fiftieth anniversary of the end of World War II. Another important official apology related to the issue of the so-called comfort women—also described as sexual slaves of the Japanese imperial military—was issued by Chief Cabinet Secretary Yōhei Kōno in 1993. Prime Minister Abe delivered another comprehensive statement of apology framed in a broader context of twentieth-century history on the seventieth anniversary of the end of World War II in August 2015. (The full text of these three statements is provided in appendix 3.) Dozens of Japanese prime ministers, foreign ministers, and ambassadors—among others—have issued statements of apology and contrition in both official and private capacities over the years, both within Japan and across Asia and the world, many at sites important to wartime or colonial-era events and incidents. Still, both in and outside Japan, significant numbers of people seek a more comprehensive and heartfelt apology from Japan for its past actions. These persistent calls have contributed to a backlash among some in Japan, described as "apology fatigue"—leading to a vicious cycle of further calls for apology.[43] It is impossible to understand the shape and dynamics of Japan's security renaissance without reference to this first historical legacy.

The year 2015 marked the seventieth anniversary of the end of World War II in the Pacific, or what Japanese also refer to as the Great East Asia War, the Second Sino-Japanese War, or simply the Pacific War. American historical memory of the conflict is bookended by two dramatic events: the surprise attack on Pearl Harbor on December 7, 1941, and the atomic bombings of Hiroshima and Nagasaki on August 6 and 9, 1945. Japan's unconditional surrender to Allied forces on the USS *Missouri* in Tokyo Bay marked the end of much more than four years of war for Japan, however. It marked the end of a period of territorial expansion and imperialism across Asia that began with the first Sino-Japanese War of 1894–1895. Indeed, one of the provisions of Japan's unconditional surrender was the reversion of Japanese territory to pre-1895 boundaries, which is the basis for one of the most volatile territorial disputes in the East Asian region today—the issue of whether the uninhabited islands that Japan administers as the Senkaku Islands and China claims as Diaoyu (and Taiwan claims as Diaoyutai) should be considered part of territory Japan should have returned as part of the Yalta peace accords. (Japan's position is that it had expanded into that territory prior to 1895, as with other parts of Japan that were incorporated into Japan's core territory earlier in the nineteenth century, including the northern main island of Hokkaido and the southern Ryūkyū chain. This issue is examined further in chapter 3.)

Japanese never fully came to terms with their fifty years of colonialism in Asia, marked by the expansion onto the island of Taiwan in 1895, the Korean Peninsula (formally colonized in 1910), and subsequently acquired territory—all of which Japan was forced to return after its defeat in 1945. A strong narrative of postwar, defeated Japan was that of Japan as a victim state: a victim of atomic bombings, of a relentless firebombing campaign prior to that, and of the Japanese public being "misled" and abused by militarists within their own government.[44] The US decision to not try Emperor Hirohito for war crimes when other Japanese wartime leaders were brought to the International Military Tribunal for the Far East (aka the Tokyo Tribunals)—as well as other US policies during the seven-year occupation of Japan—further clouded responsibility and accountability of Japan's wartime and colonial-era conduct.

Japan formally concluded peace treaties with its neighbors in a piecemeal fashion, beginning with the United States and some US allies in 1951 and Taiwan in 1952 but with South Korea only in 1965, China in 1972, and still to this day not formally with Russia (with which Japan continues to dispute possession of four islands to the north of the four main Japanese islands) or North Korea. The Cold War division of Asia, which kept Japanese largely out of physical contact with many areas Japan had possessed or invaded during its colonial period (such as North Korea, Manchuria, and parts of northern and coastal China) further impeded Japan's postwar historical reconciliation. The end of the Cold War, which happened to coincide with the death of Emperor Hirohito in 1989, offered new opportunities for Japan to consider its wartime past and to open new dialogues with neighboring countries—leading to newly published material on Japan's wartime and prewar conduct in Asia, including in memoirs from Japanese imperial-era soldiers and settlers and from survivors of Japanese aggression.

Dialogues in Japan and between Japan and neighboring states among survivors and perpetrators continue to this day, as do calls for Japan to better atone for its past conduct. In addition, today and in Japan's postwar past other Japanese have sought to portray Japan's past actions in a more positive light, repeating wartime and colonial-era claims that Japanese actions served to liberate Asia from Western imperialism and to promote economic development and modernization.

Legacy Two: Postwar Antimilitarist Constraints on Japan's Defense Establishment

> While taking silent pride in the path we have walked as a peace-loving nation for as long as seventy years, we remain determined never to deviate from this steadfast course.
>
> —PRIME MINISTER SHINZŌ ABE, CABINET STATEMENT, AUGUST 14, 2015

A second legacy of the past that deeply affects Japan's security renaissance is the set of choices Japan made in the early postwar years to embrace the US-imposed Article Nine of Japan's postwar constitution and to commit itself publicly to a war-renouncing pacifist model of postwar renewal. Many scholars have examined the politics and intellectual currents that led to Japan's postwar security policies, variously labeled antimilitarist or rooted in a "Yoshida Doctrine."[45] While the exact boundaries of this postwar security identity can be debated, what is beyond dispute is that this set of policies and practices is strongly rooted in the postwar Japanese psyche and thoroughly embedded in political institutions and practices. Confronting this second legacy requires great expenditures of political capital and innovative ideas persuasive enough to dislodge a set of policies that have kept Japan outside active international conflict for nearly three-quarters of a century, an enviable record for any great power in the international system.

Japan's security renaissance has called into question this long-standing historical legacy of postwar Japan—its antimilitarist security identity. This security identity has structured policy choices toward nonmilitary approaches to international security through its institutionalization into laws and bureaucratic practices and through regular societal feedback through elections, public opinion polling, and other forms of political advocacy (including, at times, political demonstrations).[46] Security identity is not just something elites or scholars imagine: it has been apparent in broad national conversations in Japan that have been ongoing and the subject of political battles for seventy years.[47] It remains important to examine the political and social forces that are resisting the shifts manifested in Japan's security renaissance and still possess at least the power to delay or modify the policy preferences of those seeking for Japan to play an even more active regional or global security role. Just as in the European Renaissance, Japanese society today is composed of political actors with a wide range of beliefs, many at odds with one another.

Legacy Three: The Security Alliance with the United States

What should we call this if not a miracle of history? Enemies that had fought each other so fiercely have become friends bonded in spirit.

—PRIME MINISTER SHINZŌ ABE, ADDRESS TO A JOINT SESSION OF THE US CONGRESS, APRIL 29, 2015

The military alliance between Japan and the United States that has endured for over half a century and prior security relationship under military occupation and the subsequent Mutual Defense Treaty from 1951 to 1960 provide the locus for a third set of contested historical memories that shape Japan's security renaissance. This postwar legacy is in addition to US-Japan issues related to World War II that are subsumed under the first historical legacy already discussed and that include controversies like American prisoners of war held by Japan during the war and the atomic bombings of Japan by the United States.

Postwar relations between the United States and Japan began with seven years of formal military occupation of Japan, ostensibly by the Supreme Commander for the Allied Powers (SCAP) but in the Japanese popular imagination and in actual practice by the United States. General Douglas MacArthur led SCAP and was forever seared into Japanese historical memory via an iconic photograph of him in army khakis with an open collar standing next to the diminutive emperor of Japan dressed in formal morning-coat attire.[48] The legacy continued with a vastly un-equal "mutual defense treaty" that was, in essence, the price of ending the military occupation—together with the continued occupation of Okinawa, discussed later. The treaty was signed unceremoniously by Prime Minister Shigeru Yoshida at a US military facility outside San Francisco, away from press or other observers. Japanese politicians moved to address perceived inequities in the treaty almost immediately after, culminating in a new security treaty that was signed amid what are thought to be the largest political demonstrations in Japanese history in January 1960, under the tenure of Prime Minister Nobusuke Kishi, grandfather of Prime Minister Shinzō Abe. Kishi resigned soon after the treaty was signed in contrition for the plainly antidemocratic man-ner by which the treaty was adopted in the Diet.[49] In the years that fol-lowed, the security relationship with the United States was consistently a divisive issue, in particular related to US military bases in Okinawa, territory that reverted to Japanese administrative control in 1972 but continues today to host the overwhelming majority of US bases and US military forces in Japan despite constituting less than 1 percent of total Japanese territory.[50]

Seventy years after Japan's defeat in World War II, approximately fifty thousand US troops remain stationed in Japan, one of the largest concentrations of US forces outside the United States. Beyond the troop presence, the United States maintains substantial military assets at US bases in Japan, including the only nuclear-powered aircraft carrier home ported outside the United States, the USS *Ronald Reagan*. The Japa-nese government provides nearly $2 billion per year to offset the cost of stationing US forces in Japan, with the US government spending an additional approximately $2 billion per year on nonpersonnel costs for troops stationed in Japan.[51]

In contrast to the early years of the US-Japan alliance, when even use of the word "alliance" (*dōmei*) was taboo, the alliance today is greatly augmented by the capabilities and missions of the JSDF—which, de-spite the defensive nomenclature, rivals the military prowess of all but a handful of the world's militaries. The JSDF works closely with US mili-tary forces in the region to patrol sea lanes, to provide for extended deterrence through Japan's robust ballistic missile defense capabilities (the largest such capability outside the United States),[52] and to offer disaster relief and humanitarian assistance in times of crisis regionally and globally. Japan has also begun to support global security missions together with the United States and the United Nations, including an ongoing extended contribution to counterpiracy patrols[53] and nearly ten years of logistical support for US counterterrorism activities around Afghanistan.[54] Expanded joint operations and interoperability are on the horizon, as set out in the new US-Japan Guidelines for Defense Cooperation announced in April 2015. Japan has thus become an important military partner of the United States but inevitably continues to be seen as a junior partner, with the concomitant lingering resentments that entails. Moreover, Japan's decisions to increase the capabilities of the JSDF are often portrayed in the media—and even at times by political leaders—as necessary concessions to the United States to maintain a strong alliance commitment.

Still, Japanese public support for the US-Japan alliance and American public views of Japan have been at record highs in the past several years,[55] which in itself can be seen as a demonstration of Japan's security renaissance. This high level of support can be linked to US military assistance to Japan in response to the March 11, 2011, triple disaster. Growing Japanese regional security concerns—in particular in relation to China—also surely play a role in growing support for the US-Japan military alliance.

The US-Japan relationship is much broader than a military relationship, of course. Outside of North America, Japan is the second-largest export market and source of imports for the United States, as well as the second-largest source of foreign direct investment and second-largest foreign holder of US treasuries.[56] There is a large Japanese-American community in the United States, and the cultural appeal of both states for each other is quite high—from sushi and anime in the United States to baseball and American music (from jazz to rap) in Japan.[57]

Despite the very close ties between the two states and their citizens today, the legacy of the postwar security relationship between the United States and Japan casts a long shadow over Japan's contemporary security renaissance. In the lead-up to the fiftieth anniversary of the current 1960 security treaty, political tensions were felt on both sides of the Pacific as Japanese prime minister Yukio Hatoyama—Japan's first DPJ prime minister in over fifty years—openly called for a more equal alliance with the United States, just as his grandfather had in the 1950s, and as American policy makers groused at Japan's unwillingness to contribute more to the operational aspects of the alliance. Even LDP prime minister Abe, the first Japanese prime minister to address a joint session of Congress, has used similar language in lamenting the "shackles of the postwar regime" he characterized as imposed by the United States.

These three historical legacies, while distinct, also interrelate. When Prime Minister Abe expresses the desire to "destroy the postwar regime" —referring indirectly to issues such as the US-imposed Article Nine of the postwar constitution and the verdicts of the Tokyo Tribunals—he evokes not only the complex postwar US-Japan legacy but also the legacy of antimilitarism as well as contested memories of World War II. Another example of the interrelationship among the three historical legacies is US complicity in Japan's difficulties in reconciling with its neighbors after World War II due to US concerns for stability during the occupation period and, later, Cold War desires to keep Japan firmly on the US side and away from the communist Soviet Union and China.

As with Europe's Renaissance a half millennium ago, Japanese today are engaged in vibrant and heated discussions about both the past and the future. This security renaissance is not just about policies but also about politics, process, institutions, and identity. Some of these new institutions and ideas—like the NSC, created in December 2013, or the conception of "dynamic joint defense" from the December 2013 NDPG —have not yet been the focus of sustained scholarly inquiry. While it is too early to determine definitively how they will develop, the structure and principles behind them can be examined as important components of Japan's security renaissance. Other existing institutions and ideas are being adapted by new political forces and therefore must be reconsidered vis-à-vis previous scholarship.

Chapter 2 develops the core arguments of this book in a more scholarly manner, linking international relations theory and existing scholarly literature on Japan and on security policy evolution with the idea of a security renaissance advanced in this chapter. In particular, chapter 2 builds on recent scholarship that advances our understanding of how domestic norms, practices, and identity are constructed not only through domestic processes but also through international interactions. Although this theoretical examination is rooted in constructivist approaches to identity, the goal of chapter 2 is to bridge the gap between what some view as excessively abstract theorizing in recent constructivist scholarship and policy concerns that more often are rooted in realist terminology and understandings. Chapter 2 also illustrates how the three historical legacies affecting Japan's security renaissance today have exerted a strong influence in previous periods as well and addresses some persistent myths about Japan's past security practices in the earlier postwar period, including its gradual security awakening in especially the post–Cold War period.

The next two chapters consider in greater depth how the changed regional and global environment shifted the perceptions and policy preferences of political actors in Japan, again seeking to bridge the gap between constructivist strengths at explaining identity construction and adaptation and the strengths of realist-informed scholarship at explaining and demonstrating empirically the changing nature of military threats and shifting balance of power regionally. Chapter 3 examines changing regional and global dynamics and the effect of Japan's declining relative power on its approach to military security. Chapter 4 discusses the "six prime ministers in six years" period (2006–2012), beginning with the ambitious security agenda of the first Abe administration and the substantial pushback it faced, both within his party and from outside; this chapter also explains important policy outcomes of this period and how they show substantial evolution of Japanese security policy toward a more activist role despite leadership from different political parties and from prime ministers with different political orientations. Chapter 5 turns attention to the return of Shinzō Abe and his party to power and their goals and achievements through August 2016. This chapter shows how Japan's security renaissance—a new openness and acceptance of some new approaches to security and substantial pushback on others— is laying the foundation for the next decade of Japanese security policy, as illustrated by the new national security strategy, recrafting of such long-standing policies as arms export restrictions and the ban on the exercise of CSD, and further deepening and expanding of security co-operation with the United States through revised US-Japan Guidelines for Defense Cooperation.

The concluding chapter considers Japan's security challenges in the coming decades, examining both challenging domestic circumstances such as Japan's aging demographic profile, shrinking population, and fiscal deficits, and the most likely regional and global security challenges. Japanese domestic politics remain in flux. Further surprises and unpredictable political realignments are certain. This changing domestic political landscape will continue to shape Japan's security renaissance in the coming years in conjunction with—and in interaction with—the changing dynamic regional landscape of a transformed Asia.

CHAPTER TWO

The Gradual Awakening

A review of Japan's past strategic responses to changes in its security environment shows clearly that Japanese leaders sought to develop new military capabilities and strategies over the course of the postwar period to address emerging threats and a changing security environment.

Many studies have advanced claims of a single critical turning point in this evolution, such as the end of the Cold War, the first Persian Gulf War, the North Korea missile test that overflew Japan, the September 11 attacks, and any of several crisis points with China related to the Senkaku Islands. In retrospect, however, it is clear that there was a gradual awakening of Japanese elites and later the Japanese public to the need for Japan to develop greater military capabilities and to reform outdated and cumbersome standing procedures to address newly perceived security threats. These new capabilities and strategies were greatly shaped and limited by the historical legacy of Japan's militarist and colonial past as well as new postwar historical legacies that would emerge from domestic political pressure for antimilitarist security policies and an unequal security relationship with the United States.

By the 1980s, as Japan's economic power resources developed to "economic superpower" levels (see figure 2.1), many questioned why Japan did not devote more resources to its military security in response to

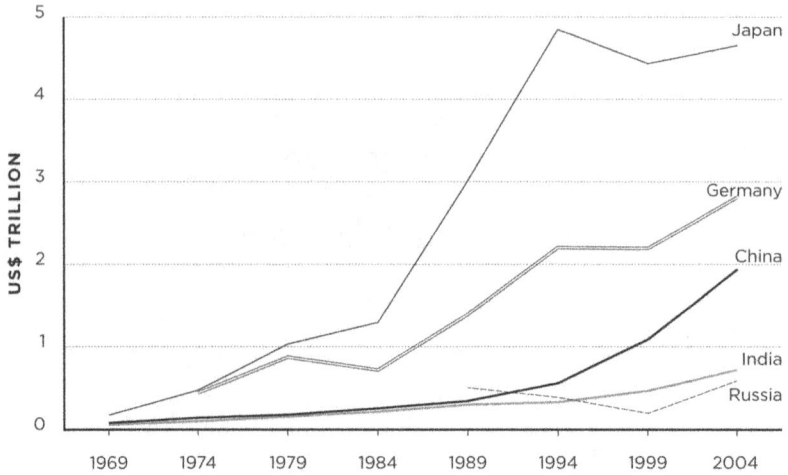

FIGURE 2.1 Japan's GDP relative to other major powers, 1969–2004. GDP in current US$ trillion; not available for Russia prior to 1989 or Germany prior to 1970. World Bank, http://data.worldbank.org/indicator/NY.GDP.MKTP.CD?page=6 (last updated July 28, 2015).

perceived threats and to question Japan's reliance on its only military ally, the United States. Japan's GDP was larger than any European state by 1974, as represented by Germany (Europe's largest economy) in figure 2.1. In 1989, when economic statistics for Russia and China became more reliable, Japan's economic size was larger than that of China, India, Russia, North and South Korea, and Taiwan *combined*. Even near the end of the period considered in this chapter, in 2004, Japan's GDP was over twice that of China's and more than that of China, India, and Russia combined.

Realist-informed international relations theory predicted that an economically rising Japan would also become a militarily rising Japan, both in terms of military spending and the ultimate great power status symbol of acquiring nuclear weapons. Neither of these predictions proved correct. Rather, Japan continued to increase military spending only in proportion to its overall economic growth (although this did lead to substantial increased spending on defense because of Japan's robust economic growth) and to rely on the US nuclear umbrella and the broader extended deterrent of US military forces based on Japanese territory.

This book does not seek to revisit these debates of the Cold War era when Japan was an economically rising state that had become the world's second-largest economy. A substantial scholarly literature exists that argues for different positions in this debate.[1] Rather, this study focuses on how Japan has adapted its security strategies for the challenges it faces in the twenty-first century based on the power resources it has available at this time—after over two decades of economic stagnation and facing the dual challenges of record-setting government debt and budget deficits together with a demographic profile that makes Japan the most rapidly aging society in recorded history.[2]

This chapter reexamines the first six decades of Japan's postwar experience, as the country sought to rebuild and with particular focus on post–Cold War steps toward the security renaissance of the past decade. There have been many excellent studies of Japan's postwar reemergence into the international order, the complex domestic politics of this period, and Japan's efforts to once again play a major international role in and to contribute to international peace and security. My own earlier work focuses on the aspect of this period related to the historical legacy of antimilitarism, arguing that Japan's postwar security identity of domestic antimilitarism took decades to emerge and be institutionalized via an intensively political process.[3] Other important works have focused on the first historical legacy of Japan's colonial and wartime era, considering the domestic politics of the so-called history issue, Japan's attempts to reconcile with various states, and the broader political science and moral questions about the nature of reconciliation in international politics in the past or in the more contemporary era.[4] Yet another set of literature has examined the role of the United States in Japan's security policy evolution and, at various points in the past several years, the state of the relationship at that time.[5] Drawing on insights from this previous work, this chapter illustrates how the original history issue of the postwar period—Japan's coming to terms with its conduct in World War II and the years leading up to it—was not resolved even by the sixtieth commemoration of the end of that war, and how two new postwar historical legacies also emerged and were codified in this period. In addition, this chapter presents a snapshot of Japan's military capabilities and security policy institutions on the eve of the important

changes that would take place in the next decade, 2006 to 2016, in order
to illustrate in subsequent chapters the substantial departure Japanese
security practices of the past decade represent from earlier decades, yet
also the continuity present in part because of the three historical legacies that have affected policy formulation throughout the postwar years.

A reconsideration of Japan's past security practices also offers an
opportunity to address two common but misleading narratives about
Japan's recent security policy evolution in relation to its past practices.
First, there is a pervasive, lingering belief that postwar Japan did not
contribute actively to international security beyond simply refraining
from war and advocating for peace. As discussed in the following, however, recent scholarship convincingly demonstrates that Japan played
an important supporting role in balancing against the Soviet military
threat during the Cold War and worked with other major powers to address new post–Cold War security threats such as piracy and terrorism
(though largely by nonmilitary means in the latter case). Second, there
is a widespread and misleading narrative that in the post–Cold War era,
Japan "normalized" its approach to military security, abandoning Cold
War–era "shackles" and leaving antimilitarist rhetoric as merely that—
rhetoric, not substantive constraints. Here again, substantial scholarship
demonstrates the effect of antimilitarist norms and beliefs on Japanese
security policy—though a robust set of counterarguments also exist for
the period 2000 to 2006, the Koizumi years.[6] This chapter first addresses
the first misleading narrative, showing how Japan built substantial military capabilities in the postwar period leading to a formidable standing
military force by 2006, the eve of Japan's security renaissance. Next, the
chapter shows how despite the impressive capabilities of the JSDF by
2006, the constraints on its use were far more than rhetorical or minor
inconveniences to be worked around and continued to be pervasively
shaped by the three historical legacies of the past.

Japan's Gradual Security Awakening

Japanese security strategy, capabilities, and institutions adapted to
changes in the regional and global security environment over the dura-
tion of the postwar period. Numerous scholars have carefully catalogued
this evolution, providing complementary explanations for foreign policy

change.[7] They disagree to some extent over principal drivers of change—in particular whether Japanese leaders implemented a "grand strategy" or were more "reactive" in their policy choices—but all agree that Japan has long sought to respond to important changes it perceived in the international environment.

The Emerging Cold War Context
and Japan's Growing Alliance Role

In the early postwar period, the nature of security threats to Japan had fundamentally changed from the prewar and wartime periods, with Japan's immediate neighbors China and Korea embroiled in civil wars and a cold war emerging between the United States and another of Japan's close neighbors, the Soviet Union. Japan's other Asian neighbors in this period were focused on achieving or maintaining their own independence in the new postwar global regime and on developing economically, posing no direct security threat to Japan; further afield, the European powers that had posed an imperialist threat to Japan earlier in the century were retreating from global empires. In terms of direct military threats posed to Japan, only the United States and the Soviet Union could be considered true military threats. In response, Japan entered into an alliance with the United States, protecting itself militarily from both direct threats.[8] Over this long Cold War period, Japan substantially increased the defensive capabilities of its JSDF in coordination with its only military ally, agreeing in a limited manner to ever-increasing demands by the United States for Japan's new postwar military forces to expand their scope of mission and level of military readiness.

After the initial outbreak of the Cold War, the spread of nuclear weapons presented a new concern globally and for Japan in particular, prompting an extended discussion in Japan of whether Japan, too, should acquire nuclear weapons to provide for its security in a new, nuclear era. There is a widespread popular misconception that because Japan is the only state to have been the victim of a nuclear attack, it did not seriously consider arming itself with nuclear weapons in the new nuclear era, but considerable scholarly research clearly shows that this was not the case. Through an extended consideration of its security options in the nuclear-armed, Cold War era, Japan—like a number of other states globally—ultimately did decide to forgo possession of nuclear weapons in exchange for protection under the US nuclear umbrella and a pledge by the existing nuclear weapons powers to limit the further proliferation of nuclear weapons and to work toward an ultimate future of a world free of nuclear weapons, a position Japan continues to advocate.[9]

Japanese security strategy therefore initially focused on building military capabilities sufficient to repel a small-scale, nonnuclear attack and expanded over time as Japan's economic power grew to developing military capabilities that allowed the JSDF to play an important supporting role in balancing the Soviet military threat in the Asia-Pacific through advanced air and sea patrols. Japan's "Basic Policy for National Defense" was approved by the Kishi cabinet in 1957 and provided the mandate "to progressively establish efficient defense capabilities in accordance with the nation's strength and situation"—but with the important limitation that this should be conducted "within the limits required for self-defense."[10] Following this policy guideline, a series of five-year plans for defense acquisition were developed and implemented. Each new five-year plan faced opposition from those seeking to limit Japan's military development, often framed around legalistic discussions of the constitutionality of each new capability proposed, in particular whether it fit under the threshold of what was "minimally necessary" to protect Japan.

Despite this persistent opposition, explained further later in this chapter, by the end of the Cold War in 1989, Japan had completed considerable investment in developing world-class military capabilities as set out in its first National Defense Program Outline (NDPO, later renamed NDPG in English) in 1978 and the related five-year Mid-Term Defense Plan (MTDP).[11] As summarized by a former US naval officer and US Defense Department official, these investments "resulted in Japan's completing a high technology air-defense and anti-submarine warfare (ASW) network highlighted by 200 F15 and 100 F4 interceptors and 60 destroyers and 100 P-3C ASW aircraft—all of which significantly complicated Soviet military planning, the essence of deterrence."[12] Another study completed in the early 1990s noted, "Over the past decade the JDA [Japan Defense Agency, precursor to the MOD] has enjoyed one of the fastest defense expenditure growth rates in the world, averaging 6.5 percent between 1980 and 1989."[13] This study also highlighted the advanced capabilities of the JSDF that resulted, writing that the JASDF at the time possessed "about 340 planes, which is similar to the number the US Air Force has defending the continental United States. The JASDF also has at its disposal some of the West's most advanced air defense systems including the Patriot surface-to-air missile that proved so effective in the Gulf conflict."[14] The study continues, "[The JMSDF] is equally impressive. In size it is bigger than Britain's Royal Navy . . . [and] . . . in numbers it is nearly three times the size of the US Seventh Fleet whose strategic responsibility covers the Western Pacific and Indian Ocean."[15]

Thus, and contrary to lingering popular belief both in Japan and abroad—due, in part, to extensive public relations from the Japanese government—Japan possessed formidable military assets by the mid-1980s *and* used many of them regularly to help monitor and contain the Soviet threat, the only serious military threat facing Japan at that time. James Auer and Robyn Lim describe "Japan's role in winning the Cold War" in a way germane to recent debates over CSD held in the Diet, writing, "Fully armed Japanese naval aircraft, alternating on a daily basis with US Navy anti-submarine aircraft, patrolled throughout the Sea of Japan, upon which lie Vladivostok and other Soviet Pacific Fleet bases. That convinced Soviet naval commanders that Japan was prepared to fight alongside the United States if necessary. Officially, the Japanese government's position was that it could not participate in CSD; Japan's actions sent a different message."[16]

Still, antimilitarist sentiment ran deep among the Japanese public and also among major political figures, and not just among members and supporters of the JSP but in the ruling LDP as well. As Japan's military capabilities grew, so did institutionalized limits on the use of these capabilities and reassurances to a concerned public that Japan's military might was only for self-defense.

Adapting to the Early Post–Cold War World

Japan also perceived fundamental changes in its security environment in the post–Cold War period and made important modifications to its security strategy and capabilities as a result. Christopher Hughes writes of two "cycles" of military modernization that took place in the period discussed in this chapter, related to new NPDOs released in 1995 and 2004 that each sought to adapt Japan's security apparatus to important changes in Japan's international environment.[17]

In the early post–Cold War period, Russia remained the only state that directly threatened Japan militarily—apart from the very limited nuclear threat posed by other, minor nuclear weapons powers and, again, apart from the threat some in Japan construed from the United States. The Russian threat was perceived to be much less than the previous Soviet threat, however—to the degree that Russia was actively courting Japanese economic assistance and making overtures toward resolving the long-standing territorial dispute between the two states over what the Japanese call the Northern Territories (see the map opposite page 1), a dispute that has not yet been resolved after over seventy years since the conclusion of World War II. At this time, in the early 1990s, Japan's defense spending was double that of China and its military capabilities vastly superior, even apart from the additional security provided by Japan's military alliance with the United States. (China did, however, possess nuclear weapons that Japan did not—part of the rationale for Japan's continued military alliance with the United States.)

As in the United States, this new, seemingly more favorable international environment led to calls in Japan for reducing military capabilities, which had been designed to counter a Soviet attack. The revised NDPO of 1995, the first revision of this document originally crafted during the Cold War, set out a reduction in JSDF personnel and heavy equipment like tanks (see table 2.1),[18] with political debates continuing over possible further reductions and even perhaps an end to permanent US bases in Japan.[19]

As the extended post–Cold War era began to unfold, however, a number of additional direct military threats to Japan emerged.[20] In the mid-1990s, North Korea began activities to develop nuclear weapons and continued these activities despite repeated efforts by major powers to stop them; by the following decade, North Korea had achieved a limited nuclear deterrent and de facto acceptance as a nuclear weapons state by these powers. In addition, North Korea's conventional missile capabilities greatly increased in a way that posed a direct military threat to Japan (though the stated intention of these new missiles was to protect North Korea from possible attack by its southern neighbor South Korea and its ally the United States). As a result, Japan developed its own indigenous surveillance satellite capabilities to monitor this newly perceived threat and worked with the United States to develop missile defense technology and to deploy an effective limited missile defense capability—departing from previous security doctrine.[21]

China's military capabilities also substantially increased in the post–Cold War period, posing a new direct military threat to Japan beyond the limited nuclear weapons threat that developed in the 1960s and that was countered via Japan's coverage under the US nuclear umbrella. As with North Korea, China's missile capabilities also greatly increased in this period, with hundreds of new missiles deployed that were capable of targeting the Japanese homeland—though the stated and generally accepted purpose of these new missile deployments was to threaten Taiwan, not Japan. A significant military escalation in the region in 1995 to 1996 over China's testing of new missiles in areas surrounding Taiwan, and the US response by transiting an aircraft carrier through the Taiwan Strait, was widely covered in the Japanese media and led to an increase in Japanese public concern about military security in the post–Cold War era.[22]

Japanese detection of a Chinese nuclear-powered submarine passing through Japanese territorial waters in November 2004 was an early touchstone of the future of growing Chinese military capabilities—including China's greater ability to disrupt Japan's sea connection to the Middle East and Europe via the South China Sea. Only in the past decade, though, has China's military technology and level of defense procurement rivaled Japan's own military capabilities—as discussed in chapter 3.

In addition to the two state-based new threats posed to Japan by North Korea and China, a number of newly perceived so-called new security threats were identified by Japan's defense planners in Japan's major defense strategy documents of the early post–Cold War period. Piracy in Southeast Asia (where the vast majority of Japan's oil imports transit) saw a marked rise in the 1990s, from 16 incidents in 1993 to 242 in 2000.[23] The JCG played a leading role in bringing the number of such incidents down substantially by 2006, and even further in subsequent years.[24] Notably, however, the JMSDF played a very limited role in such operations, in no small part due to the historical legacies of Japan's wartime past and postwar antimilitarism.[25]

In addition to a reconception of Japan's self-defense needs, Japan continued to face demands for an expanded global security contribution in the early post–Cold War period. The outbreak of the first Persian Gulf War, 1990–1991, just as the Cold War was concluding, forced Japanese political leaders to scramble to seek to adapt Japan's antimilitarist security constraints to a new international environment. The inability of Japan's political leaders to make a military contribution to the global coalition that pushed Iraq out of Kuwait created a lasting and bitter memory for numerous key decision makers in Japan's defense establishment.[26]

In response to the new instability emerging in the post–Cold War period, and contrary to the wishes of some to reduce the US presence in Japan at the end of the Cold War, the United States and Japan renewed their commitment to maintaining the alliance and expanded the roles and missions of the alliance for the new post–Cold War security environment—issuing a Joint Declaration on Security in 1996 and revised US-Japan Guidelines for Defense Cooperation in 1997, the first revision to these guidelines since their crafting during the Cold War.[27]

Post-9/11 Pressures: Moves Toward a "Normal" Japan

The September 11, 2001, attacks on the United States starkly illustrated the new terrorist threat posed by nonstate actors like Al Qaeda. Under the leadership of Prime Minister Jun'ichirō Koizumi, the Japanese Diet passed multiple "special measures laws" (short-term laws with sunset provisions) to counter this new threat while the government internally deliberated and battled over longer-term legislation that would be introduced in the following decade. The Anti-Terrorism Special Measures Law, passed in October 2001, enabled the dispatch of the JMSDF to the Indian Ocean to provide logistical support to the US and multinational coalition forces engaged in Afghanistan—operations that took place from November 2001 to January 2010 (with a brief pause at the end of 2007). The Law Concerning Special Measures on Humanitarian and Reconstruction Assistance, passed in July 2003, enabled the dispatch of the JGSDF to Iraq in limited numbers and strictly noncombat roles.[28]

More than twenty-two thousand JSDF personnel took part in support missions in Iraq and Afghanistan from 2001 to 2010, according to the MOD.[29]

Beyond perceptions of threat in the post–Cold War era, Japan also sought to increase its international contribution to global peace and stability in this period—including by making its first contributions to UNPKO and other international cooperation activities after heavy criticism for not deploying the JSDF to the multinational forces who joined in the first Persian Gulf War of 1991. The JSDF has been dispatched to fourteen countries or areas since its first overseas deployment to assist in minesweeping operations in the postconflict Persian Gulf in 1991 through 2006.[30] Bhubhindar Singh provides a detailed account of Japan's increased contributions to international security in the context of his argument that Japan was developing a new security identity as an "international state" in this early post–Cold War period.[31]

A comparison of the three NDPGs from 1978, 1995, and 2004 (see table 2.1) affords a first look at the sort of changes Japan's military forces underwent in the first fifteen years after the end of the Cold War, but

TABLE 2.1
NDPG comparison: Personnel and major equipment

	1978	1995	2004
Total JSDF personnel authorized	180,000	160,000	155,000
JGSDF Regionally deployed units	12 divisions; 2 brigades	8 divisions; 6 brigades	8 divisions; 6 brigades
Tanks	1,200	900	600
JMSDF			
Destroyers	60	47	50
Submarines	16	16	16
Combat aircraft	220	170	150
JASDF			
Air warning groups	28	8	8
Squadrons	0	20	20
Combat aircraft	430	400	350
Fighters[a]	300	350	260

Source: Adapted from Ministry of Defense, *Defense of Japan 2014*, 151–52.
Note: Some of the values are listed as approximate in *Defense of Japan 2014*.
[a]Subset of combat aircraft.

the quantitative table does not convey that the shrinking *quantities* of equipment were more than offset by improved *quality* and *institutional flexibility* of Japan's post–Cold War military forces. On the quantity side, the JSDF saw reduced personnel from 180,000 to 155,000 authorized—though the JSDF was not maintaining more than 160,000 standing troops at the time of the "reduction" of personnel. The number of tanks was halved from 1978 to 2004, JMSDF combat aircraft reduced by about one-third, and JASDF combat aircraft by about one-quarter.

On the surface, these reductions would seem consonant with a "peace dividend" from the end of the Cold War Soviet threat. However, the JSDF budget did not decline—rather, it rose to its peak to date around 2003.[32] In addition, savings from cutbacks in personnel and in some types of heavy equipment were invested in new technologies and equipment for newly perceived threats. This additional spending and redeployment of resources led to the creation of the most capable and versatile JSDF to date, one able to contribute to many more types of military missions than possible during the Cold War era—developments that were widely described in the popular press and some scholarship of the time as the "normalization" of Japan.[33]

As set out in the 1995 and 2004 NDPGs, each branch of the JSDF increased its capabilities and flexibility in this period. The JGSDF began a transition deepened in the following decade that altered parts of its regionally based brigade structure to also allow for a "rapid reaction force" that could be quickly deployed both across Japan and for overseas operations, including by utilizing new dedicated helicopter transports. The JMSDF procured additional *Ōsumi*-class transport ships with flat decks for landing of transport helicopters and rear docks for operation of hovercraft capable of landing tanks (which were used in Japan's largest HADR mission to date, after the Indian Ocean tsunami of December 2004).[34] The JMSDF also procured new destroyer-helicopter ships (DDH, also referred to as mini aircraft carriers)[35] and six Aegis-equipped Kongō-class destroyers (the cutting edge of missile defense technology developed by the United States). The JASDF continued its modernization via procurement of additional F-2 fighters and, for the first time, developed a limited midair refueling capability by procuring four Boeing KC-767 tanker aircraft;[36] in addition, the JASDF became the designated operational lead over Japan's advanced missile defense capabilities.[37]

A move toward "jointness" of operations between the three services of the JSDF is also an important institutional precursor to Japan's security renaissance of the past decade as it shows political and military leaders conceptualizing the JSDF as an actual fighting force rather than solely as an element of deterrence. Under the new joint operations posture, enacted in March 2006, a new joint chief of staff is selected from one of the three services to advise the minister of defense and prime minister on force operations while the preexisting chiefs of staff of the three services maintain responsibilities for affairs other than force operations such as human resources, training (except joint training), and buildup of defense capabilities.[38]

In sum, by the start of the twenty-first century, Japan's military forces rose to a level of capabilities that would rival all but a handful of states in the world—if these forces were enabled by an unencumbered legal or constitutional framework and by a political leadership willing to use the military in this way. Japan had not reached this point in its postwar gradual security awakening, however—and still has not, though important additional developments would take place under Japan's security renaissance of the next period. As one group of security analysts has recently written, "It is not a rhetorical flourish that Japan's constitution renounces war as a sovereign right. The JSDF are organized and equipped based upon a strategy of defensive defense, enshrined in both national and alliance policies. As such, the JSDF will remain politically and operationally constrained, small, and less capable than might be the case otherwise."[39]

Hughes describes three continuing domestic obstacles to Japan's further military modernization in this period: (1) organizational inertia (e.g., the JGSDF's clinging to its regional brigade structure); (2) budgetary restrictions (e.g., stagnant defense spending despite ambitious modernization plans and a declining share of the national government budget devoted to defense more broadly), and (3) political pressure (e.g., organized political opposition to Japan's development of new capabilities).[40] In addition to these factors, the strong legalistic tendencies among Japanese legislators when discussing defense doctrine should be noted, though this might broadly be considered a type of organizational inertia. During this period, substantial political capital was devoted to changing Japan's foundational security document—Article Nine of the postwar constitution—to provide the legal foundation for increased Japanese security roles and missions, but this effort failed.[41]

The security renaissance taking place in Japan today may lead to these next steps. In terms of capabilities, however, by the end of the Koizumi period in 2006, Japan's military forces had crossed many Rubicons that were unthinkable to most Japanese at the end of the Cold War. These milestones did not yet mark the security renaissance of the post-Koizumi period, however. In part this was due to an inability to confront the three historical legacies that were reified in the postwar period, as discussed in the following sections, and to recraft them to support security policies for a new era. These milestones do, however, represent a further gradual awakening of Japan's security consciousness and a new level of engagement with the regional and global security realms.

The Unresolved Legacies of Japanese Militarism and Colonialism

Japanese domestic politics, budgetary constraints, and Cold War concerns all helped to shape Japan's postwar defense policy evolution, but Japan's colonial and wartime experiences and conduct cast a long shadow over Japanese efforts to craft a postwar security policy. Moreover, this original history issue shaped the politics surrounding postwar security policy making to the extent that it fostered a new historical legacy shaping Japanese defense policy: the postwar legacy of antimilitarist constraints, discussed in the next section. Both within and outside Japan, memories of Japan's conduct in World War II and before profoundly shaped its postwar security planning and engagement with its neighbors and global security institutions. These memories have also led to powerful political constituencies in Japan's democracy such as the Japan Association of the War Bereaved (Izokukai) and the survivors of the atomic bombings (*hibakusha*) and activist Japanese on both sides of the debate over Japan's school textbook descriptions of Japan's wartime and colonial past.

One would expect challenges in arriving at a postwar settlement of a war that caused tens of millions of deaths and ended with atomic bombings of two major cities—but few would have expected that seventy years after the end of the war many issues central to concluding the hostilities would remain unresolved. By 2006, and indeed by 2016, Japan still had not even concluded a peace treaty with neighbors Russia and North Korea (then a Japanese colony); nor had it resolved outstanding territorial disputes connected with small but arguably strategic outlying islands with *all* its close neighbors: Russia, Korea, China, and Taiwan.[42] That these issues linger into the twenty-first century cannot but be seen as a failure in Japanese diplomacy and domestic politics and a significant shaper of Japan's security policy in the contemporary era.

This is not to say that progress has not been made—but reaching a postwar settlement of Japan's militarist past has been uneven across space and time to say the least. Even with Japan's closest ally and a country whose citizens overwhelmingly describe friendly feelings toward Japan today, there is a lack of common understanding and reconciliation of pivotal issues related to World War II, from Pearl Harbor and Hiroshima to POWs and kamikaze fighters.[43]

Thomas Berger usefully categorizes government policy related to historical reconciliation into five areas: "rhetoric (i.e., how political leaders talk about the past), commemoration (museums, monuments, holidays, etc.), education (especially school textbooks), compensation (policies aiming to help victims of past injustices), and punishment (both of perpetrators of injustice as well as policies that restrict freedom of speech and organization)."[44] Compensation and punishment were the focus of initial efforts at addressing Japan's wartime responsibility with victims of Japanese militarism. Punishment was dictated initially by Allied occupation authorities and then by the Tokyo Tribunals held from 1946 to 1948.[45] The designations from the tribunal of Class A, Class B, and Class C war criminals remain in the contemporary lexicon of those following Japanese security issues because of the enshrinement of fourteen Class A war criminals at Yasukuni Shrine in Tokyo, which commemorates Japan's war dead and has become a potent symbol of Japan's war remembrance. The museum of Japan's wartime past adjacent to the shrine is also frequently evoked in a critical way related to Japan's commemoration of its wartime past. These are just two of many examples of how issues related to Japan's manner of addressing its wartime past continue to occupy media headlines in the present—which undermines the contemporary message the Japanese government seeks to convey about the proactive contributions to peace it desires to make in the region and globally. The education area is another, with Japan's descriptions of its wartime policies and actions in school textbooks providing another source of tension between Japan and neighbors China and South Korea in particular.

Japan concluded the San Francisco Peace Treaty with the United States and several US allies in May 1951 as the first formal effort at compensation for Japan's victims, but numerous states that were victim to Japan's wartime actions were not present at this conference. Korea, a former Japanese colony, was not allowed to participate as only a semi-sovereign state at that point and in the midst of fighting a civil war. China also was not represented because of Cold War politics after the mainland "went red" in 1949, though Taiwan concluded a separate peace treaty with Japan in 1952 under US encouragement. The Soviet Union also refused to participate in the San Francisco conference. Nevertheless, Article 14 of the San Francisco Treaty awarded all Japanese overseas assets, both public and private, as reparations to the countries in which they were located, including, retroactively, to China and South Korea (despite their not being signatories to the treaty). Berger values these assets at approximately $25 billion in 1945; moreover, he writes, "The Japanese government agreed to pay an additional $1 billion to the countries it had occupied between 1941 and 1945 (Burma, Indonesia, the Philippines, and Vietnam). . . . In addition, under Article 16 of the treaty, the Japanese government agreed to pay $16 million to the International Committee of the Red Cross to help compensate former Allied prisoners of war."[46] This latter point continues to resonate today, as former POWs were not compensated directly. The first major Japanese company to apologize for use of POW labor during the war did so in August 2015.[47] Still in 2015 litigation was pending related to this issue in courts around the world, including in the United States, South Korea, and China.

Japan began formal negotiations for a postwar settlement with South Korea after the cease-fire of the Korean War in 1953—which also ended without a peace treaty (to this day)—but negotiations dragged on until successful conclusion in 1965. Japan was effectively prohibited from negotiating a peace treaty with mainland China until US president Richard Nixon's dramatic opening to China in 1971 but took quick advantage of that diplomatic turn, arriving at a joint communiqué on normalizing relations with China in 1972 and a formal peace treaty in 1978. In both cases, South Korea in 1965 and China in 1978, leaders of those countries renounced war reparations from both public and private Japanese actors and issued statements indicating a preference to focus on the future.[48]

As political leaders changed in these states (and as South Korea democratized), however, this preference did not hold.[49] In 2015, leaders from both states pressed Japan for compensation for wartime conduct and criticized its failure to address this issue in the past—despite their plainly stated renunciations of reparations in the peace treaties. Scholars have attributed this change of heart to multiple factors, including the power asymmetry between the states at the time of the treaties, the changing views of the top political leadership (including the move toward democracy in the case of South Korea), and the political points scored domestically from perceived toughness on Japan in recent years.

Japan still has not formally concluded a peace treaty with Russia, nor a formal agreement on reconciliation for Japan's past actions—initially due to early conflicts over Russia's harsh treatment of Japanese POWs at the conclusion of the war and then to Cold War politics and, in later years, to the territorial dispute over the Northern Territories. Similarly, Japan has not reached a postwar settlement with North Korea, despite concluding one with South Korea in 1965. In the post–Cold War period, North Korea's nuclear weapons development and testing and the issue of North Korea's abduction of Japanese citizens during the Cold War and failure to fully account for their fate have stalled progress toward a lasting peace.

In recent years, Prime Minister Abe is often associated with drawing Japan's past conduct into contemporary debates about Japanese security policy, but many Japanese prime ministers were challenged to confront Japan's past as they sought to craft new policies for postwar Japan. Prime Minister Nobusuke Kishi managed to satisfy the Australian political leadership with a terse general statement of "heartfelt sorrow for what occurred in the war" during his visit to Australia and Southeast Asia in the late 1950s—but still met with substantial media criticism and public protest on each leg of his trip.[50] Prime Minister Kakuei Tanaka faced intense anti-Japanese demonstrations in Jakarta and Bangkok during his visit to Southeast Asia in 1974. "In response to the 1974 anti-Japanese movements in Southeast Asia," states the 2015 Advisory Panel report on history to Prime Minister Abe, "Prime Minister Takeo Fukuda announced the 'Fukuda Doctrine,' which expressed Japan's determination not to become a military power, as well as its willingness to establish a 'heart-to-heart diplomacy' of mutual confidence and trust with Southeast Asia."[51] Prime Minister Yasuhiro Nakasone faced substantial criticism both abroad and at home in the 1980s for his role in expanding Japanese defense capabilities, including closer coordination with US military forces.

The post–Cold War era offered new geopolitical space for Japan to engage in international contributions to global peace and security as well as new expectations given Japan's higher economic status. In addition, as a coincidence in timing, Japan's wartime emperor, Hirohito, died in 1989, leading some Japanese with memories of the war to speak more frankly about their experiences after the emperor under whom they had served had died.[52] In 1999, the respected publisher Bungeishunjū even reissued a contemporary report of the controversial Rape of Nanjing that had been published as a book in 1938 but immediately banned by Japanese censors at the time.[53]

The 1990s also included the marking of the fiftieth anniversary of the end of the war and a brief period in Japan's domestic politics during which the LDP lost control over the Diet. These two factors contributed to a string of new public apologies and other efforts by Japan to address its militarist past. In August 1993, Chief Cabinet Secretary Yōhei Kōnō issued the first public Japanese government statement of remorse to the so-called comfort women. (The text of this statement is provided in appendix 3.) In conjunction with the statement, the Asian Women's Fund was established to make "atonement payments" to former comfort women, most of whom (apart from Japanese women) came from Korea, though women from a number of other states in the region and beyond were also victimized. The public-private nature of the fund—despite its pairing with a letter of apology from the Japanese prime minister—

was widely criticized in South Korea, which led to few publicly known recipients of atonement money by South Korean women, though some women from other states (in particular, the Philippines) chose to receive such monies and the apology letter.[54]

Days after the Kōnō statement was issued in August 1993, the LDP briefly lost power to an unwieldy coalition of opposition parties. The new prime minister, Morihiro Hosokawa, issued a new apology for Japan's wartime conduct, though members of his cabinet rejected it.[55] Among the contentious issues was one that was also prominent in media coverage leading up to the seventieth anniversary statement by Prime Minister Abe: whether Japan was an "aggressor" in the war. At the time of the fiftieth anniversary of the end of World War II, only a little over half of Japanese agreed in public opinion polling that Japan was an aggressor.[56] The statement by Prime Minister Tomiichi Murayama at the fiftieth anniversary of the war's end was widely described as a watershed apology—though not without its critics, both from abroad and at home. Within the Diet there was not sufficient support for Murayama's views to have the language of the Murayama statement reflected in the Diet resolution marking the anniversary of the end of the war. The brevity and much more vague language of the Diet resolution is evident. (The text of both statements is provided in appendix 3.)

By the time of the sixtieth anniversary of the end of the war, Japan's relations with China and South Korea had experienced a significant downturn under Prime Minister Koizumi, due in no small part to his repeated annual visits to Yasukuni Shrine, the first prime minister to do so since Prime Minister Nakasone in the mid-1980s. Koizumi apologized for Japan's wartime conduct during his visit to Yasukuni Shrine in 2001 and later in his sixtieth anniversary statement to mark the end of the war (provided in appendix 3), but such words did not erase the feelings held by many abroad (and some at home) that his words were undercut by his conduct. Koizumi's foreign minister, Makiko Tanaka, also reaffirmed the "deep remorse" and "heartfelt apology" of the Murayama statement at the fiftieth anniversary commemoration of the signing of the San Francisco Peace Treaty in September 2001, as have numerous foreign ministers and other government officials before and after her.[57]

That all these expressions of remorse, combined with Japan's indisputably restrained security policies of the postwar era, did not lead to reconciliation between Japan and the victims of Japanese conduct prior to and during World War II thus deserves further consideration—and in fact has been the focus of a substantial amount of scholarly research since the 1990s. One collective finding of the research is that, in a sense, there is not just one legacy of Japanese militarism on the postwar period but many—for each of the countries or areas Japan invaded or whose soldiers or civilians Japan engaged with. Thomas Berger argues in his 2012 study, "Japan's apologies have been limited in scope, challenged domestically, and singularly unsuccessful in improving Japan's relations with its Asian neighbors,"[58] but clearly there has been more success with Asian states further afield and with European and American victims. Prime Minister Abe's 2015 Advisory Panel on History also describes Japan's efforts at reconciliation as more successful with states further from Japan.[59]

Jennifer Lind argues in her work *Sorry States*, meanwhile, that many states have created positive new relationships without undergoing a round of apologies for past negative encounters. Moreover, she demonstrates in her research both the potential dangers of expressing contrition to a country's international politics as well as the negative effect such actions can have on a country's domestic politics.[60] Brad Glosserman and Scott Snyder illustrate both these potential pitfalls in their examination of recent Japan–South Korea relations.[61]

Lind's offering of the postwar US-Japan relationship as a compelling example is relevant also to the context of this book: the development of a forward-looking postwar relationship between Japan and the United States, including a security alliance, preceded any systematic set of apologies from Japan to the United States for specific conduct (such as the surprise attack at Pearl Harbor or treatment of American POWs); moreover, the United States has refrained from any sort of official apology for civilian deaths caused by the atomic bombings or for the even greater number of deaths caused by indiscriminate firebombings of dozens of Japanese cities. That both the Japanese government and Japanese firms have begun to address some of these outstanding issues in recent years can be seen as an indication of the security renaissance under way in the past decade, including a recrafting of long-standing historical legacies in response to new concerns.

Despite all these challenges (and quite a few self-inflicted wounds), Japan nevertheless did build substantial military forces over the course of the six decades since the end of World War II considered in this chapter and also began to play a greater international security role, more or less in the same period—the 1990s and early years of the subsequent decade—that demonstrations and protests over Japan's lack of sufficient apologies and contrition boomed. Sixty years after defeat, however, this issue had become only one of three major historical legacies to affect the twenty-first-century development of Japan's security posture; two new legacies would emerge in the postwar period and continue to shape Japan's security renaissance in the present.

A New Postwar Legacy of Antimilitarism

Concerns about Japan's prewar and wartime conduct in the early postwar years prompted the creation of a counterlegacy in the ensuing years: the postwar historical legacy of antimilitarism. This legacy was created and strengthened over the course of the seventy years of the postwar period and continues to be reified into new policies[62]—such as Japan's first formal national security strategy in December 2013. Yet Japan possesses substantial military capabilities for a state described as antimilitarist. The antimilitarist aspect of Japan's postwar security identity is important for understanding the evolution of Japanese security policy but can be overstated to suggest that it is only recently that Japan has played an important role on its own and in regional security. Still, these antimilitarist concerns did impose important constraints; they were not just rhetorical conceits.

Seventy years after the end of World War II, Japan's prime minister was still expected to reassure the world about Japan's postwar record and future intentions. In seeking to provide this reassurance, Abe's Advisory Panel on the History of the Twentieth Century underscores the robust antimilitarist legacy that has been created in postwar Japan, writing, "Japan has never once sought to pursue its self-interests through military action. Constant opposition to changing territories, etc. by force anywhere in the world is a sentiment that has been broadly shared and deeply ingrained among the Japanese people in post-war

Japan, and has been consistently embodied in policies of the Japanese government."[63]

Contestation over the content of Japan's postwar security identity of "domestic antimilitarism" has been an enduring facet of postwar Japan, experiencing ebbs and flows in line with substantial changes in Japan's domestic and international environment—despite continuity in the core principles upon which the identity is based.[64] This identity has been defined by three central tenets that were vigorously negotiated and contested in the period leading up to their codification around 1960 and that continue to be contested by some political actors in Japan today. They are (1) Japan will possess no traditional armed forces, (2) there will be no use of force by Japan except in self-defense, and (3) no Japanese participation in foreign wars.[65]

It is important to note that this domestic antimilitarism has never been a pacifist security identity in that it explicitly incorporates some role for a postwar military and also embeds Japan in a military alliance with the United States (including under the US nuclear umbrella). Both these aspects—*some* postwar military forces and a defense treaty with the United States—were opposed by many Japanese in the postwar period but have become widely accepted characteristics of Japanese security policy today.

In the Cold War period, two major political party actors engaged in extended negotiation and contestation over Japan's security policies. The LDP, the ruling party from 1955 through the end of the Cold War, contained members who actively sought for Japan to reemerge as a major military power, outspoken nationalists and historical revisionists (including the grandfather of Prime Minister Abe, Nobusuke Kishi, who also served as prime minister from 1957 to 1960). A majority within the party, however, sought a middle ground rooted in the security identity of domestic antimilitarism and in the US-Japan security alliance. The main opposition party, the JSP, was the flag bearer for a pacifist Japan that would not maintain any military forces (even the euphemistically named, in their view, Self-Defense Forces) and would not engage in an alliance relationship with the United States. The JSP also sought to deepen Japan's relationship with its neighbors (including communist China, North Korea, and the Soviet Union). In the middle of this period, a third party emerged, the religious-affiliated Kōmei Party, which also advocated a peace-loving agenda but expressed somewhat more conservative economic policies than the socialists and which also remained as part of the opposition.[66] Consistent and substantial voter support of opposition parties in the Cold War period greatly limited the evolution of Japan's strategic culture toward a more active military posture.

Contemporary Japanese politics resembles the Cold War era of party-based division over security policy, but the mainstream debate is no longer characterized by the extreme poles of either rejecting or accepting the very idea of the JSDF and the US-Japan alliance. Indeed, the party best known for advocating the one extreme, the JSP, is no longer a major political party in contemporary Japan. Rather, political debate over issues central to Japanese security in the past several decades has been largely about the *boundaries* of the hegemonic security identity of domestic antimilitarism, not about the core principles themselves.[67] In the latter part of the period examined in this chapter, Japanese security policy has deviated from long-standing practices in a number of areas but only to a very limited degree. For example, the JSDF was dispatched in groups of a few hundred at a time to Iraq to contribute to the US-led coalition to stabilize Iraq, but only in nonmilitary roles (and protected by the militaries of other states). In addition, strict arms export restrictions were relaxed to allow for joint production of some weapons with the United States (such as missile defense and fighter aircraft) but transfer to third parties was prohibited. This period also saw the JCG and JMSDF respond more directly to incursions into Japan's territorial waters and airspace. In these and other cases, the Cold War–era pattern of the majority party (LDP) pushing for relaxation of long-standing limitations on Japan's military forces and the minority parties (more recently led by the DPJ) initially opposing the plans but ultimately settling for a compromise remained.

In the past decade, however, the long-standing role of political parties in the process of maintaining and contesting Japan's security identity has changed. This important aspect of Japan's security renaissance is the subject of chapters 4 and 5, which examine the period of turmoil of the "twisted Diet" (2007–2012) and under the second Abe government (2012–present). In both periods, the findings from earlier work on the effect of security identity on policy making are confirmed: "policy initiatives that conform to existing interpretation of the security identity of domestic antimilitarism should proceed quickly and be relatively unhindered, absent other intervening factors such as bureaucratic politics, alliance politics, or personal executive leadership effectiveness," while "policy initiatives that conflict with the existing interpretation of the security identity should take more time, require extensive use of political capital, and often necessitate substantial political concessions to the initial intent of the policy in order to proceed."[68] However, the extent of political capital required to enact policy contrary to the security identity seems to be declining in comparison with earlier periods, and further policy initiatives in this direction appear to be forthcoming—issues discussed in greater detail in chapters 4 and 5.

The Complex Postwar Legacy of the U.S.-Japan Security Alliance

That the United States was central to the development of Japan's postwar security policies is undisputed and widely known,[69] but the complex nature of that role is often underappreciated or misunderstood on both sides of the Pacific.[70] At its core, the alliance is a trade of protection (of Japan) for bases (for the United States in Japan)—it is not a trade of like things and thus is by its nature unequal. Beyond the specific terms of the security treaty, however, the complex relationship deeply influenced both the shape of Japan's postwar military forces (as the shield to the American sword) and the way in which Japan's military power was perceived by Japan's neighbors given its integration (or, as some viewed it, containment) within the US-Japan alliance.

This complex relationship continues, and continues to shape Japan's security renaissance in numerous ways large and small. Still, while discussion and modest steps toward reconceptualizing the alliance into a regional and global partnership in practice were apparent by the period discussed in this chapter, the implementation of a transformation of the alliance into a truly regional and global partnership has begun to be implemented only in the past decade, as signified in particular by the new 2015 US-Japan Guidelines for Defense Cooperation and the passage of a package of security legislation in the Diet in September 2015 to implement one of the most important parts of the new guidelines, CSD operations of the JSDF overseas.

Despite what many Americans see as a "free ride" that Japan got in the postwar period by allying with the United States,[71] many Japanese on both the left and the right either outright opposed or expressed mixed feelings about the alliance from the very start of Japan's return to independence after the end of the seven-year postwar military occupation led by the United States. This opposition or ambivalence continued to be expressed by some throughout the postwar period. The security relationship between the two states was not even routinely referred to as an "alliance" (*dōmei*) until after the Cold War had ended; numerous politicians and other officials were publicly chastised—or even fired—for doing so previously.

Many on the left viewed the alliance as a negative, militarizing influence that ran counter to mainstream public will and at times even undermined Japan's postwar democracy. In the 1950s and 1960s, it was widely believed by the left that the United States provided covert funding for the LDP, which reduced votes for the JSP in national elections and perpetuated the dominance of a conservative elite beholden to US interests—rumors confirmed in the post–Cold War era by declassified documents and interviews granted by numerous Americans who were conduits for such support.[72] Even apart from such rumors, those opposed to participation of wartime-era conservatives in the postwar government blamed the United States for the Cold War–inspired "reverse course" of the occupation that led to the release from prison of numerous suspected war criminals, including Nobusuke Kishi (who was being held as a suspect for Class A war crimes as the former minister of munitions in the Tōjō cabinet), who would later become the prime minister who rammed through the passage of the new US-Japan Security Treaty by questionable practices in 1960.[73] Most broadly, many on the left saw the United States as dragging Japan into a cold war with the Soviet Union in which they believed Japan could remain neutral under different political leadership.

Conservatives also saw a deepening alliance with the United States as problematic. Some chafed at the long-term—seemingly permanent—presence of US troops on Japanese soil; others at having to parrot what they saw as a mistaken narrative of what led to the war and Japan's defeat (the museum connected to Yasukuni Shrine presents a quite different narrative more palatable to those conservatives); still others objected to the increasing "interoperability" between US and Japanese military forces as an erosion of Japanese autonomy.[74] Moreover, naturally it was the United States that disarmed Japan in the first place and imposed through the occupation countless other reforms that political conservatives found objectionable—and that conservatives today in Japan are still seeking to reverse. Article Nine of the postwar constitution is one long-standing target, but there is a range of other issues such as removal of "patriotic education" from school curricula and the relegation of the status of the emperor to only a "symbol" of the state. The LDP's "draft constitution" circulated to the general public to garner support in 2012 shows the persistence of political conservatives' efforts to reverse occupation reforms even after over half a century.[75]

Conservatives did address some of their concerns vis-à-vis US-imposed reforms after the occupation ended, such as rehabilitating some political figures prohibited by the occupation forces to serve in elected office (including Nobusuke Kishi) and greatly reducing the "footprint" of US bases on the main Japanese islands (leading to today's concentration of US forces on Okinawa). Later successes include the reversion of administrative control of Okinawa to Japan in 1972 and the buildup in military capabilities in the 1980s. The 2015 Advisory Panel on History to the Abe government reflected on the importance of such policy successes vis-à-vis US-Japan relations, writing, "The fact that Okinawa remained under US occupation was perceived as a symbol, which left people with an impression that the relationship between Japan and the United States was not an alliance but rather a relationship of the defeated and the victor, respectively."[76]

Despite these many concerns of both the left and the right about a long-term alliance relationship with the United States, the alliance—and broader US-Japan relations, which exist well beyond just the formal military alliance—provided enough positive benefits to be championed by the ruling party and sustained through decades of challenges. The alliance allowed Japan to spend less on its military than it otherwise would have and limited political confrontation at home and abroad related to Japan's reemergence as a global actor in the postwar era. Given Japan's alliance with the United States, Japan was able to resume an international role in the early postwar period that was entirely nonmilitary, allowing Japan decades of interactions with its neighbors and other great powers in economic, cultural, and diplomatic arenas to rebrand Japan's international reputation. Despite opposition to the alliance in particular from the pacifist left, it is ironic that essentially owing to the alliance Japan has not sent its military forces into combat abroad since Japan's surrender in 1945—a feat achieved by no other major state in the world over such an extended period.

One central dynamic of the complex security relationship in the postwar period was over dual concerns of abandonment or entrapment: on the one hand, Japanese feared that in the case of an actual attack on Japan, the United States would not come to Japan's aid as promised (abandonment); on the other hand, Japanese feared that because of its military alliance with the United States Japan would get drawn into regional or global conflicts that it otherwise could avoid (entrapment).[77] Here two central provisions of the 1960 security treaty still in effect are important to understand: Article Five of the security treaty provides for the immediate defense of Japan (including areas administered by Japan but the subject of territorial disputes), while Article Six states that a coequal goal of the treaty is the maintenance of international peace and security in the Far East and that US troops and equipment located on bases in Japan can be used for that purpose.[78] In short, some Japanese fear abandonment of Article Five obligations while others fear entrapment from Article Six obligations. By contrast, the United States has at times feared entrapment by Article Five—being drawn into a Japan-China military conflict over the Senkaku Islands, for example—and abandonment by Article Six, Japan's prohibiting US engagement in a regional conflict from bases located in Japan. During the Cold War, Japan's deepening military cooperation with the United States to contain the Soviet naval threat was downplayed to the public in part because of its antimilitarist legacy but also owing to widespread Japanese public concern of Japan's being entrapped by what they feared as US Cold War–era adventurism.

Another central dynamic of the complex postwar relationship was the security-economic linkage; in particular, growing US concerns about Japan's rising economic power and the implications this had for US industry and the related view that Japan was not contributing enough to the military aspects of the alliance.[79] In the United States such concerns were widely known among the US public, fueling the belief that Japan made few military contributions to the alliance and that Japan was getting a "free ride"—and, indeed, Japan did spend much less on defense as a percentage of GDP than did the United States and most NATO allies during the Cold War. In Japan, the general public was well aware of US demands for Japan to do more—to contribute more money to alliance maintenance (such as the so-called sympathy budget Japan created in 1978 under US pressure to offset the cost of US forces based in Japan[80]) and for the JSDF to play greater roles within the alliance framework and to develop greater capabilities.

This complex dynamic of asymmetric concerns and unmet expectations on both sides continued into the post–Cold War period, even though Japan's contributions to the alliance greatly increased despite its relative power being on the decline as its economy stagnated for first one then two decades in the period while China and other states in the region grew robustly. The 1990s required Japan and the United States to recraft the alliance, since the primary threat the alliance had been envisioned to counter, the Soviet Union, had literally ceased to exist. Other threats remained (including from Russia), however, and new threats were emerging in the post–Cold War world. As a result and after several years of study, the alliance was reimagined for the post–Cold War order under the same security treaty but under new US-Japan Guidelines for Defense Cooperation adopted in 1997.

The evolution of the US-Japan alliance, and the complex nature of the relationship overall, can be viewed through the lens of the development and evolution of these guidelines, first published in 1978. This planning document sets out specific roles and missions for US and Japanese military forces both in peacetime and in the event of a military emergency at a level of detail not publicly seen in other US alliances, even among NATO allies. The 1978 guidelines marked a turning point in the security relationship toward what increasingly came to be seen as—and publicly referred to as—an alliance. The 1997 revision of the guidelines to reshape the alliance in order to respond to the challenges of the post–Cold War world greatly influenced the development of Japan's defense institutions and capabilities. The jump from the 1997 guidelines to the 2015 guidelines are another indication of the security renaissance taking place in Japan today, as outlined in chapter 5.

Elements introduced in the 1997 guidelines continue to resonate in Japan's security debates in the contemporary period and therefore should be noted here. The April 1996 Joint Declaration on Security that paved the way for new 1997 guidelines expressed concern over a "regional contingency" (shūhen jitai) such as on the Korean Peninsula or related to Taiwan and set out the concept that the guidelines were concerned with "situations in areas surrounding Japan" (SIASJ, pronounced "sigh-es-jay" in Washington and Tokyo circles); it would no longer be the case that the JSDF was purely for the defense of Japan within its own territorial space, while US forces would use bases in Japan for other security contingencies in the region acting on their own. Japanese political leadership at the time steadfastly refused to specify the exact boundaries of this "area"[81]—which subsequent to the guidelines' being adopted was applied as far away as the Indian Ocean.[82]

Another issue central to the guideline revision in 1997 was the status of US forces in Okinawa. The concentration of US forces on that small island and their proximity and influence on the local population were major concerns expressed by residents of Okinawa at the time,[83] ones that still present significant challenges to the US-Japan relationship. This issue further complicates the complex legacy of the US-Japan postwar relationship because it essentially adds a third party to the relationship—that is, one must view "Japan" through the lenses of "Tokyo" and "Okinawa."

By the end of this period, and on the eve of what would emerge as Japan's security renaissance, the US-Japan relationship exhibited record levels of security cooperation and was widely reported to be on a trajectory for further deepening in the short term. The Bush-Koizumi years (2001–2006) were a time of unprecedented cooperation in the alliance—including Japan's first dispatch of the JSDF to provide support for combat operations of other military forces overseas (though, importantly, Japan's logistical support was not framed in this way—but it is effectively what the JSDF was doing, on a very limited scale and with many restrictions). The JMSDF was dispatched to the Indian Ocean to provide fuel for, first, US military vessels and then for vessels of other countries working together in an ad hoc US-led coalition to fight terrorism around Afghanistan. Personnel and equipment of the JMSDF and JASDF also provided limited support for US operations around Iraq, and then, from 2004 to 2006, the JGSDF was dispatched to Iraq in limited numbers to provide humanitarian and reconstruction assistance within Iraq.[84] JSDF officers have been stationed at US Central Command in Tampa, Florida, since 2001—a development unimaginable a decade prior. These developments thus form an important step in Japan's gradual awakening to respond militarily to regional and global security concerns.

Still, many limitations on the JSDF remained in this period and were the subject of heated debates in the Diet and in the broader public sphere. Public opinion was firmly against the deployment of the JGSDF to Iraq, which was achieved in no small part because of the leadership and high popularity of Prime Minister Koizumi (not unlike what Prime Minister Abe would later achieve in 2013–2015). Once troops were dispatched despite the public opposition, support for the operation grew— based, it would seem, in part on a rally 'round the flag effect but also on the many restrictions put on JSDF operations in Iraq (including having to be protected by the military forces of other states given the severe restrictions placed on JSDF use of weapons).[85] Thus, while the legacy of the US-Japan alliance did push Japan further than it had gone before, the competing postwar legacy of antimilitarism continued to exert a strong countervailing influence on Japan's security policy evolution in this period.[86]

The Bush-Koizumi alliance deepening ended with the 2006 "roadmap for the future," which envisioned a new stage that, if implemented (as is beginning to take place presently), would reflect what this book calls Japan's security renaissance. Numerous points of this "roadmap" were at least partly implemented in the past decade and its future cemented in new US-Japan Guidelines for Defense Cooperation adopted by the two states in April 2015.

In sum, over the course of half a century, Japan's military capabilities have expanded and the United States and Japan have engaged in more joint missions and training, but the imbalance in the alliance remains, and remains a political touchstone in Japan. The rise of the DPJ to power in 2009 brought these long-simmering (and sometimes boiling) concerns to a head once again. Despite the return to LDP rule from 2012 to the present, and the again growing closeness in the alliance under the new 2015 guidelines, the complexity of the relationship remains, and remains a major long-term shaper of Japan's security renaissance.

This chapter has discussed how Japan's postwar security policies gradually evolved in "pre-Renaissance" Japan—a period in which certainly Japan's military capabilities rose steadily, its contributions to regional and global security emerged and expanded, and a broader societal discussion began in the post–Cold War period on whether Japan's long-standing postwar security policies were appropriate for Japan's future. The endpoint of these discussions, however, and resulting constraints on Japan's military capabilities and roles outside Japan were firmly rooted in the postwar continuities influenced by the three postwar historical legacies discussed in this chapter, and in particular the postwar legacy of antimilitarism.

Japan has now entered a new period. This period has been sparked by significant changes in Japan's strategic environment, including the declining relative power of Japan vis-à-vis other actors. The next chapter explains how a changed international strategic environment has contributed to a new phase of domestic political contestation and policies in relation to Japan's appropriate military posture. The remaining chapters then examine how this changed international environment has already contributed to new security practices in the years following the political leadership of Prime Minister Koizumi, including the first administration of Shinzō Abe (2006–2007), the three years of DPJ rule (2009–2012), and in the second Abe administration (2012–present).

CHAPTER THREE

Japan's Relative Decline and New Security Challenges in a Multipolar Asia

Japan's regional environment has shifted more dramatically in the past decade than generally conveyed with common descriptors like China's rise, the North Korea threat, or a power shift in Asia. These catchphrases are accurate but stress continuities over several decades—Chinese economic growth, North Korean military provocations, the economic and military growth of other East Asian states—rather than significant milestones and "game changers" since 2006. There have been many such game changers, however, and Japanese are well aware of them. Japanese media and political campaigns regularly debate issues such as the scale of China's rise and how Japan should respond, the pros and cons of restarting nuclear power reactors to address Japan's spike in energy imports after the March 2011 tsunami and nuclear disaster, how to most effectively address the growing nuclear, missile, and other threats posed by North Korea, and how to tackle the challenges of Japan's population decline in recent years as part of what demographers call a super-aging society. Japan's security renaissance is driven, in part, by these debates over appropriate responses to Japan's relative decline in Asia.

China's economic size has nearly *tripled* since 2006. In 2010, China surpassed Japan to become the world's second-largest economy, a significant psychological milestone for citizens of both states. North Korean military provocations escalated beyond testing missiles and nuclear weapons (which also continued) to provocative military operations in this period, with the sinking of a South Korea submarine and shelling of a South Korean border island, under the direction of a new and little known third-generation dynastic leader who was only twenty-nine years old when he assumed power in 2011. South Korea, Australia, and ASEAN as a regional unit all significantly increased their regional security engagement in this period as well, indicating a move away from the China-Japan regional rivalry apparent since the 1990s toward a more complex, multiactor regional economic and security environment. In 2011, the United States announced a recommitment to the region through a multifaceted strategy to "rebalance" US diplomatic, economic, and military assets to the region. In 2012, total defense spending in the Asian region as a whole (including beyond East Asia) surpassed the next-highest region, Europe, for the first time—$287.4 billion for Asia versus $259 billion for Europe—accounting for 20 percent of total defense expenditures in the world.[1] Spending on defense has continued to rise in the region since then, with Chinese increases as the principal driver of the total reported increase. According to a 2014 report by the Stockholm International Peace Research Institute (SIPRI), "Military spending in Asia and Oceania increased by 5 per cent in 2014 and by 62 per cent between 2005 and 2014, reaching $439 billion in 2014 at current prices and exchange rates. . . . In 2014 the growth of 9.7 per cent in China's expenditure dominated the regional trend, with the overall increase in the rest of the region standing at just 1.2 per cent."[2]

Japan's evolving international environment interacts with Japan's domestic politics and conceptions of its security identity in a dynamic fashion. It is not simply that a changing international environment directly leads to security policy change in Japan. Japan's security renaissance is sparked by Japan's changing interpretation of its security needs and perceived efficacy of different approaches to security in a shifting world—in particular Japan's declining relative power in relation to China and other regional actors, the persistence and escalation of the North Korean and Chinese military threats, and a global shift toward more cooperative security practices via formal institutions, expanded "minilateralism," and globalized production networks. These regional and global changes have inspired new thinking in Japan that roots Japan's security in an expanded regional and global contribution—including through an expanded US-Japan alliance and new security partnerships with other regional actors. Changing international conditions thus interact with domestic conceptions of security identity and also alter the domestic political landscape. These domestic effects of a changed international environment are examined in chapters 4 and 5.

This chapter describes the changed regional and global security environment Japan's leaders and citizens have perceived since 2006, and begins to discuss how Japan's security renaissance can be seen in new Japanese security policies and practices in the region. Further examination of Japan's changing security policies and practices of the past decade follow in chapters 4 and 5, linking more explicitly the interaction between a changing international environment and changing domestic politics at home.

In response to the perception of an increasingly insecure region, Japanese security planners have crafted a three-tiered response: (1) increase Japan's own military capabilities, including by reforming the legal framework and strategic deployment limiting the use of these forces; (2) deepen security cooperation and planning within the existing US-Japan alliance framework, including formal revision of the US-Japan Guidelines for Defense Cooperation; and (3) seek new security partners in the region, both friendly states and multilateral institutions.[3]

China's new behavior and resources mark the most dramatic change in this period but represent only one of many changes Japanese security policies have sought to address. There is a rising economic prosperity in the region overall, leading to a relative decline of Japan economically and militarily—though in both areas Japan remains a regional giant. This is a striking change from the time Japan entered into the 1951 Mutual Defense Treaty, when only the United States and Japan could be seen as important regional actors, with the Soviet Union about to emerge as a third.

The same sort of old and new regional security concerns discussed in chapter 2 continue to challenge Japan's security, but several are growing more severe and perceived as more immediate, such as the possibility of unprovoked military action by North Korea against Japan and the dramatically escalated territorial dispute with China over the Senkaku Islands that many Japanese believe could lead to a Chinese military attack. Moreover, Japan's resource dependence spiked after the devastating tsunami of March 2011 and resulting meltdown at the Fukushima nuclear power plant led to a shutdown of all fifty-three of Japan's nuclear power reactors. Oil and gas imports rose sharply as a result, shifting Japan's trade balance into a deficit for the first time since the early postwar years. The huge increase in oil and gas imports deepened Japan's concerns over vulnerable shipping routes through the contested South China Sea and pirate-prone coastline near the Gulf of Aden and heightened awareness of Japan's resource dependence among the general public.

The US rebalance to Asia is another shift that Japan's security planners have sought to adapt to, largely by following a similar strategy. Japan's rebalance in this period involves a deepening of the US-Japan alliance and expansion of security partners in the region.

Rising Regional Prosperity and the Relative Decline of Japan

Japan is no longer the standout economic giant with an anomalously diminutive military posture. Rather, it is a long-stagnating state with rising security challenges and significant future challenges facing its domestic economy and society. Meanwhile, across the region—well beyond China—states are experiencing robust economic growth, a growing middle class, and rising military spending as a result. The security environment is therefore getting more complex as more states have grown into middle-income states and completed a first phase of postindependence state formation. While China's increased military-related activities in the region have driven Japan's recent expansion of JSDF and JCG capabilities and roles, Japan also perceives independently a national interest in helping to shape and create linkages with the growing military infrastructure developing across Southeast Asia, Oceania, and South Asia. For example, Japan has an interest in shaping codes of conduct to avoid unintentional escalation or accidents at sea and to promote personal ties with growing officer corps of regional states through educational exchanges and joint exercises. Japan actively promotes following the rule of law in its diplomacy, which includes a stress on international law of the sea. While China and others often describe such behavior as "balancing" China, the reality is much more nuanced. Moreover, apart from the strictly military balance and security concerns in the region, Japan's economic decline

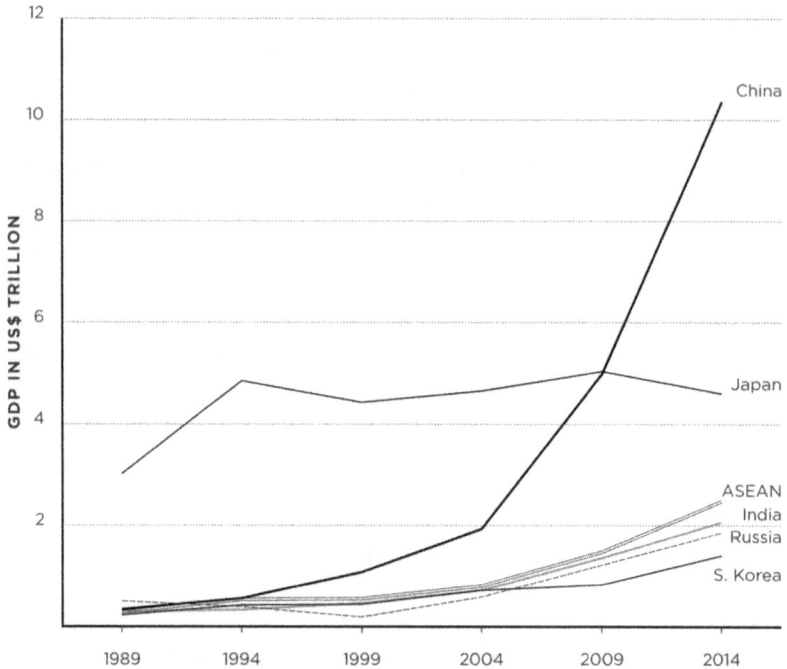

FIGURE 3.1 Japan's GDP in comparison with its neighbors, 1989–2014. World Bank, *World Development Indicators*, http://wdi.worldbank.org/table/1.1.

relative to other states in the region also has security implications for Japan—both directly and psychologically.

Figure 3.1 shows Japan's GDP size relative to its neighbors since 1989 in five-year increments. In 1989, Japan's was the second-largest economy in the world, after the United States. Its GDP of just over $3 trillion was almost twice the *combined* GDP of China, Russia, India, South Korea, and all ten ASEAN countries. In 2014, China's GDP alone was over twice that of Japan's and the remaining economies combined were about 70 percent larger than Japan's. The Japanese economy is still well over twice the size of the Russian or Indian economies (in real terms, not using PPP) and almost twice the size of the combined ASEAN economies, and Japan's per capita income is vastly higher than that of any of these states. However, all these economies have been growing faster than Japan's economy and are likely to continue to do so (except, perhaps,

Japan's Relative Decline and New Security Challenges

Russia), further narrowing the economic gap between Japan and its neighbors.

The growth burst from 2004 to 2014 is especially striking—with China leading the way by far, but total ASEAN GDP also doubling in this ten-year period and South Korea's GDP increasing by over 50 percent. By contrast, Japan's economy in this period declined in dollar terms. In yen terms, the Japanese economy has been more or less stagnant for the past two decades—with recent modest growth offset by a decline in the value of the yen relative to the dollar (a decline that also complicates multiyear comparisons of Japanese military spending, as we will see later in this chapter). Looking over a longer, twenty-year period, from 1994 to 2014, Japan's average annual growth rate was an anemic 1.21 percent versus China's rate of 9.2 percent; in between this stagnation and boom, India grew at 6.2 percent, Malaysia 5.7 percent, and even more mature economies like South Korea and Taiwan managed a strong 5.4 percent and 4.4 percent, respectively.[4]

In part as a result of increased economic size, states across the region are also spending more on their militaries—just as Japan did when it was growing economically. In the past decade, Asia imported the largest number of weapons outside the Middle East.[5] Still, military spending by Japan and China dwarfs other military spending in the region, even though Japan spends only 1 percent of its GDP on defense (see figure 3.2). Russia also spends mightily (above Japan in recent years), but only a small fraction of its spending is devoted to Asia. The United States remains far and away the largest military spender, with its stated rebalance policy to Asia likely to lead to even more resources devoted to the region in future years (though, as we will see later in this chapter, US military spending has been declining overall since 2010).[6]

Japanese defense documents do not express concern over growing military spending in the region apart from China and North Korea but do call for adequate training of new military forces and more broadly express concern about a potential arms race in the region that links to China's greatly increased military spending. Japan also shares security concerns with many states in Southeast Asia and so now has new potential partners—and is planning for further partnerships as these states continue to grow.

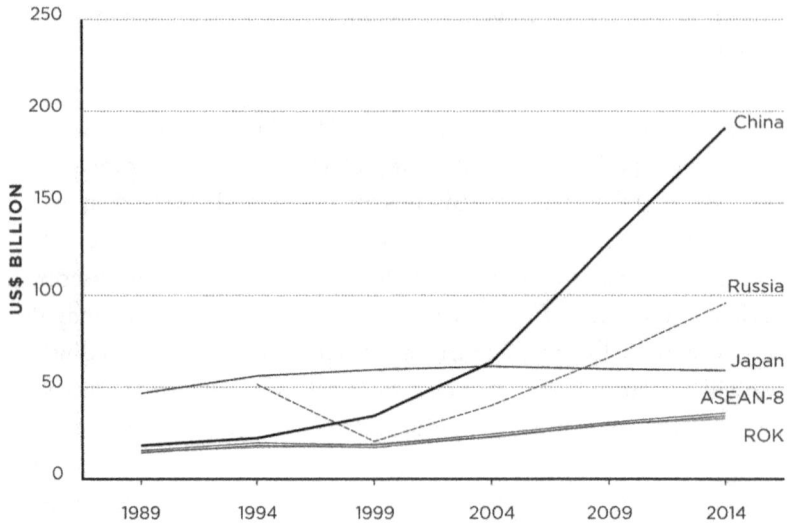

FIGURE 3.2 Japan's defense spending in comparison with its neighbors, 1989–2014. ASEAN-8 does not include Myanmar and Laos because of unavailability of data for some years and does not include data for Vietnam in 1999 (and thus is ASEAN-7 for that year). International Peace Research Institute, SIPRI Military Expenditure Database, 1988–2015, http://www.sipri.org/research/armaments/milex/. Constant 2011 US$ billion.

Despite Japan's relative economic decline, its economic size still dwarfs that of Southeast Asia—larger than the combined ASEAN GDP by about one-third, despite having less than one-quarter of the combined ASEAN population. Moreover, despite relative decline, Japan is expanding its security role in the region—both bilaterally and through multiple regional institutions. Clearly, therefore, relative decline does not directly translate into any single response in security strategy. Policy is mediated through politics, as discussed further in chapters 4 and 5. Japan's new security roles are often underappreciated but are important. For example, Japan is hardly mentioned in Robert Kaplan's best-selling *Asia's Cauldron*—which captures the tensions surrounding the South China Sea in an otherwise engaging manner—except in reference to the legacies of World War II.

Looking forward, Japan's relative economic decline seems inevitable owing to its challenging demographic future and complex economic challenges caused by a shrinking, aging population. Japan's birthrate sank below replacement level in 1975—over forty years ago—and as a

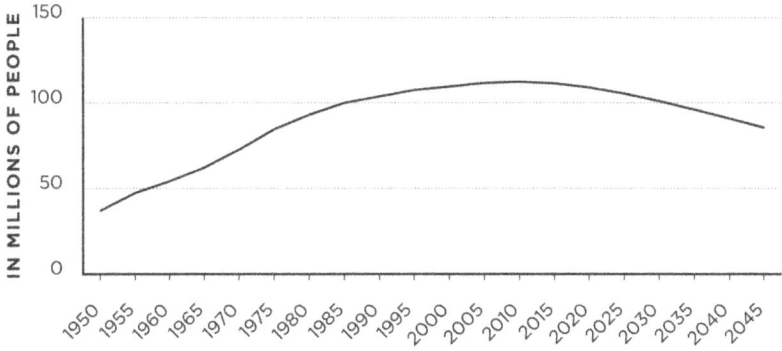

FIGURE 3.3 Historical and projected total population for Japan, 1950–2045. United Nations, Department of Economic and Social Affairs, Population Division, *World Population Prospects: The 2012 Revision*, http://esa.un.org/unpd/wpp/index.htm.

result its *total* population has begun to decline, a development that will accelerate more sharply in the next decades according to projections from the United Nations Population Division (see figure 3.3).

To date, population decline in Japan has been quite modest—about a million out of a population of around 127 million—but this decline will accelerate in the coming years, with the population expected to fall below 120 million in the 2020s and below 100 million (a psychological milestone) around 2050. This demographic reality—one essentially impossible to reverse in the short term given human life spans—makes the prospects of positive economic growth seem quite dim. Indeed, just maintaining the current size of the economy with a smaller population will require per capita economic growth—but relative to other countries in the region, especially the growing populations of some Southeast Asian nations, Japan's economic size is almost certain to decline. By 2040, the population of the Philippines is expected to exceed that of Japan, and Vietnam will be roughly the same size at around 100 million.[7] Indonesia, already the second-largest in population in East Asia after China, is expected to grow to a population of around 300 million. These countries are all likely to see overall growth in their GDPs as their workforces increase, just as Japan did in its high-growth period in the 1960s to 1980s, when its working-age population also grew. These demographically growing countries are also countries, coincidence or not, where Japan's new regional security outreach has been most robust.

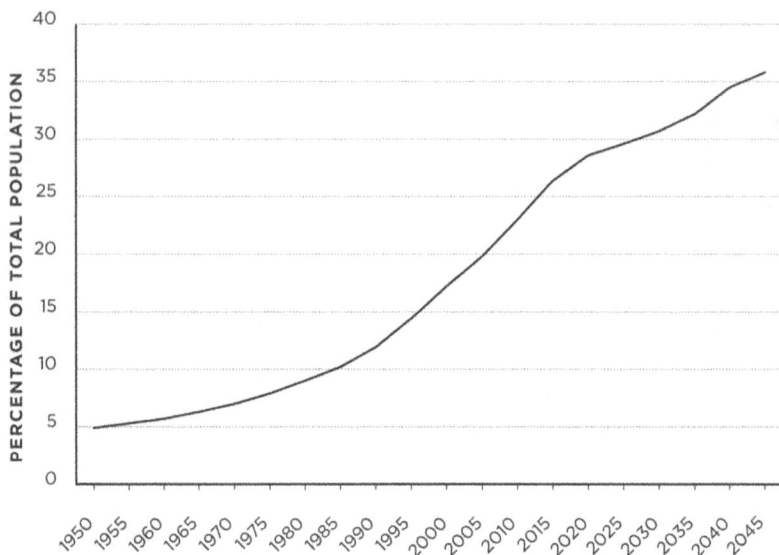

FIGURE 3.4 Historical and projected population of those sixty-five and greater, Japan, 1950–2045. United Nations, Department of Economic and Social Affairs, Population Division, *World Population Prospects: The 2012 Revision*, http://esa.un.org/unpd/wpp/index.htm.

Japan's shrinking population is only part of the demographic challenge it faces. In addition, its remaining population is getting older (see figure 3.4). In fact, in the language of demographers, Japan is already one of just three countries in the world called a super-aged society—one where more than 20 percent of the population is over sixty-five years old. Japan was at 26 percent in 2015, followed by Italy at 22 percent and Germany at 21 percent.[8]

This difficult demographic picture has contributed to Japan's dismal public finances. Despite an international image as a country of obsessive savers and prudent financial managers, Japan now has the highest rate of government debt in relation to GDP of any economically significant country in the world—higher than Greece, Ireland, Italy, and even all but a handful of developing countries (see table 3.1). This fiscal reality suggests significant limits on the possibilities for the future of Japan's security renaissance.

There has been an active and at times quite divisive debate in Japan over immigration as a possible solution to Japan's demographic

TABLE 3.1
Japan's government debt as a percentage of GDP, calendar years
1999–2014

1999	2004	2009	2014
129.0	166.3	188.7	231.9

Source: Ministry of Finance, http://www.mof.go.jp/budget/fiscal_condition/related_data/
  sy014_26_02.pdf.

challenges. While immigration could perhaps provide a partial solution, demographically speaking—quite apart from the politics—it would be practically impossible to resettle enough immigrants in Japan to offset the effects of Japan's aging society. By one estimate, Japan would need to import over *ten million* immigrants *per year* to keep the same dependency ratio of working-aged population to elderly.[9]

Japan is not the only country in East Asia to face these challenges, however—which itself poses its own set of security implications. In the 2020s, South Korea and Taiwan will also join the ranks of the super-aged. In 2015, South Korea was the most rapidly aging society in the world.[10] By contrast, Japan's growth rate of the aged has passed its peak. By 2040, China and the United States are expected to be among the fifty-five countries that will join the ranks of the super-aged.[11] In China, the working-age population (aged fifteen to fifty-nine) began to shrink just after China became the world's second-largest economy in 2010. This decline is expected to substantially accelerate in the 2030s.[12] Unlike Japan, China does not yet have a fully developed social safety net for the elderly. This may prove to be an advantage by not immediately leading to the crushing fiscal realities Japan is currently facing related to its super-aged society, but it may also lead to increased social instability. China also faces other demographic obstacles such as its male-female imbalance that some have connected to future security threats.[13]

In sum, Japan's economic size relative to other regional states is almost certain to decline further, as is Japan's overall population. This is a starkly different security environment than Japan faced at the end of World War II or at the end of the Cold War—and even at the start of the first Abe administration in 2006. And yet Japan today still enjoys substantial military capability advantages over other regional states because of many decades of investment in technology and training, extensive sharing of technology and training with the United States, and still boasting one of the largest defense budgets in the world.

The website Global Firepower ranked Japan's overall military capability in 2015 as ninth in the world, after the United States, Russia, China, India, the United Kingdom, France, South Korea, and Germany.[14] Turkey is listed as number ten. Note that these rankings do not factor in nuclear weapons; in addition, comparing military capabilities across all areas is a notoriously difficult endeavor given important subjective measures such as level of technology and training. Still, it seems beyond dispute that Japan's military forces in terms of capabilities overall would fall behind the United States, Russia, and China and above most other states in the world apart from the short list mentioned in the Global Firepower list.[15]

In terms of a specific military conflict, however—such as a naval battle between Japan and China or Japan and Russia—JSDF capabilities and training could match even the larger Russian or Chinese forces in some scenarios and certainly constitute a significant deterrent. The JMSDF has increased its number of submarines and Aegis-equipped destroyers in the past decade and has plans to increase the number of combat aircraft and ISR capabilities. The JASDF possesses the fifth-largest number of planes of any air force in the world and among the very highest level of technology. In addition, of course, Japan is a formal military ally with the United States, which is treaty obligated to defend Japan if it is attacked. Thus, while Japanese power may be declining in relative terms, in absolute terms Japan's military capabilities are stronger than ever and likely to grow further (if modestly) in response to new and emerging threats, discussed in the next section.

New Regional Security Concerns and Deepening Prior Concerns

East Asia is a geographically large, densely populated, diverse area with a range of security concerns as wide as in the world as a whole. Moreover, increasingly the international relations of East Asia are connected to the more western and southern parts of Asia to create a larger, more dynamic system. In particular for Japan, India has begun to feature prominently in security discussions and strategy. In addition, the Asia-Pacific conception of East Asia also broadens the scope of security concerns and opportunities. Japan's new security partnership with Australia and participation in new multilateral security institutions has expanded the East Asian region from the perspective of military security. This expanded security region faces both long-standing and new security challenges.

Four of the world's ten largest standing armies are in East Asian states (China, North Korea, South Korea, and Vietnam).[16] The border between North and South Korea remains the most militarized border on the planet. The legacy of a China divided by the civil war that concluded in 1949 with the victory of the People's Republic on the mainland and Republic of China on Taiwan also remains a dangerous conflict flash point, despite declining overt military tension in the past decade. Russia maintains the second-largest nuclear weapons force in the world after the United States, and the number of Chinese nuclear weapons has been increasing rather than decreasing. Despite the formal end of the Cold War, Russian planes and ships continue to test the boundaries of Japan's territorial space, requiring regular scrambles by the JSDF.[17] In Northeast Asia—Japan's immediate neighborhood—the Cold War never fully ended, while new post–Cold War threats have emerged.

Familiar Cold War–era conflict flash points have taken on new dimensions in the post–Cold War era and in the past decade. In North Korea, Supreme Leader Kim Jong Un has ratcheted up tensions with close neighbors even further, alienating even its longtime patron, China. North Korean actions have been a principal driver of Japan's evolving security policies since the mid-1990s and continue to feature prominently in Japan's defense strategy documents as a primary rationale for strengthening Japan's military capabilities and for adapting long-standing institutions and practices. Japan's concern over Chinese military capabilities has also substantially evolved from the Cold War era even as the long-standing concerns over China's nuclear and conventional missile capabilities remain. In the period of focus of this book, China's growing military capabilities and actions have become the primary military threat identified by Japanese security planners—and therefore further discussion of the new "China threat" to Japan is the subject of its own section just following.

As Robert Kaplan has observed, "Europe is a landscape; East Asia is a seascape."[18] Maritime security has long been a primary concern of Japan's defense planners, which necessarily involves the Asian region—the transit area for the vast majority of Japan's imports and exports. In recent years Japanese defense planners have framed many of Japan's security concerns around the idea of "threats to the global commons"—which includes freedom of navigation on the high seas and through shared straits but also shared airspace, outer space, and cyberspace. Japan's dependence on the sea for its security and prosperity is among its oldest security concerns, but as technology changes and new actors have emerged in the international system, the specific nature of Japan's concerns regarding the maritime commons has evolved. During the Cold War, Japan expanded its contributions to the US-Japan alliance to include patrols of up to one thousand nautical miles of sea lanes from Japan to protect against the Soviet threat. In the 1990s, Japan made headlines by contributing to regional antipiracy operations around the Strait of Malacca in Southeast Asia, working with Singapore and Indonesian partners in particular. A decade later, Japan again made headlines by contributing to anti-piracy operations in the Gulf of Aden off the coast of the Horn of Africa. In this latest stage, under Japan's security renaissance, Japan has begun to work with countries in Southeast Asia to bolster their coastal defenses in response to China's aggressive maritime claims, which Japan sees as potentially compromising the free passage of goods and oil bound for Japan through this shared maritime space.

Geography creates an especially important role for the JMSDF, one of world's largest and most capable navies. The JMSDF is well prepared to play an enhanced role in protecting the maritime commons as the service less discredited after World War II,[19] and one with a long history of international cooperation with the US Navy throughout the Cold War and post–Cold War years. More recently, the JCG also has expended greater energy and resources both in Japan's territorial defense and in providing assistance in protecting the maritime commons in Southeast Asia—to the degree that it has been described as a "fourth branch" of Japan's postwar military forces.[20]

China factors closely into these security concerns—as both a potential contributor and potential spoiler. As a potential contributor, China's expanded blue water navy and other maritime forces contribute—as Japan does—to anti-piracy operations in Southeast Asia and around the Gulf of Aden. In the medium term, China's expanded blue water capabilities could contribute to the sea lane protection in East Asia currently provided largely by the United States with assistance from Japan. China figures as a spoiler, however, in the rivalry between it and Japan—and with the United States—and in its consequential competition for influence in multilateral security institutions. Moreover, China frequently sacrifices low-level security cooperation to express displeasure over other concerns, such as Japanese prime minister visits to Yasukuni Shrine, Japanese textbook descriptions of historical events, or US arms sales to Taiwan.

China's Leading Role in Japan's Security Renaissance

China's resurgence in the region is the biggest change to Japan's security environment in the past decade and poses the largest long-term challenge to Japanese security—and, arguably, to global security. China has risen to a level of "existential threat" in the eyes of some Japanese—paralleling language used to describe the Soviet threat to the United States in the context of the Cold War. Chinese military forces have possessed the ability to strike Japan with both conventional and nuclear weapons for half a century. In terms of defense planning, it is Japan's alliance with the United States that protects Japan from this threat through the doctrine of extended deterrence. China possessed approximately 175 immediately usable nuclear warheads plus another 65 in reserve in 2010—and is expected to greatly expand that number in the next decade.[21] Moreover, China is seeking greater resilience of its nuclear weapons in the event of an attack by building mobile underground facilities to prevent a successful first strike. Although China has a formal pledge not to use nuclear weapons against nonnuclear states like Japan, escalating military tensions between Japan and China naturally lead Japanese defense planners to question this pledge.

It is ironic that Japanese security concerns over China have played such an outsized role in Japan's security renaissance since China has repeatedly criticized Japan's increased defense capabilities, international security contributions, and deepened military alliance with the United

States—which, arguably, China itself has brought to fruition. In this way, Japan-China security relations exhibit a classic security dilemma.

Japan's relationship with China is multifaceted, however, with deep economic and social ties despite growing military tensions.[22] Tourism between the two countries is booming: more than 3.5 million Japanese visited China in 2013, up 70 percent from 2000 to 2010; more than 1 million Chinese have visited Japan, and many more are expected after visa restrictions were relaxed in 2011.[23] According to another study, the number of Chinese tourists to Japan is predicted to increase from 1.4 million in 2010 to 3.9 million in 2020.[24] Japan has even become a popular location for Chinese elite to buy second homes.[25] The countries are deeply connected economically, with much of Japan's modest economic growth in the past decade attributed to Japanese trade with and investments in China and Chinese economic growth undergirded by Japan's substantial foreign direct investment (FDI) in China (which has declined in percentage terms in recent years but remains the largest source of FDI apart from Hong Kong and Taiwan).[26]

Japan enjoyed largely peaceful relations with China for roughly two thousand years, until the end of the nineteenth century, and Japan's religious, literary, and broader cultural traditions have been pervasively shaped by the interactions between the two states.[27] On one of many visits of Chinese leaders to Japan, Premier Wen Jiabao remarked in a speech in the Diet in 2007, "The length, scale and influence of China-Japan friendly exchanges are rarely seen in the course of world civilization. These exchanges are our shared historical and cultural heritage which we should hold in great value, enrich and pass on from generation to generation."[28]

The period from the start of the first Sino-Japanese War of 1894 to 1895 (which resulted in the Japanese colonization of the island of Taiwan) to the conclusion of the second Sino-Japanese War in 1945 created a vivid and difficult fifty years of troubled memories, however. Still, after Japan's reopening to China was possible as a result of US normalization with China in the second phase of the Cold War, Japan quickly reestablished positive relations with its close neighbor and provided massive economic development assistance to China (in lieu of reparations for the damage it cased in World War II) in the subsequent three decades. As Sheila Smith writes in her fascinating study of China's impact on

Japanese domestic politics, "The last forty years of Japanese-Chinese diplomatic relations have rested on a simple premise: economic interdependence would be the path to postwar reconciliation between the peoples of both countries."[29]

Unfortunately, however, this premise turns out to have been flawed. As economic interdependence deepened, China became more demanding about historical reconciliation issues, and its overt military challenges to Japan also increased. As Denny Roy has framed in his study of China's contemporary rise, "China is not only a rising great power, it is a *returning* great power."[30] This fact has great import to Japan's relations with China given the difficult past between the two states in the long twentieth century. In international politics, the powerful write history, or rewrite it.

Japan experienced the most tense relations with China since the end of World War II from 2010 to 2016, but periods of tension are certainly not new between the two states. Moreover, the period of focus in this book, 2006 to 2016, began with quite *positive* relations: it is not the case that Japan-China relations have been on a continuous downward spiral. It is often forgotten in examinations of Prime Minister Abe's recent tenure as prime minister that when he first came to power in 2006, his rise was overtly welcomed by China as a potential for a reset in relations after the difficult Koizumi years, particularly since Abe publicly pledged not to visit the controversial Yasukuni Shrine as prime minister—the practice restarted under Koizumi that contributed to a deep chill in Japan-China relations under Koizumi's tenure.

Prime Minister Abe made his first foreign visit as prime minister to China to signal the importance he attached to that bilateral relationship, and on this October 2006 visit he signed a joint communiqué, titled "Sino-Japan Relations of Top Priority," that promised a cooperative solution to the East China Sea boundary and resource issue, joint research in history, and a range of new exchanges and areas of cooperation.[31] Premier Wen Jiabao visited Japan in April 2007, the first by a senior Chinese leader since 2000. During the visit, Wen acknowledged Japanese apologies for past wartime conduct and expressed appreciation for Japanese economic assistance over the years.[32] That same year, China became Japan's largest trading partner.[33] In May of the following year, President Hu Jintao visited Japan to sign the "China-Japan Joint

Statement on All-round Promotion of Strategic Relationship of Mutual Benefit."[34] The following month, Japan and China signed an agreement for cooperative development of the Chunxiao gas field in the East China Sea. Prime Minister Jun'ichirō Koizumi and US president George W. Bush were famously photographed throwing a baseball during Koizumi's visit to the United States in June 2001; Prime Minister Yasuo Fukuda (Abe's first-term successor) and Chinese premier Wen re-created this image in December 2007 in Beijing. This iconography illustrated that Japan and China were indeed "playing ball" after the difficulties of the Koizumi years. By August 2010, on the eve of an annual Japan-China friendship meeting, the *China Daily* published a front-page article hailing the best relations between the two countries ever. And then things began to fall apart. . . .

The Territorial Dispute Over the Senkaku Islands

Just days after the Japan-China friendship meeting lauded in China's state-run media, a small Chinese fishing trawler operating in the East China Sea entered waters that Japan considers part of its EEZ and was directed by the JCG to leave. The ship did not comply, collided with the JCG vessel, and the crew of the ship was arrested and taken to nearby Japanese territory to be prosecuted for damaging a JCG vessel.[35] Chinese officials were enraged at the "abduction" of Chinese citizens in this manner, issuing harshly worded diplomatic protests and responding with a series of actions that greatly escalated the dispute during the ensuing month. The initial arrests and the Chinese response altered the status quo beyond return, even after the crew was allowed to return to China the following month. Nationalist agitators in both countries (in addition to others in Taiwan, which also claims the islands) as well as ordinary citizens pressed their governments to better protect the sovereignty of their national territory, leading to a series of intensified interactions between the JCG and a range of public and private Chinese ships and aircraft in the years that followed, and that continue to this day.

The territory in question is what the Japanese call the Senkaku Islands, or, technically, islets: five small uninhabited islands and three large protruding rocks, with a total area of about four square miles, located to the southwest of the Japanese main islands and the outlying

Ryūkyū island chain. These islets are roughly equidistant from populated Japanese islands and Taiwan and also close to mainland China; they are roughly one thousand miles from Tokyo. As a practical matter, as in the so-called Fishing Trawler Incident of 2010, the maritime space around these islands is central to the dispute—waters rich in fishing resources and possibly undersea minerals, oil, and gas.

This territory has been "administered" by Japan (a term important to the US-Japan Security Treaty) since 1895, apart from the period of US occupation of Japan and administration of the Okinawan islands (1945–1972). One of the islands was used as a firing range for US forces in the early postwar period. In the early twentieth century, a small Japanese fishing village was located on one of the islands, which remained in private hands until it and two other of the islands were purchased by the Japanese government (aka, "nationalized") in 2012 to keep them out of the hands of Japanese nationalists seeking to escalate the dispute, a second major spark of escalation in the evolving crisis in Japan-China relations. China (and Taiwan) maintain that these islands are administratively part of Taiwan and thus should have been returned to Chinese control at the end of World War II when Japan agreed to relinquish all territory it acquired in its long campaign of territorial expansion dating back to the first Sino-Japan War, which included the Japanese withdrawal from the island of Taiwan. Japan's position is that the islands were integrated into Japanese territory unrelated to its first war with China, following international law of the time.[36] The United States does not take a position in this sovereignty dispute but has repeatedly stated that the US-Japan Security Treaty is crystal clear that any territory administered by Japan is included in the US security guarantee provided to Japan under Article Five of the treaty. This position was even publicly restated by President Obama himself during a visit to Tokyo in April 2014.

The most substantial and urgent threat perceived by Japan in connection with China's reemergence and military rise remains over China's claims to the uninhabited Senkaku Islands. China's increasingly assertive claims to this territory and actions to challenge Japan's administrative control over them constitutes the principal driver of Japan's increased military capabilities and reform of long-standing practices and institutions that have limited Japan's effective use of its military power.

For example, significant shifts in JSDF posture from the north to south-west of Japan, development of "jointness" between the three services of the JSDF, and development of amphibious assault capabilities set out in the 2010 NDPG and expanded in the 2013 NDPG are all directly the result of the increased perception of threat from China.

China Challenges Beyond the Senkaku Islands

The nature of the Chinese military threat to Japan has changed dramatically as China's economic rise has fueled huge increases in China's military spending, capabilities, and activities. In the area of military security, China poses both a direct territorial challenge with rising military and quasi-military escalation and a broader challenge related to its growing capabilities and the implications for the security of the Japanese main islands, of joint US-Japan forces in Okinawa, and the security of the sea lanes through the South China Sea, which both Japan and China rely on as a lifeline for energy imports and trade. China surpassed Japanese defense spending in 2004.[37] Moreover, China's defense spending is dramatically higher if adjusted for PPP—$400 billion in 2011, over four times the real dollar value.[38] Japan's annual defense white papers and the annual *China Security Reports* produced by the MOD's National Institute for Defense Studies convey growing explicit concern about China, in contrast to the vague expressions of concern conveyed in defense white papers prior to 2006.

The increased Japanese concern about a China threat is based on increasingly provocative Chinese military and quasi-military actions, which are widely covered in the Japanese media and documented annually in Japan's defense white papers. For example, the transit of Chinese naval vessels through the Tsugaru Strait (between the main Japanese islands of Honshu and Hokkaido to the north) and the Miyako Strait (between Okinawa and Miyako Island chain to the south) took place over a dozen times from 2006 to 2014. In April 2010 Chinese military helicopters buzzed Japanese destroyers that were tracking ten Chinese naval vessels en route to the Pacific via the Miyako Strait, leading to a formal diplomatic protest by the Japanese government. In January 2013 Chinese naval vessels locked fire-control radar on JMSDF vessels in the

East China Sea on two separate occasions, again leading to diplomatic protests by the Japanese government. (Chinese officials deny that these latter incidents took place at all.)

Bjørn Grønning has described Japan engaging in "counterbalancing" behavior to China's reemergence, rooting this both in "Japanese perceptions of aggressive Chinese behavior" and in the changing balance of military power in the region in China's favor. He writes, "Japan's balancing has manifested itself both internally through a comprehensive revision of the JSDF's force posture and military capabilities and externally through efforts to strengthen the Japan-US alliance framework."[39] Jeffrey Hornung, too, has argued that Japan "has shifted away from its traditional engagement policy toward first a soft hedge, followed by a harder hedge that continues to this day."[40]

China's own defense planning documents—which are widely criticized as lacking sufficient transparency—acknowledge China's quest for a blue water navy, transitioning away from coastal defense to "far sea defense." Chinese defense planners also frequently refer to a strategy of "asymmetrical warfare" to challenge the United States, including plans to develop "carrier killer" ballistic missiles and EMP attack capability.[41] In January 2007, China destroyed one of its own weather satellites—an act that demonstrated to itself and the world its ability to destroy the type of satellites that US forces rely on for weapons and troop guidance. Such Chinese statements and actions underscore a dilemma Japan faces in its attempts to respond to China's increase in military capabilities: while Japan is seeking to respond to China's new muscle, China is seeking to develop forces capable of deterring the much more powerful US military. In this sense, Japan is caught in the middle—though, of course, it benefits from its security relationship with the United States.

Beyond these hard military challenges, China also poses a broader threat to Japan's global economic competitiveness, its regional economic leadership, and its soft power—particularly since Shinzō Abe's return to power, when China began a coordinated global propaganda campaign to paint Abe as a dangerous ultranationalist and Japan as the provocative and unpredictable military power in the region. The milestone of China surpassing Japan as the second-largest economy in the world in 2010 led to countless media stories in Japan about the rising China challenge, which were only in part about China's growing military challenge; recall that that year began as one of celebration of several years of improving Japan-China relations, including new rhetoric from the recently elected DPJ leadership about a new era of closeness in Japan's relations with the region, including China (policies discussed further in chapter 4).

Japan's complicated relationship with China is not merely a bilateral phenomenon, though. It is closely linked to other relationships. Both Japan and China view their relationship with each other through a prism that includes the United States. Japan fears the emergence of a "G2" relationship between the United States and China that excludes Japan, possibly even jeopardizing the US-Japan alliance—despite abundant US official reassurance that the G2 concept exists only in the imagination of certain thinkers outside government. China sees Japan's power greatly amplified by the US-Japan alliance and has increasingly sought to disrupt the harmony of the alliance to weaken both US and Japanese power in the region.

Japan-China relations are also manifested through a competition over influence in Southeast Asia and Oceania—in terms of soft power but also direct economic ties and increasingly over military ties, with Japan now in a deep security partnership with Australia and with growing military ties to the Philippines and Singapore, and to Vietnam and Indonesia. Most of the states in the region traded substantially more with Japan than with China at the start of the twenty-first century but now are larger trade partners with China. In sum, as Glosserman and Snyder have provocatively captured the contemporary zeitgeist, "China is everything Japan is not: large, dynamic, confident, possessed of a nuclear arsenal, with a permanent seat on the United Nations Security Council, and prepared—if not anxious—to play a leading role in the region and the world."[42]

And yet China's high level of defense spending vis-à-vis Japan does not translate directly into military superiority vis-à-vis Japan—at least not presently. Even though China's military spending is now more than double Japan's (and perhaps many orders of magnitude more in real terms), China still needs to make up for decades of minimal investment in defense—both in terms of the accumulated stock of weapons over time and technology and practice with the new technology.[43] In addition, as a continental power and a nuclear weapons state, it has vastly greater demands on its budget compared with Japan. China has land borders with fourteen countries plus sea borders with several others. In addition, China has no formal military allies—and not even any significant informal allies; even Russia privately considers China a military threat, despite cooperating with China on multiple fronts, and North Korea is arguably more of a drain on China's security writ large than contributor (apart from the land buffer it provides from US forces in South Korea). Thus, there are reasons to consider the military balance between Japan and China to be closer than as some pessimists portray it and also numerous reasons to expect moderation in China's military posture in the coming years.[44] Two factors that remain especially salient to the argument of this book are addressed in the following sections of this chapter and in the following chapters; they are (1) that regardless of an objective analysis of China's threat to Japan, Japanese themselves perceive a rising threat and are taking numerous actions to address it; and (2) that the United States plays a complex role in moderating or exacerbating Japan's already complex relationship with China.

The relationship between the contours of the international system and the impulses in domestic politics is not unidirectional. The starting point of much international relations theory rooted in realist scholarship posits that changes at the international system level create strong pressures on domestic leaders to adapt policy. The scale of change in Japan's region in the past decade certainly has created many such pressures to act—though even at this level ample scholarship exists in both the realist tradition and the newer constructivist tradition demonstrating that such change must be *perceived* by domestic actors as a cause for concern.[45] In the case of China, Japanese at many levels perceive a China threat and seek to better prepare Japan against it.[46] At the same time, decisions at the domestic level can affect the nature of the system—as we see with China's decisions to greatly increase its military spending and to press more assertively its territorial claim over the Senkaku Islands. Japan's security renaissance of the past decade has also greatly altered regional security dynamics.

Japan's security renaissance is driven by more than China. East Asia's economic rise has created a multipolar environment well beyond even a US-Japan-China strategic triangle. Japan's response to this increased complexity together with its relative decline is quite similar to that of its primary alliance partner, the United States: deepen the US-Japan alliance to handle a broader range of issues and seek out new security partnerships. Like Japan, however, the United States is also losing power relatively in Asia as its investments flatten and China rises.

US defense spending dwarfs that of others in the region, including China.[47] Yet as seen in figure 3.5 and as summarized by SIPRI, "Since reaching its highest recorded peak in 2010, US military expenditure has

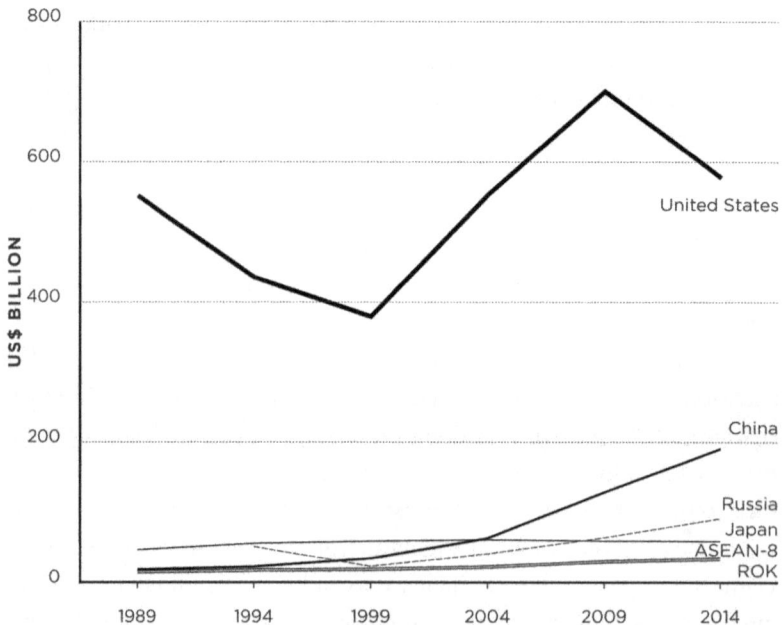

FIGURE 3.5 US defense spending in comparison with East Asian states, 1989–2014. ASEAN-8 does not include Myanmar and Laos because of unavailability of data for some years and does not include data for Vietnam in 1999 (and thus is ASEAN-7 for that year). International Peace Research Institute, SIPRI Military Expenditure Database, 1988–2014, http://www.sipri.org/research/armaments/milex/. Constant 2011 US$ billion.

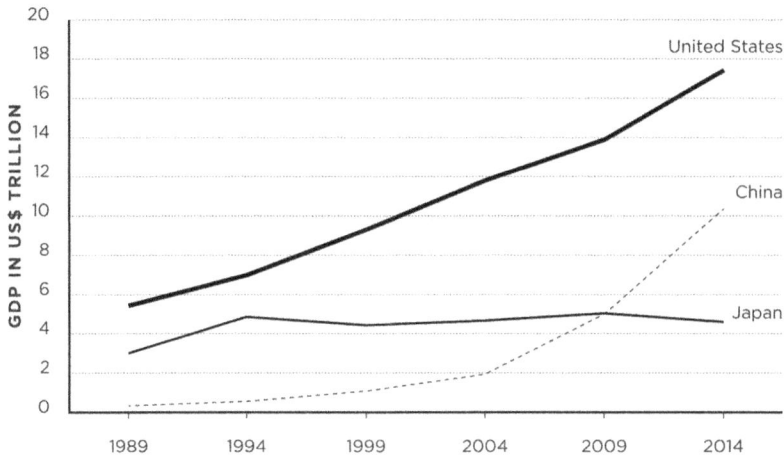

FIGURE 3.6 Japan, US, China GDP, 1989–2014. World Bank, *World Development Indicators*, http://wdi.worldbank.org/table/1.1.

decreased by 19.8 per cent in real terms [by 2014]. The USA's share of world military expenditure remains high at 34 per cent, but it is declining steadily year on year as the USA reduces its spending and other states increase expenditure."[48]

Economically speaking, the relative decline of the United States and Japan together is even more striking than a comparison of military spending alone. As shown in figure 3.6, in 1989 Japan and the United States were the two largest economies in the world, with Japan's GDP amounting to 55 percent of US GDP. In 2014, Japan was number three in the world with a GDP totaling only 26 percent of the US GDP, less than half the percentage share of the US economy only twenty-five years later. Moreover, the Japanese economy was roughly eight times the size of the Chinese economy in 1989 but less than half the size in 2014; in 2014, the size of the Chinese economy was about 60 percent of the US economy, more than Japan's share in 1989.

The US Rebalance to Asia

The US-Japan alliance is not the only part of US Asia policy, of course —though it is arguably the most important pillar. Rather, simultaneous with Japan's security renaissance, the United States also sought to deepen its engagement with Asia through what would come to be called the rebalance strategy of the Obama administration. It is not the case, of course, that the United States was uninvolved in East Asia before the rebalance strategy. Indeed, as discussed in chapter 2, the US-Japan relationship in the Bush-Koizumi years of 2001 to 2006 was a time of great closeness and deepening of the US-Japan alliance. In addition, in a line widely thought to refer obliquely to China's growing power in the region, the final Quadrennial Defense Review of the Bush administration in 2006 stated, "[The United States] will attempt to dissuade any military competitor from developing disruptive or other capabilities that could enable regional hegemony or hostile action against the United States or other friendly countries."[49] Rather, the perception of the United States by the end of the Bush years in 2008 was that the United States had become distracted by a large number of other international challenges: nearly a decade of war in Afghanistan and Iraq, weathering and devising strategies to address the worst international economic recession in almost a century (referred to as the Lehman shocks in Japan, as an indicator of where the root of the problem was seen), and growing discord at home about the best ways to meet the foreign policy challenges of the twenty-first century. Moreover, there was a widespread perception across Asia, including in Japan, that the Bush years reflected a unilateralism to US actions that did not make the United States a true part of the region. In addition, the United States was no longer the largest trading partner with most states in the region and had not been so for at least a decade in most cases.

President Obama looked to the Pacific from the start of his presidency (2009–2016)—even before, as he was born in Hawaii. Obama dispatched his secretary of state, Hillary Clinton, to make her first overseas trip to Japan and other places in Asia in February 2009, less than a month after he assumed office. She returned to Asia in July of that year for the ARF, and again in November for the APEC (Asia-Pacific Economic Cooperation) ministerial meetings. President Obama also visited Japan in his first year in office, in November 2009, and also attended the APEC Economic Leaders' Meeting that month. He met newly installed prime minister Yukio Hatoyama in New York City at the opening of the UN General Assembly in September 2009, just weeks after Hatoyama had become prime minister. Another of Obama's early goals, "a world without nuclear weapons," was a point of bonding between the Japanese left and Obama and a later source of disappointment as he moved away from a focus on that goal.

Beyond the Japanese aspect of the US rebalance, the US-China Strategic and Economic Dialogue met for the first time in July 2009, in Washington, DC, and has continued annually ever since. At the June 2013 "Sunnylands Summit" President Obama met the newly installed Chinese president Xi Jinping. At a June 2009 summit between Obama and South Korean president Lee Myung-bak, a US–South Korea "Joint Vision for the Alliance" was released—using similar language ("joint vision") to the US-Japan joint statement released in April 2015. US-ASEAN outreach also boomed in the Obama years, with the United States signing the Treaty of Amity and Cooperation with ASEAN in July 2009, serving as an important symbol appreciated by regional leaders. Later US outreach to Myanmar and deepening relations with Vietnam also indicate the depth of renewed US interest in the region—even before the escalation of the South China Sea territorial disputes drew the United States even closer to Vietnam and to the Philippines.

Across these cases, the United States and Japan shared many common interests and coordinated together in ways that further shaped Japan's security renaissance. Japan alone cannot keep pace with China's increased military capabilities but can address them in tandem with the United States and other partners—a core aspect of Japan's 2013 national security strategy. Similarly, US strategy to manage China's rise includes working more closely with existing US allies and forging new partnerships. Thus, there is much overlap and potential for cooperation in recent US and Japanese security strategies.

To realize these important synergies, however, there is a need for changes in the US-Japan alliance as a result of a rising China. In the past, as Sheila Smith has noted, "the alliance spent very little time on the possibility that Japan might become engaged in a direct conflict with China."[50] Rather, alliance planning was concerned with Japanese support of US forces over a Taiwan or a Korea contingency. At the same time as the United States seeks to recraft its alliance with Japan to respond to the new security environment—as seen in the April 2015 US-Japan Guidelines for Defense Cooperation—the United States is also seeking to craft a new relationship with China to jointly address regional and global security challenges. Also as Smith has observed, "the biggest challenge for US policymakers will be developing a cooperative relationship with Beijing while not undermining the United States' close alliance with Tokyo."[51]

This interconnectedness between Japan's Asia outreach and US efforts to outreach to Asia has been discussed by T. J. Pempel in a broader regional context. Pempel has concluded that if the United States continues its recent policies of deeper engagement with Asia, it will help Japan avoid having to decide on a preference in its overall foreign policy, the Asian region or the US-Japan relationship.[52] As I argue in chapter 4, the DPJ's perceived need to make this choice—at least under the first DPJ prime minister, Hatoyama—greatly complicated its policy making.

Japan's New Regional Security Partnerships

One challenge of the Japanese strategy of broader engagement in the region, and a similar challenge to what the United States faces, is to expand these partnerships without causing increased tensions with China over China's fear that it is being "contained" by hostile states. Yet recent escalation of tensions in the South China Sea further concerns Japan about potential lapses in the sea lines of communication through that area and thus further encourages partnerships with regional states that seek to push back against Chinese claims, in particular the Philippines and Vietnam.

Another manifestation of Japan's security renaissance is that Japan has added a military dimension to its bilateral relationships with a number of states in the region—not just provision of assistance or participation in joint exercises that have a security dimension (such as support for coast guards or anti-piracy operations) but also direct cooperation with the militaries of states other than the United States. Such security cooperation has proceeded furthest with Australia, where Japan issued, in 2008, its first-ever "Joint Declaration on Security Cooperation" with a state other than the United States and, in 2010, its first-ever ACSA with a state other than the United States. After Japan further relaxed arms export restrictions in 2014, Australia was at the top of a short list of states that would likely enter an agreement for the export of Japanese military equipment, such as Japan's advanced diesel submarines that are especially useful in areas around the shallow South China Sea (though the submarine deal itself did not come to fruition).

India has also emerged as a new security partner for Japan, though not as closely as with Australia. The JMSDF joined US-India naval exercises off the coast of Okinawa beginning in 2007 and multilateral exercises that also included Australia and Singapore later that year, and in 2012 it conducted its first-ever joint naval exercises with India and has continued them annually since that time. Moreover, as with Australia, India stands to benefit from Japan's relaxation of its arms export restrictions. The case of India is perhaps the best example of what Corey Wallace has described as Japan's embrace of "the full spectrum of security tools in order to achieve its longer term foreign policy goals by assisting future candidate middle and great powers in sustainable political and economic development."[53] In addition to regular visits between the prime ministers of both states and talk of deepened security cooperation, the two states signed an information-sharing agreement to protect the exchange of classified military information and created a framework for the transfer of defense equipment and technology in December 2015. Looking farther into the twenty-first century, as India becomes the most populous country in the world and assuming that its economy continues to grow steadily, India may become the naval power in the region of most importance to Japanese security. India may also become the next economy to surpass Japan's, possibly within the next decade—and already has in terms of PPP.

Japan's earlier forays into security cooperation beyond the United States included promotion of the ARF as a way to handle traditional security issues multilaterally and provision of ODA for the training of regional coast guards (though not, pointedly, naval forces).[54] In 2012, however, the MOD announced that it would, for the first time, provide noncombat military equipment and supplies to the militaries of other countries in Asia, including the Philippines and Vietnam, for the purpose of capacity building. Japan has held bilateral talks with defense officials of numerous states in the region on an expanded and more substantive basis in this period.[55] The new JSDF chief of the Joint Staff Office even chose to visit the Philippines in the midst of the standoff between the Philippines and China over the disputed islands in the South China Sea. Wallace writes, "While Chinese boats were still surrounding the Scarborough Shoal in July, the Philippines and Japan signed a 'Statement of Intent on Defense Cooperation and Exchanges' which indicated that the two sides would continue to hold high level exchanges at all levels of the defense establishment—ministerial, official, and uniformed—and that the two sides would also conduct 'training activities and exercises on the occasion of the mutual ship visits between the PN and the JMSDF.' "[56] Japan also provided patrol boats and an advanced maritime surveillance system to Indonesia from 2006 to 2009 and agreed to hold high-level annual defense dialogues beginning in 2012. It has provided greater defense-related assistance to Vietnam, Malaysia, Thailand, and Myanmar as well. In addition to this new military connection with multiple states in the region, Japan continues to engage in strengthening its economic and cultural ties with the region, in no small part in recent years as a further mechanism to balance rising Chinese influence.[57]

Growth in multilateral approaches to security in East Asia in the twenty-first century also enhances Japan's growing security contributions to the region and complements long-standing Japanese approaches to East Asia in other issue areas. In the past decade, annual meetings of the ARF, ADMM+, the EAS, and Shangri-la Dialogue have become important facets of the regional security environment and ones that Japan has deepened its participation in to ensure that its interests are represented.

Japan's security environment changed between 2006 and 2016 in ways that a wide and diverse range of Japanese saw as requiring a shift in existing policies and practices. Several long-standing concerns have deepened and new concerns have arisen. Moreover, looking forward the likelihood is that current concerns will deepen. The future security environment, of course, is unknowable—but defense planners must prepare for the most likely contingencies and also have backup plans for managing less likely game changers. In its comprehensive "strategic net assessment," a Carnegie Endowment for International Peace study argues that a full-scale military conflict between Japan and China is unlikely but that China's "coercive power" is likely to grow in ways that will negatively affect Japan.[58] Overall, though, despite rising tensions in some areas, the broader story of developments in East Asia in the past decades is one of overwhelming growth in cooperation, including institutional networks of cooperation that have undergirded, indeed fostered, the substantial economic growth the region has enjoyed in recent decades.[59]

Chapter 4 examines how the shifting international environment is filtered through Japan's recent democratic politics, including examination of the effect of turnover of power to the DPJ and back to the LDP, and further considers changes to Japan's security policies and practices as a result of international factors discussed in this chapter and in light of the domestic political environment that characterizes Japan's security renaissance.

CHAPTER FOUR

Domestic Power Transitions and Japan's Evolving Strategic Posture, 2006 to 2012

Japan has experienced two historic power transitions in the past decade that have underpinned Japan's security renaissance, one international, one domestic. As discussed in chapter 3, Japan's regional security environment was fundamentally transformed as China's economic rank surpassed that of Japan's, China's military spending ballooned, and other states in the region pursued new strategies to adjust to this regional power transition. Equally important to Japan's security renaissance, however, Japan also experienced a power transition at home—with the collapse of public support for over five decades of conservative rule under the LDP and the victory of the rival DPJ in a historic Lower House election in August 2009—the first time since the LDP was created in 1955 that another political party won more seats in a national election than the LDP.[1]

The primary reasons for this domestic power transition are rooted in domestic issues but are linked to Japan's place in the world and its broader security practices. Moreover, this domestic power transition formed an essential component of Japan's security renaissance, marking the first time since Japan's defeat in World War II that the ruling party and primary opposition party shared a broad consensus on Japan's appropriate military security policies and practices—despite substantially different approaches to the three historical legacies that continue to shape Japan's security renaissance. As discussed in chapter 2, there were important political and policy precursors to Japan's security renaissance in earlier periods, but the six years examined in this chapter cemented Japan's security renaissance in place, setting the stage for a further series of enhanced military capabilities and practices that would be implemented under the subsequent government of Shinzō Abe after his (and the LDP's) return to power in December 2012. Contemporary reporting on Japanese security policy evolution under the second Abe administration that began in December 2012 often ascribes the primary impetus for change to Abe himself, but as demonstrated in this chapter, the root of much of Japan's security renaissance lies in the period 2006 to 2012, which included five prime ministers in addition to Abe.

In these years, the political opposition that came to power adopted a new NDPG that shifted the JSDF southward toward China, increased its capabilities, enhanced Japan's participation in global counterpiracy operations, continued Japan's role as the largest funder of Afghanistan reconstruction efforts beyond the United States, and led to greatly escalated military tensions with China over the disputed Senkaku Islands. Security cooperation with regional partners such as Australia, India, and ASEAN countries also reached unprecedented levels in these six years. While Prime Minister Abe pushed practices further in this direction upon his return to power in December 2012, there is every reason to think that Japan's security policies, and its security renaissance, would have proceeded similarly under DPJ prime minister Yoshihiko Noda (who lost power in the December 2012 election to the LDP) or a future DPJ prime minister. In sum, to fully appreciate the extent of Japan's security renaissance, one must consider security policy change beyond Shinzō Abe—which requires a close examination of the period between his two terms as prime minister, an aim of this chapter.

The six years from September 2006 to December 2012 did not unfold as observers of Japanese politics or security policy expected. In September 2006, popular LDP prime minister Jun'ichiro Koizumi passed the baton of leadership to his anointed successor, Shinzō Abe, who had been instrumental in crafting security policy in the Koizumi administration first as deputy chief and later as chief cabinet secretary. Koizumi resigned despite his continued strong popularity, and it was expected that Abe would build on Koizumi's efforts to expand Japanese security capabilities and activities.[2] Although among prime ministers in the preceding fifteen years, only Koizumi had managed to serve for more than three years, many expected that Abe would continue in Koizumi's footsteps in this area as well and would serve at least three years as prime minister, further adding continuity to Japan's recent efforts to adapt its security policy and practices for the challenges of the new century.

The year that followed, however, departed greatly from the expected script: in July 2007 (after Abe had been in office only ten months) the LDP lost control of the Upper House (the less-powerful house of Japan's parliament), which created a divided government, or what the Japanese media termed a twisted Diet (*nejiri kokkai*), for the first time under the postwar constitution that established in 1946 the current division of power between the two houses of the Diet.[3] In September 2007 Abe resigned as prime minister, reportedly for health reasons, though pressure to resign after the poor showing in the Upper House election and the low popularity ratings of his cabinet also surely contributed to this decision. In the following two years, two more LDP prime ministers (Yasuo Fukuda and Tarō Asō) also served for only one year. Then, in a historic moment in postwar Japanese politics, the LDP lost the Lower House election to another party for the first time since the LDP was formed in 1955, to the rival DPJ. As with the first Abe government, however, the DPJ also enjoyed less than one year of control of both houses of the Diet, losing control over the Upper House in July 2010. The period of the twisted Diet and annual turnover of prime ministers continued until December 2012, when Abe led the LDP to an electoral victory in the Lower House and returned to the prime ministership. An LDP victory in the subsequent July 2013 Upper House election offered the likelihood of LDP control over both houses of the Diet until at least July 2016 (the next required national election, of the Upper House), together with its coalition partner, the Kōmei Party. An early surprise Lower House election in December 2014 further cemented LDP-coalition control of the Diet.

The six-year period considered in this chapter features the debut of Prime Minister Abe's security agenda, in his first term as prime minister. Moreover, beginning in September 2009, these years offer only the second opportunity in the entire postwar period to examine whether security practices created and institutionalized under the LDP would endure after a new political party took over the reins of power, the first being the short-lived anti-LDP coalition government of 1993–94 that lasted only nine months.

Substantial media reporting predicted great breaks from past security practice during these tumultuous years of political turnover—from revision of Article Nine of the constitution under the first Abe administration to a wholesale recrafting of the US-Japan military alliance under the first DPJ Hatoyama administration. However, while the period indeed saw many important changes in Japan's security practices, it did not see substantial success in implementing policies contrary to the long-standing historical legacies of policies rooted in antimilitarist security practices and the US-Japan alliance.

Contrary to expectations, the once-opposition then ruling-party DPJ embraced the vast majority of the security policies and approaches previously adopted by the LDP, marking a historic moment in Japanese security politics, a moment where the ruling coalition and opposition coalition expressed substantial agreement about the general contours of Japan's security policies. Although some individual politicians of both major parties continue to disagree with some aspects of their party's mainstream positions, the consensus compromise legislation and practices illustrated striking continuity of outcomes—despite many instances of concern expressed that this would not be the case.

Growing concern over Japan's regional security environment was evident throughout this period, in particular Japan's growing sense of insecurity vis-à-vis China. The first concerted policy responses to military concerns of a rising China were developed internally in the LDP governments of Abe, Fukuda, and Asō and crafted into a new draft NDPG in 2009. Before this new NDPG could be formally adopted, however, the LDP lost control of the Diet, and the DPJ took over the reins of power. Over the course of the next year, as discussed in chapter 3, the security situation vis-à-vis China worsened, with China's GDP surpassing Japan's to become the second-largest economy in the world and the first of what would become a series of escalating disputes over control over the Senkaku Islands in the fall of 2010.

In sum, what was expected in this period vis-à-vis security policy was twofold: (1) different LDP prime ministers would have different policy priorities given their different faction ideologies in the LDP and

(2) opposition parties in control would alter the guiding parameters of Japanese security policy in important ways. What resulted in this period, however, confounded expectations: despite some different policy priorities of different prime ministers, there was much continuity in the area of security policy outcomes. Moreover, the years of opposition control (three years of DPJ-led governments) led to the most significant changes cementing Japan's security renaissance in the six-year period of frequent turnover examined in this chapter, laying the foundation for further security policy innovation in the second Abe administration, examined in chapter 5.

The 2010 NDPG adopted by the DPJ government in December marked a substantial change to Japan's long-standing regional security posture —to the extent that it was widely characterized both within and outside Japan as a dramatic break from the past. Indeed, although the new NDPG released by the Abe government in December 2013 received substantial coverage as another example of Abe's push to craft a more active security role for Japan abroad, it is the 2010 NDPG that introduced most of the core concepts that the 2013 NDPG seeks to further advance—such as "dynamic defense," increased capabilities for the JSDF, the "southwestern shift" of the JSDF to respond to the increased China threat, relaxations on arms export restrictions and joint weapons production, and the strategic use of ODA for military-related purposes.[4]

How can we explain these surprising outcomes? Two primary drivers take center stage: First is the growing impact of a changed international environment—which was a factor in the previous decade but grew much stronger in the decade of Japan's security renaissance.[5] Second, the historical legacies of the postwar period strongly influenced leaders from both parties in their efforts to address challenges emerging from a changed international environment. The postwar antimilitarist legacy provided a well-trodden path difficult to deviate from, one that was popular with the public and highly institutionalized—constraining political actors on the right and on the left. The postwar historical legacy of struggles with inequality in the US-Japan alliance also played a strong role. The United States continued to strongly push Japan to enhance military capabilities and deepen cooperation with the United States within the alliance framework. The United States also served as a bulwark against the DPJ government, at times secretly in coalition with senior bureaucrats who opposed the new policy initiatives of the DPJ and working together with the LDP opposition. This behind-the-scenes work contributed to the downfall of the first DPJ government of Yukio Hatoyama. Later, though, strong coordination with the United States assisted the next DPJ prime minister, Naoto Kan, two times: over the 2010 Fishing Trawler Incident related to the Senkaku Islands and coping with the triple disaster of March 2011. DPJ attempts to alter the long-standing postwar dynamics over history issues related to Japan's colonialist and militarist periods also were not as successful as many expected them to be given the priority the party placed on addressing long-lingering history issues in its campaign manifestos.

Beyond the strong influence of the three historical legacies, three additional explanatory factors are evident in this period: (1) changing public and elite opinion linked to the dramatically changed international environment; (2) continuing stresses on the old party system after the implementation of the new electoral system in the 1996 election, one decade earlier, which led to a large rise of so-called floating voters (unaffiliated with any party) and a pummeling of the LDP faction system (including by Koizumi and as a result of a series of other institutional changes); and (3) weak or inexperienced leaders more influenced by experienced and entrenched interests. Each of these factors is examined in this chapter as facets of the developing security renaissance during these important six years.

Disagreement over Japan's future security policies was not the central issue leading to the frequent turnover of political leadership in the six-year period examined in this chapter, but it did play a contributing role. The next section explains the broader context for the annual leadership turnover seen in these six years and for the historic domestic power transition to DPJ rule in 2009. This next section also includes a brief overview of the institutional structure of Japan's parliamentary style of democracy, which creates more frequent leadership turnover than a US-style presidential system. Next, efforts of the first Abe administration to alter long-standing constraints on Japanese security policy are explained, offering an argument for why such efforts failed, followed by consideration of the efforts of Abe's two short-term successors, Yasuo Fukuda and Tarō Asō. Then the chapter examines the important domestic power transition to DPJ rule and its effect on Japan's security practices—beginning with the challenge the first DPJ prime minister, Yukio Hatoyama, posed to the US-Japan alliance legacy and continuing through the subsequent two DPJ prime ministers, Naoto Kan and Yoshihiko Noda. The chapter concludes with a summary discussion of how Japan's security renaissance was cemented in this period, offering a transition to the further transformation of Japan's security posture from 2012 to 2016 in the second Abe administration after the return of LDP rule.

Leadership Turnover and Security Policy Change: Confounding Expectations

Japan's parliamentary system creates more frequent leadership turnover than the US presidential system. With Lower House elections mandated at least every four years, on a date chosen by the prime minister, the incentive for the ruling party is to lock in support when public opinion is favorable and to weather periods of low support. This logic had led to Lower House elections being conducted on average every 2.6 years in the postwar period 1946 to 2015.[6] While the timing of Lower House elections is not directly related to turnover of prime ministers, there is a correlation between the two—with standing prime ministers frequently resigning after a poor showing in a national election, or even before an election if public opinion suggests that the party needs to present a new face and image to voters prior to the election. In addition, prime ministers may resign at other times because of a poor showing in an Upper House election (where half the seats are elected every three years), declining support rates, a political scandal, or other factors. Thus, the average term of a prime minister in postwar Japan is less than the average time between Lower House elections, only 2.1 years.[7] This makes the annual turnover of prime ministers from 2006 to 2012 exceptional but not unprecedented; for example, Japan had nine different prime ministers in the first decade of the post–Cold War era from 1989 to 1999.

Postwar Japan has seen only six prime ministers who served over twice the average term length of 2.1 years: Shigeru Yoshida (over seven years), Hayato Ikeda (about four and a half years), Eisaku Satō (about eight years), Yasuhiro Nakasone (about five years), Jun'ichirō Koizumi (about five and a half years), and Shinzō Abe (five years in December

2016). It is notable that each of these prime ministers is known for accomplishments in foreign policy. For example, the Yoshida Doctrine developed during Yoshida's seven years in office is widely considered to have delineated the boundaries of postwar Japanese foreign policy.[8] Ikeda successfully shifted Japanese public attention away from the contentious security treaty revision demonstrations of 1960—thought to be the largest public demonstrations in Japanese history—and onto a focus on high economic growth that would later be described as the "economic miracle." Satō shared a Nobel Peace Prize for his antinuclear weapons policies and successfully brokered the return of Japan's Okinawan islands to Japanese administrative control in 1972, twenty years after the occupation of the rest of Japan had ended. Nakasone could be seen as setting the stage for Japan's more active security policies in the post–Cold War era, expanding JMSDF patrols to one thousand nautical miles from Japan and coordinating Cold War strategy closely with US president Ronald Reagan. The Koizumi era, as discussed in chapter 2, is the focus of numerous studies related to Japan's so-called normalization.

In the seventy years from 1945 to 2015, Japan has been governed by thirty-three different prime ministers, including two who returned to power after serving previously (Yoshida and Abe). Twenty-two of these were members of the LDP, all but six of the twenty-eight prime ministers who have served since the LDP was created by the merger of the Liberal and Democratic Parties in 1955. Seventy years of experience with leadership turnover shows that changes in prime minister frequently led to changes in Japan's overall foreign policy agenda—from moves to the left (such as under Prime Ministers Miki and Murayama) to moves to the right (such as with Prime Ministers Kishi and Nakasone). It does not require a change in party in power to see change in Japan's security policies because a change in prime minister can take place at any time.

In the period prior to 2009 and after 1955, however, the LDP was in power for all but nine months. In the one brief nine-month period that the LDP was out of power, there was substantial concern among managers of Japan's security about a possible fundamental reordering of Japan's security practices. This short period ended too quickly to test what the impact of a non-LDP government would be in the area of security policy, however. Thus, with no substantial experience of non-LDP rule over the vast majority of the postwar period, there was worry in the Japanese defense establishment and in the United States of the possible effect of the rise to power of a DPJ government as LDP popularity plummeted under Prime Minister Asō in 2009 and a Lower House election was imminent. In the United States, some of this worry was owing to the minimal outreach by the United States to the DPJ prior to its rise to power. There is also some evidence that the DPJ itself resisted the minimal outreach that was pursued, which in itself concerned the United States.

By contrast, the expectation in the waning months of the Koizumi period was that Abe would continue and deepen the security policies of his predecessor and mentor, further pushing the envelope of antimilitarist principles and further strengthening the US-Japan alliance based on a template announced with great fanfare in 2006 in a Koizumi-Bush joint statement. There was even talk of constitutional revision of Article Nine—as set out in the LDP draft constitution circulated in November 2005, which followed the model of proposing a specific alternative as the right-of-center *Yomiuri* newspaper had in 1994.[9] While there were some initial moves in this expected direction, ultimately this is not the path that transpired under Abe and his LDP successors.

Later in this period there was also the expectation that two years after Abe's resignation when the DPJ came to power, the DPJ rise would lead to a fundamental reimagining of the US-Japan alliance and of Japan's security posture more broadly. While, again, there were some initial moves in this direction, this also is not the policy direction that was taken. Instead, the DPJ governments institutionalized Japan's security renaissance in 2010 with the dual acts of adopting a new NDPG and reaffirming Japan's commitment to the US-Japan alliance on the occasion of the fiftieth anniversary of the current security treaty, laying a template that Abe would expand upon after his and the LDP's return to power in December 2012.

Abe 1.0 and His Successors: Declining LDP Support and New Security Initiatives

The three LDP prime ministers to follow Prime Minister Koizumi were not able to expand substantially his security legacy, despite trying. Abe 1.0

(his first attempt at prime minister) tried the hardest and failed the most dramatically. Fukuda took a different approach, more influenced by the postwar antimilitarist legacy, but was fundamentally constrained by the policy paralysis caused by the twisted Diet and the effects of the global financial crisis. Asō advocated policies similar to Abe's but faced a serious challenge to party control and a forced Lower House election at a time of extremely low public support.

Abe began his term as prime minister as the anointed successor to the popular Koizumi. It can be difficult to follow such a popular leader, but Abe benefited from continued high popularity of the LDP as well. Where the LDP, and Japan as a whole, was not popular was with close neighbors China and South Korea. An early challenge and goal of Abe's was to repair the diplomatic damage Koizumi had caused with these two states. Abe also faced growing tensions with North Korea from a position of strength in public opinion over his avowed dedication to the abduction issue with North Korea.

Abe came from an illustrious political background. His father, Shintarō Abe, was Japan's longest-serving foreign minister and early in his career an aide to his father-in-law, Prime Minister Kishi. Shinzō Abe often invokes his grandfather Kishi's legacy—but less often alludes to his other grandfather, Kan Abe, who also served in the Diet.[10] Even more than when Abe returned to power in 2012, Abe's outspoken nationalist views were a matter of great media and public interest at the time Abe became prime minister in 2006. As chief cabinet secretary under Koizumi, Abe was at the forefront of LDP members advocating a more "balanced" view of Japan's past history, and he frequently criticized the 1993 Kōnō statement on the comfort women issue and efforts to introduce more detail about Japan's brutal wartime conduct into history textbooks. He was also an outspoken advocate for constitutional revision of Article Nine and of a renaming of the JSDF to something akin to a National Defense Force.[11]

From his first days in office, Abe sought to further advance the security-related legacies of the Koizumi era, including increased military capabilities, a deepened US-Japan alliance, and greater global role for the JSDF.[12] The MOD was established in the first months of the Abe government (from the former Japan Defense Agency) as a result of legislation passed at the end of the Koizumi administration.

In terms of a broader security strategy—before Japan yet had a formal national security strategy document—Abe sought to advance Japan's security interests in two ways. First, his administration advocated an "Arc of Freedom and Prosperity" of outreach to Australia, Southeast Asia, and India based on "shared values"—a not-so-subtle exclusion of China.[13] As he would in his second administration from 2012, Abe traveled widely to promote these policies. He signed a milestone agreement with Australia for security cooperation and laid the groundwork for a similar deepening of security ties with India. He was the first Japanese prime minister to address NATO. Second, Abe pursued what Daniel Sneider and others have called the Japanese dual hedge, "to maintain the security alliance with the United States while seeking to draw China into a regional and global economic and security structure."[14] Outreach to China and South Korea was not the sole purview of DPJ advocacy. As discussed in chapter 3, Abe's first foreign trips were to China and South Korea—before even the United States, a departure from standard practice noticed in Washington and across the Asian region.

Abe also attempted to formally revise Article Nine of Japan's postwar constitution, succeeding in a necessary first step of passing legislation in the Diet that set out the procedure whereby the required second step to constitutional revision, a national referendum on the proposed change, would take place. A national referendum of any kind has never been conducted in Japan, and so there were no procedures in place as to how it would take place if necessary. Even the legislation to set out the formal process for future change caused alarm among many Japanese, and a compromise in the legislation was included such that it would not take effect for a year after passing (at which point, it turns out, Abe was no longer prime minister).

Many of the policy achievements of the second Abe administration (the subject of chapter 5) were raised in his first term in office but not accomplished. For example, the idea to create a National Security Council passed in a different form in December 2013; recommendations from the expert commission Abe assembled to examine the legal basis for national security, especially the issue of CSD, were adopted by cabinet decision in July 2014 and a package of legislation in September 2015; and implementation of policies based on the US-Japan joint security declaration of 2006 were enacted in new US-Japan Guidelines for Defense Cooperation in April 2015. In this sense, Abe's first term in office can be seen as setting the agenda for what would become Japan's security renaissance, building on an agenda set under Koizumi.

Abe also sought in this first term to respond to new security challenges posed by Japan's changed regional environment and also to affronts to the historical memories of World War II perceived by his right-wing supporters. Here he was constrained by the strong postwar antimilitarist legacy and also made little headway in changing the narrative in historical memories of World War II. Abe did manage to continue the modest level of Japan's increased global presence enacted under Koizumi and put Japan-China relations on a better track, which was further cemented by his successor, Fukuda. During Abe's reign, Chinese premier Wen Jiabao visited Tokyo and spoke to the Diet in a way that explicitly minimized Japan's wartime atrocities vis-à-vis China and focused on the future in a way that foreshadowed how Abe's approach to discussing Japan's history would emerge when he returned to become prime minister in 2012 (and which the Chinese at that time would harshly criticize).

However, Abe showed insufficient attention to economic policy and pursued an overly ambitious security agenda—likely the result, at least in part, of political inexperience, a lesson he learned from for his later term as prime minister. Growing public discontent over Abe's apparent aloofness to the concerns of everyday Japanese—opponents derisively called him *obotchan* (a reference to a spoiled child)—led to a major election upset just ten months after Abe assumed power.

The LDP loss of the Upper House in the July 2007 election dramatically altered the prospects for Abe's agenda. The DPJ won a stunning 50 percent of the seats contested in the election (half the seats were not up for grabs in the staggered six-year terms of the Upper House), leaving the DPJ tantalizingly close to a majority on its own but in any case holding enough seats to thwart the LDP from passing legislation without the cooperation of parties other than its standard coalition partner, the Kōmei Party. The LDP won only 30 percent of the seats. (See appendix 2 for more on the election outcome.) As a result, a new era in Japanese politics had begun: the era of the twisted Diet—for the first time in postwar Japanese history. While common in the United States, this new, divided government required significant rethinking of Abe's political agenda.

The DPJ promptly exercised this new power in the security arena by refusing to renew JMSDF refueling support for the US-led antiterrorism coalition that had been operating from the Indian Ocean since 2001, leading to a brief suspension of a JMSDF role while new constraints on JSDF action overseas were negotiated. The DPJ's policy cohesion, especially in the area of security policy, however, was uneven at best due to the patchwork way it became the primary opposition party.[15] The DPJ was founded in 1996 from several disparate groups, including former members of the JSP and the LDP—archrivals in the previous "1955 system" discussed in chapter 2. Yukio Hatoyama, a former fourth-generation LDP politician whose grandfather had served as the first LDP prime minister, and Naoto Kan, formerly of the Democratic Social Federation, cofounded the party—and, fittingly, would become the first two DPJ prime ministers thirteen and fourteen years later, respectively, as seen in the next section. Mergers in 1998 and 2003 expanded the ranks of the DPJ. In 1998, the DPJ absorbed six small opposition parties and enlisted some former members of the splintered New Frontier Party, transforming itself into the "new" DPJ. In 2003, Ichirō Ozawa's Liberal Party merged with the DPJ. As such, the DPJ began its history with incumbent candidates of diverse career and social backgrounds.[16] By 2003, the DPJ had risen to become the primary opposition party to the LDP.

After two months of trying to advance his agenda under the new political circumstances of a twisted Diet, Abe resigned for health reasons in September 2007. He returned to backbencher status in the Lower House and passed the baton of leadership to his LDP colleague, Yasuo Fukuda.

A common pattern seen in LDP leadership turnover over the previous fifty years is a shift in policy priorities with a new prime minister. In the area of security policy, Fukuda's orientation was more similar to other centrist and left-leaning prime ministers of the past, seeking greater regional outreach and an economics-first diplomacy along the lines of his father, former prime minister Takeo Fukuda—who, in the late 1970s, had advocated for what is now called the Fukuda Doctrine of economic development and closer diplomatic and cultural ties with Southeast Asian states. Yasuo Fukuda continued Abe's policy of outreach to China, as noted in chapter 3—including visiting Beijing in his first three months in office and literally "playing ball" with Chinese premier Wen. Much fanfare was made of a "historic" cooperative agreement over the East China Sea—but details were scant, and in subsequent years the agreement was largely abandoned.[17]

At the same time, however, Fukuda was forced to try to manage the twisted Diet, which led to paralysis in multiple areas of domestic policy and also to strains in US-Japan relations. In particular, the agreed-upon plan to relocate the Futenma air station in Okinawa was stalled and the suspension of JMSDF refueling operations in the Indian Ocean because of DPJ opposition in the Upper House caused tense exchanges with Washington. More broadly, this policy gridlock led Washington to question the global role Japan had paid at least lip service to under Koizumi, with Japan's intransigence criticized in several high-profile reports.[18] Fukuda, too, would serve as prime minister for only one year, resigning amid declining popularity and concern in the party about required Lower House elections less than one year away.

Under Prime Minister Tarō Asō, public distaste for the LDP continued unabated. The global financial crisis of autumn 2008 and the winter of 2009 posed an additional serious setback for a resurgence of the LDP in the polls, as Japanese exports plummeted and Japan once again entered into recession. Asō expressed many of the foreign policy preferences of Abe, including deepened outreach to Australia and India and a values-based diplomacy concept based in a "security diamond" concept. Under Asō's leadership, the LDP completed a draft of an ambitious plan to recraft Japan's broader security strategy to respond to new international circumstances, a new NDPG, and also made a renewed commitment to the United States to make progress on Okinawa base realignment after Democrats came to power in the United States, with the January 2009 inauguration of US president Barack Obama. On Secretary of State Hillary Clinton's first trip abroad, to Japan, Asō assured Clinton that Japan was fully committed to moving ahead with deepening the US-Japan alliance in ways set out in the 2006 roadmap issued under Koizumi four years prior but not substantially pursued.

The Asō government did not last long enough to implement either plan, however. After multiple delays to calling elections in the Lower House because of repeated declines in LDP popularity in opinion polls,

Asō was forced to call an election at the very end of the four-year term of the Lower House. A DPJ victory seemed assured—but few predicted the complete rout of the LDP that took place.

The DPJ Challenge to Japan's Long-Standing Yet Evolving Security Practices

The DPJ's win in the Lower House election of August 30, 2009, was historic—the first time another party gained more seats in the Lower House since the LDP was formed in 1955—and it was a landslide: the DPJ won 64 percent of the seats (with roughly 45 percent of the vote—see appendix 2). What the Lower House landslide could not change, however, was the result of the 2007 Upper House election, in which the DPJ fell just a hair shy of an outright majority on its own and thus required a coalition partner to govern both houses of the Diet after the Lower House election win. After just over a week of political wrangling, the DPJ announced a coalition with the tiny SDP and formed its historic non-LDP cabinet a week later—including Japan's first non-LDP minister of defense in over half a century. This coalition with the SDP forced the DPJ repeatedly to compromise on security legislation in a way similar to how the LDP would later have to compromise with the Kōmei Party to pass legislation in its coalition formed after the December 2012 election.

The initial euphoria of a landslide election result and an opposition rise to power quickly turned to a fundamental challenge of DPJ governance without governing experience, however. This was exacerbated by the DPJ campaign pledge of "politician control over bureaucrats" (*seiji shudō*) and a lack of a formal process of political handover (since a handoff from one party to another party also had not happened in half a century). One example of many such challenges was the lack of an official system of classifying information as secret or sensitive, an issue controversially addressed by the later Abe government with the Designated State Secrets law of December 2013. At the time of the transition, numerous senior bureaucrats expressed concern over what sort of information about Japan's security policies could be shared with the senior leadership of the DPJ-led government. The issue of the so-called secret agreements (*mitsu yaku*) with the United States related to the possible discretionary US introduction of nuclear weapons into Japan during the Cold War (despite Japan's official three principles on nuclear weapons that would preclude such introduction) is one example that earned widespread media attention, and an official inquiry panel set up by the DPJ when numerous senior and retired bureaucrats and former LDP officials steadfastly refused to provide the new DPJ government with documents related to the issue.[19]

Still, on the positive side, the DPJ-led coalition controlled both houses of the Diet, ending for a time the period of the twisted Diet. Managing the coalition proved to be a major challenge, however, particularly cooperation with the SDP over security-related policies. The SDP is the successor to the JSP, which changed its name in 1996. At the time of the name change, many members defected to join the newly founded DPJ, partly for ideological reasons but also as a practical means of winning in the newly introduced SMD in the Lower House.[20] One of the primary ideological concerns of the SDP was protecting the "peace constitution"—continuing a thread from the JSP past.[21] Research into DPJ candidates shows that by the 2000 election, there were fewer former JSP members among the DPJ ranks than candidates who were former LDP or Sakigake politicians.[22] However, even though the number of former JSP members had shrunk, they were disproportionately senior in the DPJ:[23] although former JSP members made up less than 4 percent of DPJ Diet members after the 2009 election, roughly 10 percent of appointments to the Hatoyama cabinet went to former JSP members, rising to nearly 17 percent of appointments to the subsequent Kan cabinet.[24] This led to a significant voice for Japan's long-standing antimilitarist policies in the new DPJ government.

Weston Konishi groups DPJ members at the time into four main foreign policy schools: "realists (those who favor a strengthened defense policy and US-Japan alliance), pacifists (those who want to maintain constitutional restrictions on security policy and do away with the US-Japan alliance), centrists (those who do not have deep foreign policy convictions but who tend to lean toward the realist school by default), and neo-autonomists (those who want a strong defense policy in order to gain greater strategic independence from the United States)."[25] The coalition building across these groups, and with the SDP in the early days of DPJ governance, would illustrate the next step in Japan's security renaissance: crafting a broad consensus on Japan's future security direction beyond the single long-ruling LDP. The senior DPJ leadership was fraught with challenges to managing the coalition and intraparty rivalries, particularly over the security divide in the DPJ and the more left views of the SDP. The DPJ experienced a change of fortune in February 2010, however, thanks to the defection of an LDP Diet member, giving the DPJ control of the Upper House without the SDP and allowing the DPJ to rule in both houses on its own. The DPJ-SDP coalition formally ended in May 2010.

In the end, the DPJ period served to further reify and even expand LDP-era security practices rather than lead Japan in a substantially new direction. This was certainly not the intention of the party, however, which assumed power on a far-reaching reform agenda that challenged and offered alternatives on a very wide range of domestic and international policies of the LDP in addition to challenging important processes by which policy was formulated and implemented.[26]

A substantial body of scholarship on DPJ-era foreign policy is only just emerging. The limited work that has appeared to date has focused on explaining DPJ ideas about foreign policy, including those articulated before the DPJ assumed power in September 2009, and also DPJ efforts to alter some long-standing practices in security policy.[27] By contrast, this chapter seeks to draw attention to the results of DPJ-era security policy—the legacies left by the DPJ as the LDP reassumed political power in December 2012 and the broader importance of the DPJ era to Japan's security renaissance. Already by 2009, a switch in power away from LDP to opposition was *not* expected to lead to the sort of change that the JSP coming to power in the Cold War period may have led to—such as dissolving the US-Japan alliance or disbanding the JSDF. Still, as framed by Konishi, major figures in the DPJ advocated a set of views that coalesced around three primary goals for change in Japan's security practices under the LDP: (1) a more equal alliance with the United States, (2) closer ties to China and other Asian states, and (3) a more proactive diplomacy in conjunction with the United Nations, including UNPKO.[28] The importance of the changed international security environment—particularly Japan's new position vis-à-vis China—was signaled early by the Hatoyama administration's early outreach to China, the sharp escalation of tensions with China over the Senkaku Fishing Trawler Incident of the fall of 2010 under Kan, and the resulting severe tensions over the Senkaku "nationalization" in the summer and fall of 2012 under Noda. At the same time, the long legacies of Japan's struggles to come to terms with the legacy of World War II and the colonialist period, its postwar antimilitarist past, and inequality in the US alliance were also strongly evident in these three years of DPJ governance.

Hatoyama's Challenge to the US-Japan Alliance Legacy

As the DPJ's first prime minister, Hatoyama entered office with a range of expectations that would have been impossible for anyone to fully satisfy because of both the incompatible campaign promises and the strong expectation among many voters that the DPJ would act in stark contrast to previous LDP governments. In the area of foreign policy, Hatoyama was known to be a leading proponent of a more assertive and autonomous Japanese diplomacy that sought to hedge against a growing expectation of US decline.[29] Another difficulty of the early Hatoyama period was the awkward "dual power structure" between Hatoyama and fellow DPJ leader Ichirō Ozawa.[30] Ozawa likely would have served as the first DPJ prime minister had he not been embroiled in a campaign finance scandal that led him to resign as president of the DPJ just months before the party rose to power.[31]

Hatoyama posed numerous early challenges to the US-Japan alliance legacy. He refused to commit at the time he assumed office to LDP-era agreements to implement US base relocation in Okinawa, saying he needed to review the facts on the ground. To this, explains Christopher Hughes, Hatoyama faced "a near brick wall of US resistance to certain aspects of its attempts to rearticulate the basis of the bilateral alliance."[32] In addition, as with Abe before him, Hatoyama chose to meet with Chinese president Hu Jintao before meeting with US president Barack Obama (whom he met first on the sidelines of the opening of the United Nations in New York in September and then again during Obama's visit to Japan in November). Moreover, the Hatoyama government alienated bureaucrats in Japan and the United States through its awkward outreach due to a lack of personal connections in the bureaucracy and among senior political leadership abroad and, more broadly, to the DPJ policy of *seiji shudō*, stressed in its campaign manifesto for the purpose of centralizing decision making in the cabinet and prime minister's office rather than in conjunction with senior bureaucrats. Information released through WikiLeaks shows that Japan's powerful bureaucrats sought to maintain strong US-Japan ties in the early days of the DPJ government when the DPJ leadership was seeking to exert stronger control over the bureaucracy, a central aspect of the DPJ election platform.[33]

Hatoyama's stated goal of "equidistance" with China also did not go as planned. Despite the fanfare of the Ozawa-led DPJ Diet member visit to Beijing to meet President Hu in December 2010—where Hu reportedly shook hands with six hundred DPJ Diet members and staff—China's more assertive behavior both in the economic sphere in response to the global financial crisis and in the military sphere in terms of military spending and the East and South China Seas pushed the DPJ and Japan to move on earlier LDP-era plans to develop a closer military relationship with the United States. Plans for announcing concrete measures toward a deeper US-Japan alliance at the sixtieth anniversary celebrations of the alliance in January 2010 were thwarted, however, by the tensions between the Hatoyama government and the United States generated by disagreements over Okinawa and Hatoyama's own rhetoric and management style.

Japan under Hatoyama did continue from the outset, however, the recent LDP governments' policy of seeking opportunities to diversify Japan's strategic partners beyond the United States—which resonated with the neo-autonomous ambitions of some DPJ members such as Hatoyama and Ozawa. This policy would later be reified as a core aspect of Japan's first formal national security strategy issued in 2013 under Abe. At a summit meeting in New Delhi, Prime Minister Hatoyama and Indian prime minister Manmohan Singh agreed to enhance security cooperation between the two countries. Japan also signed an ACSA with Australia for peacetime security cooperation—the first such agreement Japan has signed with a country other than the United States.[34] The DPJ also continued to work toward a greater contribution to UNPKO and legislation to enable that—building on the legacy of DPJ senior member Ichirō Ozawa's long push for Japan to make an expanded security contribution in this area (which dated back to his influential call for Japan to become a "normal nation" in his 1994 best-selling book).[35]

Despite the many shortcomings and the tensions apparent in the period of Hatoyama governance, his administration does go down in history for its ultimate embrace of the US-Japan security relationship—a fundamental turning point for Japan's former opposition party stance. The January 2010 Clinton-Okada joint statement on the fiftieth anniversary of the security treaty was not the gala celebration many had imagined just a year earlier, but it did mark the occasion with promises of further alliance deepening. The first MOD annual white paper to be issued under the DPJ government explicitly noted the significance of the first DPJ defense minister's issuing the white paper, with Defense Minister Toshimi Kitazawa giving in its introduction his personal view that a DPJ minister issuing the white paper "will give it an even greater significance than [in] ordinary years." This first DPJ defense white paper essentially continues the same themes as the introduction to the previous volume under LDP rule, noting that "the security environment surrounding Japan is growing increasingly severe" and stressing the importance of Japan's making an international contribution to security given that "Japan relies on foreign countries for most of its resources and food." Further, his introduction promises a new NDPG within the year and that "the Ministry of Defense and the SDF continue to evolve on a day-to-day basis while expanding the range of activities further."[36]

In looking back on the nine months of rule of the first DPJ prime minister, who represented a party voted to power in a landslide, it is clear that multiple, overlapping factors contributed to Hatoyama's, and his party's, inability to implement policies that substantially changed the direction of security policy of the previous LDP governments. Domestic policy and political and institutional issues factored highly in their failures, but the three historical legacies evident for decades of LDP rule—the antimilitarist legacy, the US-Japan alliance legacy, and the unresolved wartime history legacy—as well as the shifting international environment, clearly impacted Hatoyama's agenda and shaped what successes he had.

A New Security Posture and Alliance Deepening Under Kan

Naoto Kan, the second DPJ prime minister, did not face the same expectations for change as his predecessor, after the public had experienced ten months of rocky DPJ governance and had been exposed somewhat to the difficulties of transformational governance reform. Despite the end of the twisted Diet in May 2010, the DPJ ability to pass legislation in its first Diet session in power was extremely low.[37] As a result, the DPJ scaled back some of the institutional reforms implemented early in the Hatoyama period. Of particular relevance to security policy coordination, the DPJ sought to reincorporate the bureaucracy into the policy-making process. It was too little, too late, however: voters shifted support to the LDP and other parties in the July 2010 Upper House election held just a month after Kan took office.

The LDP secured 42 percent of the seats contested in the July 2010 Upper House election, the largest percentage of any party in that election. The DPJ won only 36 percent of the open seats, though they retained their share of the half of the seats from the 2007 election that were not up for grabs in 2010. (See appendix 2 for voting and seat percentages won by other parties.) Less than two months after the DPJ's pummeling in the Upper House election, however, the party benefited from a rally 'round the flag effect related to the first Senkaku crisis, the Fishing Trawler Incident, in September 2010. Despite the apparently poor handling of the incident by the DPJ, the perception of Chinese overreaction to Japanese policy had the effect of boosting Kan's popularity. In addition, Kan had just emerged victorious in a leadership battle in the DPJ presidential election (on September 10), where once again Ichirō Ozawa was pushed aside as the possible next DPJ prime minister.

Some internal DPJ efforts to alter the long-standing course of Japanese security policy were further thwarted by the return to a twisted Diet for only a second time in Japanese history (and a second time in two years). This required greater cooperation with the LDP in order to pass legislation and afforded an excuse for Kan to reach out to the LDP over security issues, leading to resumed discussion of the DPJ's implementing the new NDPG draft completed under Asō in 2009 but not able to be enacted by the LDP before its loss of power.

The September 2010 Senkaku Fishing Trawler Incident further pushed Kan and the DPJ to consider security policy initiatives developed in the waning years of LDP rule. The China threat hit home, leading to changed public opinion related to China and security and stressing among the public the importance of the US-Japan alliance, in particular Article Five of the security treaty, which promises US protection of all territory administered by Japan. The DPJ under Kan also continued outreach to new security partners. For example, Foreign Minister Seiji Maehara's first overseas bilateral meeting with Australia in November 2010 accelerated discussion of an advanced information-sharing agreement to facilitate increased defense cooperation with that nation.

The December 2010 NDPG emerged from over a year of DPJ internal discussion and debate over Japan's proper security course, which had resulted in the expulsion of the pacifist-leaning SDP from the ruling coalition and, in addition, the abrupt resignation of Prime Minister Hatoyama. In this new NDPG, which is widely reported to be quite similar to the draft prepared by the LDP in 2009, Japanese defense policy made substantial progress toward goals originally articulated in the Koizumi period that arose from multiple discussions with US alliance counterparts and in subsequent internal discussions in Japan's own defense establishment (particularly in the MOD and the Cabinet Office). On the one hand, some long-standing themes in DPJ statements about its preferred Japanese security outlook were articulated in the new NDPG, such as increased indigenous defense capabilities and enhanced capabilities that could contribute to sea-lane defense and to UNPKO. Deeper outreach to new security partners in the region such as Australia, India, and South Korea—policies initiated under previous LDP rule but also long supported in DPJ statements while in opposition—was also enhanced in this important DPJ security document. On the other hand, increased rhetoric suggesting the need to militarily confront China and to deepen the US-Japan alliance in ways that set aside earlier rhetoric of "equality" marks a significant change in DPJ policy when compared with the Hatoyama government.

The 2010 NDPG formally abandoned the "basic defense force" concept introduced in the 1978 NDPO in favor of a "dynamic defense" force concept. Similarly, "dynamic deterrence" was planned through an increase in operational activity such as ISR. This document shows conceptual linkages to US goals to respond to China's growing capabilities, such as the air-sea battle concept—clearly due to close coordination between Japanese and US defense planners. The document also introduced the idea of gray-zone disputes, defined as confrontations over territory, sovereignty, and economic interest that do not escalate into wars—as discussed in earlier chapters of this book.

Under the new NDPG, the JMSDF was set to expand its submarine fleet from sixteen to twenty-two boats, upgrade to the *Hyūga*-class destroyer, and upgrade P-1 long-range patrol aircraft. Japan's amphibious warfare capabilities were also strengthened, including a dedicated unit in the JGSDF that has been training with the US Marines in annual exercises at Camp Pendleton in California since 2013 and before that in Guam and on remote Japanese islands in the southwestern island chain.

Less than three months after the adoption of the new NDPG in December 2010, another major event would challenge the DPJ in its crisis-management skills and further nudge the Japanese public and political elites toward greater support for the JSDF and the US-Japan alliance: the triple disaster of March 11, 2011. The momentous logistical challenges of disaster-relief activities in the wake of the earthquake and tsunami starkly illustrated the benefit of advance planning for contingencies in the alliance framework and the value of interoperability of US and Japanese military forces. "Operation Tomodachi" ("friendship" in Japanese) mobilized an estimated twenty-four thousand US military personnel, twenty-four US naval ships, and nearly two hundred US aircraft that all worked with the largest deployment of the JSDF in its history—over a hundred thousand troops. Extensive news coverage of these joint efforts—and their success in rescuing many Japanese victims of the disaster and rebuilding vital infrastructure—pushed public support for JSDF and the US-Japan alliance to all-time highs.[38]

Support for the DPJ government, however, was another matter. As with the Hatoyama experience, public support for the DPJ under Kan experienced a steady decline from initial enthusiasm when he took over the reins from deeply unpopular Hatoyama to only 20 percent support by January 2011.[39] The triple disaster further weakened the DPJ, and while Kan survived a no-confidence vote in the Diet in July 2011, he resigned soon after.

Looking back on the fifteen months of the second DPJ government, one begins to see how resilient Japan's long-standing security practices had become—despite multiple stresses and changes in power. Moreover, and perhaps more importantly, one begins to see the mechanisms by which they are reinforced for new circumstances. These trends would continue under the final DPJ prime minister of this period, Yoshihiko Noda.

Noda's "Normalcy" and the Fall of the DPJ from Power

In sharp contrast to Hatoyama, Yoshihiko Noda came from the conservative wing of the DPJ. That his father was a former JSDF officer caused some on the left in his party to treat him with suspicion, and others in the LDP and bureaucracy to offer him the benefit of the doubt. Noda benefited from an early boost of support—over 50 percent in *Asahi* polls and more than 70 percent in *Yomiuri* polls[40]—but as with the previous five prime ministers, there was a quick decline exacerbated by the policy gridlock of the twisted Diet, leading to early elections in December 2012 (instead of as late as August 2013 allowed under the four-year-maximum terms of the Lower House). By what would be the final year of DPJ rule, Sneider argues, "The Noda administration, in the view of critics within the DPJ itself, had in many respects brought Japanese foreign policy back to the positions of the conservative Liberal Democratic Party–led governments that preceded—and succeeded—its coming to power."[41]

In his fifteen months in office, Noda helped to develop the US-Japan alliance relationship to LDP-era closeness, building on the post–March 11 bump in popularity among the general public, initially seen in the last months of the Kan government. DPJ policy regarding controlling bureaucrats was further scaled back, also building on Kan government policies and leading to more effective security planning and US-Japan alliance deepening. Still, numerous crises continued under DPJ rule—both domestic and international—and tensions continued to mount on a number of fronts.

On one front, tensions grew during the summer and fall of 2012 over the so-called nationalization of three of the Senkaku Islands by the Noda government—which China derided as a disruptive change in the status quo and the Noda government explained as an effort to maintain the status quo. Japanese nationalist agitators instigated by then Tokyo governor Shintarō Ishihara sought to purchase the privately owned islands for the purpose of further asserting Japanese sovereignty (such as by erecting structures or offering tours), which Noda sought to avert by arranging for the islands to be purchased by the central government.

This action sparked a return of anti-Japanese rioting in several Chinese cities and widespread damage to Japanese-owned factories and businesses in China—similar to the large-scale riots seen in the Koizumi period and to a lesser extent after the Fishing Trawler Incident of 2010. It also led to a new status quo related to Chinese activities around the Senkaku Islands, sparking a new era of regular Chinese entry into the territorial waters of the islands and occasional overflights of their airspace. This new status quo continues and is closely monitored by the JSDF and JCG—and is used as one of the major justifications for the further shift of JSDF resources to the southwest (closer to the islands), as seen in the next steps of Japan's changed defense posture discussed in chapter 5.

On another front, tensions with South Korea over history issues continued from the previous Kan administration. Kan's August 2010 statement of remorse on the occasion marking Japan's colonization of the Korean Peninsula one hundred years ago had only sparked further calls for apologies and compensation, contrary to what many in the DPJ had expected by this new apology statement and also related gestures such as the return of some Korean cultural treasures that had been taken to Japan during the colonial period. In August 2011 the Korean Constitutional Court ruled that the previous Korean government's failure to negotiate on the comfort women issue was unconstitutional—reopening the reparations issue from World War II that Japan firmly asserts was settled in the 1965 agreement to normalize relations between Japan and South Korea. The following August, South Korean president Lee Myung-bak visited Takeshima (the disputed islet between Japan and South Korea that South Korea controls), a first for a Korean president, further disrupting the status quo over history issues. In the midst of these two milestone incidents, Korean (and Chinese) criticism of Japanese textbook portrayals of Japan's wartime conduct continued at a high rate.

Noda struggled to sustain diplomatic engagement with China and South Korea through both bilateral and formal trilateral dialogue that had managed to continue through the tensions and leadership transitions among the three states since the beginning of the period examined in this chapter, transitions that also included the destabilizing rise to power of the third-generation Kim Jong Un in North Korea.

In the midst of these tensions, public support for the DPJ was waning. It appeared that the public was fed up with too many crises and missteps. In July 2012, Ozawa and forty-eight of his supporters defected from the DPJ in opposition to the Noda government's plan to increase the consumption tax and formed the People's Life Party, which later merged with other parties to become the Tomorrow Party of Japan.[42] As the deadline for the next Lower House election neared in the minds of the DPJ leadership, the LDP emerged newly resurgent under Shinzō Abe after a contentious election for the LDP presidency in September 2012. With LDP leadership renewed, there was a strong LDP push for an early election, leading to a brokered deal for a December 2012 election as a DPJ compromise to push through legislation in the twisted Diet.

Noda dissolved the Lower House on November 16, 2012—prompting additional defections from the DPJ. By the time of the December 16, 2012, election, three new parties had been formed: Your Party (YP), the Japan Restoration Party (JRP), and the Tomorrow Party. The LDP won big (294 seats of 480), and the DPJ was decimated, winning just 57 seats.[43] As Sneider has summed up this final stage, "Undoubtedly, driven in large part by the actions of the Chinese government and to some extent by events on the Korean peninsula and elsewhere in the region, the DPJ went through a return to greater realism, whether reluctantly, as some have suggested, or even resentfully. Still, the DPJ represented a significant development in the evolution of postwar Japanese foreign and security-policy thought."[44]

How can we explain the shift in DPJ policy to the right? And why the changed parameters for security policy enacted under Noda? As discussed in chapter 3, over the course of the six years discussed in this chapter, Japan's international environment continued to shift dramatically. The rise to power of the Democrats in Japan coincided with a rise of Democrats in the United States. Moreover, the US rebalance and reengagement with Asia gave new impetus to Japan's strategy of deeper engagement with the region—including militarily. In addition, China's increased assertiveness related to the Senkaku Islands, the South China Sea, and greater military capabilities overall, together with continued North Korean provocations and capability increases, pushed the DPJ to respond with new security policies. Sneider has argued that this significant development was "an attempt, however limited, to shift the paradigm away from the doctrine of total dependence and subordination to American strategic policy"[45]—but an alternative argument, looking back on the DPJ period, is that the more significant development of this period was that of a consensus among the major ruling and opposition parties (in particular the LDP, DPJ, and Kōmei) about the core direction of Japanese security policy for the twenty-first century: continuing in its mooring in antimilitarist practices and the US-Japan alliance while seeking to play a limited but expanded international role within the confines imposed by Japan's incomplete reconciling with the legacies of its militarist era.

In an early look back at the DPJ ruling period, Sneider writes, "The DPJ indeed 'learned' some powerful lessons about the obstacles to trying to shift Japanese foreign policy away, even slightly, from the well-established moorings of the established order."[46] "But," he continues, "it would be mistaken to assume that the core beliefs of the DPJ and the profound shift in Japanese policy that they imply have simply faded from the scene."[47] Indeed, contending schools of thought in Japan about the proper course of Japanese security policy have been evident throughout the postwar period. As discussed in the next chapter, the rise of the once antimainstream conservative faction in the LDP now led by Prime Minister Abe is a significant development in Japanese domestic politics with a deep influence on future Japanese security policy, but certainly it does not symbolize a new unanimity of beliefs in Japan related to military security of that ideological bent.

One finding from an examination of the three-year experience of DPJ rule, however, is that domestic political factors play a substantial role in how political coalitions form over security policy, independent of evolving public opinion over security issues and of changes in the regional security environment. Scholarly analysis demonstrates how these three factors—domestic politics and institutions, public opinion, and changes in the regional security environment—in fact interact deeply and thus cannot be fully examined independently.[48] Still, a first-order analysis can be conducted as if these three factors were independent variables, and it shows clearly that turbulently shifting domestic politics in the period 2006 to 2012 played an important role in how Japan's security policies evolved toward maintained continuity, rather than the discontinuity sought by some in the DPJ, leading to the further institutionalization of Japan's security renaissance in the six-year period "from Abe to Abe."

Conclusion: The Institutionalization of Japan's Security Renaissance from 2006 to 2012

Japanese politics appeared to have ushered in the new century with a newfound stability under the five-year reign of popular prime minister Jun'ichirō Koizumi from 2001 to 2006. After Koizumi, however, Japan returned to its 1990s experience of frequent turnover of political leadership and, as in the interlude of 1993 to 1994, a brief fall of the long-ruling LDP from power. Despite seven different prime ministers in as many years—spanning a range of positions on the left-right spectrum—Japan's security policies developed over this period toward increased capabilities, expanded roles within the US-Japan alliance, and greater international engagement. Changes in the international environment occurred together with—and contributed to—Japan's long-stagnating domestic economy and worsening budgetary and fiscal woes, prompting voters to pursue new political approaches to both domestic and international challenges, further institutionalizing Japan's security renaissance.

Looking back at the brief three-year DPJ period, it is clear that not only did the DPJ not fundamentally alter Japanese security policy but, conversely, acted to reify long-standing policies enacted under over half a century of LDP rule. This finding differs from the picture of DPJ rule painted by informed analysts at the time of DPJ rule. For example, Christopher Hughes has written, "[the DPJ] has also initiated, whether deliberately or inadvertently, a process of longer-term shift, and drift, in Japan's strategy. The DPJ is now thought to be diverting Japan from the trajectory laid down by the LDP—a trajectory that in recent years, and especially under the premiership of Koizumi Jun'ichiro, has generally been viewed as setting a benchmark to be emulated of close US-Japan alliance ties and concomitant Japanese international proactivity."[49]

While the DPJ currently is a mere shadow of its former self and is trying to reinvigorate the party under new leadership after the 2016 Upper House election, the underlying views that DPJ leaders expressed related to the three postwar historical legacies remain salient. The international environment Japan faces continues to evolve at the rapid pace seen since the beginning of DPJ rule in 2009; the leadership of the DPJ is also changing from DPJ founders such as Hatoyama, Kan, and Ozawa to a new generation whose foreign policy views have been shaped in part by the more recent international environment Japan faces.

Four major effects on Japan's security practices can be seen in the period "from Abe to Abe." First, there was a much wider public discussion of appropriate security practices to address Japan's shifting international environment. The period started with widespread expectation of further "normalization" continuing from the Koizumi period. The stresses on the political system of that period were underappreciated, however, leading to a wider public discussion of Japan's appropriate security roles in the new century and a pause in further moves down the path that Koizumi had laid. Moreover, there was growing public perception that other important issues were being neglected: economic growth, the dismal fiscal position, and even basic competency issues in governance (like losing millions of pension records and repeated scandals involving cabinet members). Fifty years of LDP rule had created the impression of an ossified and out-of-touch party.

Second, new strategic thinking was implemented in this period to move away from the Cold War–era defense posture and to respond comprehensively to the primary challenge of China's rise and more broadly to the dramatically changed regional and international environment. In particular, the 2010 NDPG set out a comprehensive strategy for implementing this new thinking, demonstrating remarkable continuity from the LDP to DPJ (and, as discussed in chapter 5, with the new LDP government in the second Abe administration). The strategic posture shift away from the Soviet threat in the north to the China threat in the southwest, enhanced military capabilities, and expanded cooperation with the United States and with other security partners were all important new legacies from this period.

Third, despite periods of tension, the US-Japan alliance was reaffirmed and revitalized in the years 2006 to 2012. The relationship stood ready for next steps of alliance deepening under revised US-Japan Guidelines for Defense Cooperation negotiated by the second Abe administration in the next period (examined in chapter 5). The March 2011 triple disaster and Operation Tomodachi response played an important role in deepening public support for the alliance, as did US support for Japan related to Japan's escalating confrontations with China.

A fourth legacy of this period is the increased international security activities Japan engaged in beyond the US-Japan alliance: the new strategic partnership with Australia, enhanced security cooperation with South Korea, deeper engagement with regional security institutions, and increased out-of-area activities (in particular anti-piracy efforts of both the JCG and the JMSDF).

A number of important and far-reaching changes to Japan's security practices have been implemented in the years since 2006, but these changes do not mark a fundamental shift in the principles that guide Japanese security policy. Given the scale of change in Japanese identity in this period as defined in relational terms, such as vis-à-vis China or South Korea,[50] one might expect greater policy change in this period than actually seen. Challenges posed to the historical legacy of anti-militarism by the first Abe administration in 2006 to 2007, for example, were substantial but not realized in actual policy outcomes. Similarly, challenges posed to the historical legacy of the US-Japan alliance by the Hatoyama administration in 2009 to 2010 were also substantial, and also ultimately unsuccessful in altering the direction of change in Japanese security policy related to US-Japan alliance deepening. Altering the long-standing historical legacy of lack of historical reconciliation over World War II and events prior also proved difficult to achieve, despite concerted efforts by successive prime ministers in this period.

This chapter has sought to highlight the new domestic political dynamic that emerged in the tumultuous period 2006 to 2012 and its broad effect on Japanese security policies and practices. The renaissance in security practice and discussions of security practice that took place in this period laid the foundation for further change implemented by the second Abe administration beginning in December 2012.

CHAPTER FIVE

The New Conservative Mainstream and New Security Policies Under Prime Minister Shinzō Abe, 2012 to 2016

Prime Minister Shinzō Abe's return to power in December 2012 returned Japan to international attention with his popular "Abenomics" economic policy platform and his oft-repeated motto that "Japan is back." Abe projected a refreshing new image of Japan as revitalized and confident. His own political comeback was seen by many as an inspiring metaphor for Japan's potential comeback. Abe's security policies have received special attention because of his outspokenly nationalist views on controversial history issues, the company he keeps (including many historical revisionists in his party and civil society institutions), and rising tensions with rival China and fellow US ally South Korea. In addition, the sheer number of new security policies enacted under Abe attracts attention and scrutiny.

This chapter explains these numerous new security policy developments as a response to the changed international environment Japan faces and as a result of changed domestic politics in Japan, but in each case also structured and limited by the three important historical legacies under which Japan's leaders must operate—illustrating how Japan's security renaissance is both forward looking and backward looking. The legacy of Japan's wartime and colonial past became closely associated with Abe, rightly or wrongly, and his efforts to address this history were widely covered. The postwar legacy of antimilitarism sharply hindered and shaped the policies enacted over these years, and the politics surrounding them. The complex postwar legacy of the US-Japan relationship also continued to shape Abe's policy preferences in multiple ways, from the landmark 2015 US-Japan Guidelines for Defense Cooperation to the continued challenges of strident opposition to the concentration of US military forces in Okinawa. Abe himself will surely exert a lasting legacy on Japan's security future as one of the longest-serving prime ministers in Japan's history, but his great efforts to advance Japan's security renaissance is only one factor that contributed to the scale of change seen during his time in office.

Many of the prominent new security policies enacted in this period mark a culmination of policies initiated by previous administrations, including those of the rival DPJ as well as Abe's own previous and short-lived administration (2006–2007). It seems likely that any prime minister, not just Abe, would have enacted a similar policy program in response to Japan's changed international environment—and, indeed, as argued in chapter 4, the three prime ministers of the DPJ ruling period set important precedents that Abe followed.

Still, Abe himself is part of the explanation for the sheer number of prominent developments in the area of military security in the first three years of his administration. His high popularity in the first years of his second term in office—and political savvy—enabled him to advance policies across many areas simultaneously. It was a comeback that rivaled his grandfather's rise to prime minister in 1957, only a decade after being imprisoned for suspected war crimes and blackballed from political office by the Allied occupation authorities. As with his grandfather Nobusuke Kishi, some of Abe's security policy reforms also elicited huge public protests, at times drawing out over a hundred thousand demonstrators in front of the Diet building and Prime Minister's residence,[1] reminiscent of the protests in those locations in 1960 over the revision of the US-Japan Security Treaty, though on a much smaller scale. Even former prime minister Murayama, albeit a former socialist prime minister, joined the protests in July 2015 over the Abe government's package of security legislation, saying to the media, "I stood up out of a sense of crisis."[2]

Important developments in security policy, institutions, and practices were numerous and far-reaching in the first three years of the second Abe administration: the crafting and adoption of Japan's first formal national security strategy, creation of the NSC, new NDPG, new US-Japan Guidelines for Defense Cooperation, enactment of an official state secrets law, legislation implementing a reinterpretation of the constitution to allow Japan to participate in CSD with the militaries of other states in limited circumstances, further relaxation of restrictions on weapons exports, recrafting of ODA doctrine to allow for defense-related aid, and increased military spending for the first time in a decade.[3] Debates over enactment of this full agenda illustrate well the international and domestic drivers of security policy change as well as the continued challenges of reconciling Japan's present goals with the legacies of its past.

The Domestic and International Politics
of Abe's Return to Power

The return of the LDP to power in the December 2012 Lower House elections resulted in large part from the collapse in public confidence in the ability of the DPJ to rule effectively, much as the DPJ's rise to power three years earlier had been largely the result of public discontent with the LDP broadly as opposed to discontent over any one specific policy or set of policies. One data point from the December 2012 election starkly illustrates that the LDP did *not* enjoy a sudden new boost in popularity despite the "landslide" outcome in terms of seats gained: the LDP actually received *fewer* votes in the 2012 election than it had in the 2009 election that brought the DPJ to power in 2009. Rather, what accounts for the huge increase in LDP seats in 2012 is the fracturing of the opposition, a marked decline in voter turnout, and the effect of the electoral system. Due to the effect of single-member electoral districts on translating percentage of vote to percentage of seats, the LDP secured 61.3 percent of the seats in the Lower House election in 2012 with only 43 percent of the vote in the SMD and 27.6 percent in the PR districts. (See appendix 2 for a breakdown of the votes in recent elections.) By contrast, the DPJ secured only 11.9 percent of seats despite gaining 22.8 percent of the votes in SMD and 16 percent in PR districts. When comparing the percentage of LDP votes across elections, one sees that the LDP gained more than double the number of seats in 2012 from 2009, with only about a 5 percentage point higher vote draw in the SMD and only 1 percentage point higher in the PR districts, and fewer actual total votes. Certainly many voters would have been aware of Abe's hawkish views—after all, he had served as prime minister six years earlier—but support for these views cannot be assumed to be a primary cause of Abe's and the LDP's electoral success. Thus, Abe's election—and the LDP return to power—cannot be seen as an example of a sudden surge of popular support for positions to the political right. Rather, it is the broad continuity of security policies and trajectory between DPJ and LDP rule that illustrates Japan's security renaissance of the past decade.

Security policy issues arguably factored into public concern with DPJ rule in the general sense of awareness of Japan's eroding national security status in relation to such issues as the growing fear of military confrontation with China and concerns over the reliability of the US-Japan Security Treaty commitments that emerged at the start of DPJ rule, but security policy issues were not the primary drivers of the change in political power. To a large degree, the particularly assertive security policy views of Abe were incidental to his return to power—though they would ultimately cast a long shadow on perceptions of his time in office. Rather, the LDP campaigned on the need to restore Japan's economic health, linking even security-policy strengthening to Japan's economic revitalization.

Upon assuming office, Abe set out three "arrows" of economic policy that would come to symbolize this goal, which the media has embraced as Abenomics. Abe's success in revitalizing Japan's moribund economy was critical to his popularity in his first year in office and allowed a simultaneous pursuit of security policy innovation.[4] The Japanese economy and stock market posted impressive gains in Abe's first year in office. Looking forward, success with Abenomics will continue to be a necessary condition for further security policy innovation, including in terms of sustaining necessary public support, maintaining respect and support in the Asian region, and simply paying for the new defensive capabilities and roles that the Abe government seeks to enact.

Abe's return to power in December 2012 led to the same sort of media firestorm and concerns about rising nationalism in Japan and a dramatic break with Japan's long-standing security practices as when Abe took office in September 2006. The similarities between the first and second Abe terms as prime minister did not end there. In December 2012, as in September 2006, Abe would face a scheduled Upper House election in July of the following year that would affect his ability to pass new legislation. And as in September 2006, Abe made a number of statements in his first six months in office from December 2012 that made headlines around the world for the concerns they raised about Japan's rightward policy moves—which the *New York Times* and *China Daily* alike described as "hypernationalism." Unlike his first experience as prime minister, however, Abe successfully led his party to gains in the Upper House election and, less than one year after assuming office, succeeded in implementing several major pieces of national security legislation. These new developments are notable and important. They do not, however, connote a dramatic break from Japan's past practices but rather reflect an adaptation of past practices to a new international environment—an adaptation that was greatly influenced by domestic politics, particularly the LDP's coalition partner, the Kōmei Party.[5]

Here it is important to note the unique sort of coalition the LDP has formed with Kōmei, which is unlike political coalitions common in European democracies due to Japan's unusual electoral system, which includes both individual constituencies and PR seats in both houses of the Diet. As a small party, Kōmei has little hope of securing seats in the individual constituencies such as the SMD in the Lower House or the prefectural constituencies in the Upper House, but it can (and does) attract voters in the PR vote. As part of the coalition agreement with the LDP, Kōmei instructs supporters to vote for LDP candidates in the SMD in exchange for greater power in the coalition and a few designated SMD seats in urban constituencies. This boost to LDP candidates in individual constituencies arguably led to the LDP landslide win of seats in 2012 and 2014.

As an illustration, consider the LDP-Kōmei return to power in 2012. In that election, Kōmei won 11.83 percent of the PR vote but only 1.49 percent of the SMD vote. (Vote percentages are provided in appendix 2.) Since each voter in Japan casts one vote in each system, one must ask where the missing 10.34 percent of the Kōmei vote in the SMD went (i.e., the difference between 11.83 in PR and 1.49 in SMD). If most Kōmei supporters followed party leader instructions to vote for the LDP candidate, that alone accounts for more than half the vote differential between the DPJ and the LDP in the 2012 election. Put another way, had those votes gone to the DPJ, the LDP and the DPJ share of the vote in the SMD would have been roughly equal, dramatically altering the balance of seats—much beyond what one would expect by just looking at the small vote share Kōmei itself draws.

Kōmei's pivotal role in boosting LDP vote share in SMD helps to explain why Abe conceded so much of his security agenda ambitions to Kōmei preferences despite Kōmei's holding presently only roughly 7 percent of the seats in the Lower House versus the LDP's roughly 61 percent. Another reason is that with Kōmei in coalition, the LDP has the necessary two-thirds majority to override opposition in the Upper House, where the LDP held a very narrow majority until the July 2016 election that could be jeopardized by defectors in the LDP and by procedural rules in the Upper House.

International developments in Japan's regional environment also assisted Abe in achieving his long-standing agenda for security policy innovation. China pursued an increasingly assertive set of policies related to its claims to the Senkaku Islands from shortly after Abe's previous term as prime minister, and this aggressive agenda further escalated shortly after Abe assumed office for the second time. In addition to regular incursions into the territorial waters of the Senkaku Islands, Japan and China exchanged harsh words in Abe's first month back in power over an alleged radar lock of a Chinese fighter plane on a JMSDF vessel, an act that might have escalated into a shooting conflict had it not been handled with restraint. That the Abe government chose to respond to this provocation with a harshly worded diplomatic protest and criticism of China in the Diet and not with military force or even economic sanctions belied the war-mongering reputation ascribed to Abe. In addition, China's actions elsewhere in the region, in particular in the South China Sea with rival claimants to islands there, the Philippines and Vietnam in particular, further fueled concern in Japan over China's military intentions, lending credence to Abe's call for Japan to increase its military spending, to develop new capabilities, and to adapt existing security practices to a more hostile environment. North Korea's continued military provocations in Japan's neighborhood also facilitated an expanded security agenda—as both had in the period of DPJ rule.

Developments in the national security environment beyond Japan's immediate region also facilitated the Abe government's agenda of developing greater military capabilities and streamlined security practices. Under the previous DPJ government, Japan's NDPG of 2010 had set out the new concept of gray-zone conflict in the context of fears over the Senkaku dispute, but in the world beyond Japan's immediate neighborhood instances of gray-zone conflict actually emerged during Abe's second term. In particular, Russia's stealth invasion of Crimea and eastern Ukraine in 2014 alarmed many Japanese for the parallels they imagined in the context of how stealth Chinese paramilitary forces might invade the Senkaku Islands—with seeming US acquiescence to Russia's actions stoking fears that US action in a Senkaku dispute would similarly be limited to rhetoric.[6] US attention to renewed conflict in the Middle East also created concern in Japan that the stated rebalance of US military forces to Asia would not be forthcoming.

Important New Security Institutions and Practices, 2013 to 2015

The speed and skill with which the second Abe government enacted a series of changes to national security policies and practices was remarkable, especially since similar efforts his first cabinet made in this area were markedly unsuccessful in 2006 to 2007. Undoubtedly part of these achievements was due to lessons learned in effective governance and policy making from his first experience, a second chance few elected leaders are granted. The changed nature of the political opposition also surely played an important role, however, with a popular new political party rising to the right of the LDP, the JRP (Nippon Isshin no Kai), and the dovish challenge of the left wing of the DPJ and SDP in decline. In addition, as discussed in chapter 3, the international environment Japan faced had notably deteriorated in the six years since Abe had last served as prime minister, leading to further impetus for policy shift—though, as discussed later in the chapter, policy responses informed by the postwar legacy of antimilitarism continued to be preferred by the majority of the Japanese public.

Even in his second attempt to enact sweeping security legislation, however, Abe and his supporters did not get everything they wanted. Indeed, part of his success in his second term was the result of asking for less. For example, in his first term in 2006 to 2007, the Abe government sought to formally revise Article Nine of Japan's constitution to allow for expanded military roles for Japan beyond strict self-defense. His government did achieve passing legislation that established the formal process for the required national referendum to revise the constitution but lost control of the Upper House in the meantime, making the national referendum legislation moot (at least for the time being). In the new Abe administration, Abe sought the lesser goal of *reinterpreting* the constitution to allow for Japan to play new roles in CSD and succeeded in this attempt—though he had to compromise even further in terms of the scope of the reinterpretation. This reinterpretation was implemented in two phases: the cabinet issued its decision to pursue this approach on July 1, 2014, and legislation to enact this reinterpretation was approved in the Diet in September 2015 after discussions in the party and coalition in the spring of 2015 and deliberation in the Diet in the summer of that year. New thinking related to military security was evident in this period, including willingness across political parties and societal actors to reconsider old taboos. Still, the three important historical legacies of the postwar period limited Abe's success in making further changes and altered the scope of the resulting changes his government was able to enact.

Establishment of the NSC and Related Legislation

The new NSC and publishing of a formal national security strategy are important indicators of Japan's security renaissance. They indicate a new willingness to consider approaches to managing Japan's national security that transcend old taboos, and they enlarge Japan's broader approach to security in their own right. Under the NSC, the Japanese government for the first time has a standing body—the National Security Secretariat (NSS)—that seeks to coordinate aspects of Japan's military security strategy across government and not just at a time of crisis.[7] It also has a formal counterpart to the US National Security Advisor in the position of the secretary-general of the NSS, the first of whom being the former chair of the advisory panel that led to the establishment of the NSC, former senior MOFA official Shotarō Yachi.

Japan has long considered security in a comprehensive manner, integrating issues like energy security and economic security, and was a global leader in the push to consider human security in the post–Cold War era[8]—but this new approach is different: it explicitly includes military advisers into the process of crafting Japan's security policies and considers more explicitly military power as an aspect of broader foreign policy objectives. The Japanese government previously had a body called the Security Council, established in 1986 as one of Prime Minister Nakasone's attempts to strengthen Japan's security bureaucracy, but it was not a standing body and lacked a secretariat to provide analysis and policy suggestions independent of its constituent ministries; moreover, as noted in the *East Asian Strategic Review 2014*," "the mere fact of its meeting was considered newsworthy" for the former Security Council.[9]

At the core of the new NSC format are the secretary-general of the NSS, two deputy secretaries-general, the roughly seventy staff members of the NSS drawn from across government, and the regular meetings of the "Four-Minister Meeting," consisting of the prime minister, the chief cabinet secretary, and the ministers of foreign affairs and defense. Under Abe, this Four-Minister Meeting is held roughly every two weeks, serving as what Japanese defense planning documents describe as "the control tower for foreign and defense policies concerning national security."[10] In addition, a "Nine-Minister Meeting" is also part of the institutional structure and is intended to provide a venue for broader consultation on national security issues that would benefit from a broader range of input from ministries such as METI and the Ministry of Land, Infrastructure, Transport, and Tourism (which has oversight over the JCG). The *East Asian Strategic Review 2014* offers China policy as an example of an issue where broader coordination may be desirable, citing the case of the rare earths export ban imposed by China at the time of the 2010 Fishing Trawler Incident related to the Senkaku Islands dispute.[11]

Through the NSC and its roughly seventy-member secretariat, members of the JSDF are playing a larger role in Japan's national security planning. This is happening, of course, under civilian control of the MOD, cabinet, and Diet oversight—but this is new for Japan, and it is happening largely without significant opposition (as opposed to the huge public protests over other parts of Abe's security policy agenda). In practice, Japan has begun to use its military prowess—in particular its advanced technology and practical working knowledge and training —as one new fledgling arm of its foreign policy. "Seamless" is one of the primary buzzwords of the NSS, the 2013 NDPG, and the US-Japan defense guidelines in the context of different branches of the military working together more effectively—but the concept is also applied to Japan's new seamless approach across government to considering military capabilities in its broader foreign policy.

Several practical complications had to be confronted and addressed to move toward this more seamless approach to Japan's crafting of its military-security policies. One was the pervasive bureaucratic stove-piping endemic in the Japanese government system and the related and strong rivalries among Japan's powerful ministries. The question of who would be represented in the Four-Minister Meeting, for example, generated years of discussion and debate—including over arriving at the final number of four. This was not primarily about defense politics, however, but rather bureaucratic politics. The creation of the NSC also marked another step forward for the MOD, which had risen to ministry status only in January 2007 (under the first Abe administration). At the same time, however, the MOD also lost some bureaucratic power in the new institutional arrangements vis-à-vis uniformed officers of the JSDF, which technically are supervised by the MOD but have greater latitude to affect policy within the NSC framework.

A second practical complication to operating a cross-ministry coordinating body for national security is the expanded need to share information across ministry boundaries. One challenge to this process is simply the bureaucratic rivalries just alluded to, but another, which invokes Japan's wartime legacy, is the need to designate state secrets in order to protect information security among a wider group of individuals across ministries and agencies.

In the years leading up to and including World War II, the Japanese government increasingly designated information as state secrets as a way to silence and even imprison opponents to the fascist-militarist regime that hijacked Japanese democracy in those years. Even the suggestion of creating such a government-wide system of secrets with criminal penalties for divulging such information to the media or general public generated substantial opposition at multiple times in the recent past, including when the DPJ floated the idea when it was in power. This practical imperative also evokes the complex postwar US-Japan legacy, given that the United States has long been pressuring Japan to address the information security gap in its policy-making structure.[12] Within the JSDF and MOD the United States succeeded in getting the Japanese government to create higher penalties for release of classified information from those organizations, but no such system had existed across ministries until the specially designated secrets (SDS) law passed in the Diet—under great opposition in the Diet and among the general public—in December 2013 with an implementation date of December 2014. As explained in the 2014 defense white paper: "In order to protect information on Japan's defense and foreign affairs, as well as the prevention of designated harmful activities (e.g., counter-intelligence) and terrorism, which requires special secrecy, the act stipulates: (1) designation of Specially Designated Secrets by head of administrative organs; (2) security clearance for personnel that handle Specially Designated Secrets in duty; (3) establishment of a framework for providing or sharing Specially Designated Secrets within and outside administrative organs; and (4) penalties for unauthorized disclosure of Specially Designated Secrets."[13]

Introduction of this legislation into the Diet resulted in the first extended battle over Abe's national security agenda, both in the Diet and on the streets. In what would prove to be a precursor to the even larger demonstrations and divisiveness in the Diet over new security legislation introduced in the summer of 2015, activists employed a wide range of new social media tactics together with old-school demonstration tactics popular in the 1960s student-led movements protesting Japan's involvement with US military action abroad. The new SEALDs student group illustrates this combination of tactics and also how the renaissance in security attitudes in contemporary Japan remains rooted in the past.[14] One result of this activism was a one-year period added to the legislation to develop a set of policies that would protect civil liberties and promote transparency, though this addition did little to quell the opposition, who continued to characterize the legislation as having been rammed through the Diet and not adequately addressing civil liberties concerns. Also foreshadowing themes that would reemerge with the introduction of new security legislation in the Diet in the summer of 2015, concerns over the constitutionality of the proposed legislation would play a central role in the protests—including condemnation by the Japan Federation of Bar Associations.[15] Moreover, evoking Japan's militarist past was also evident, such as in a statement by former Nobel laureates that included the charge that "the Abe government's political stance bears a close resemblance to the prewar Japanese government's clamping down on freedom of speech and thought and rushing into war."[16]

In sum, the creation of the NSC and passage of the SDS law show a continued ambivalence among the general public over new security practices. There was a tacit acceptance of the need for the NSC but strong opposition to the secrets law. A changed domestic configuration of power allowed for the passage of both, however—though the Abe government did pay a short-term price in its popularity with the passage of the latter.

A Formal National Security Strategy, New NDPG and MTDP

Japan's first formal national security strategy, the new NDPG, and related MTDP adopted in December 2013 in conjunction with the establishment of the NSC are other important indications of Japan's development of greater military capabilities and operational processes as part of its security renaissance.

The national security strategy document, which sets out a comprehensive outline of the security challenges Japan should consider and Japan's strategic thinking in terms of policy responses, is framed in terms of "proactive contributions to peace" but devotes the bulk of its policy prescriptions to three aspects of strengthening and expanding Japan's defense capabilities and roles: (1) the JSDF and other government institutions related national defense, (2) the US-Japan alliance, and (3) other "partners for peace" in the region and beyond. From this broad template, numerous specific policy initiatives follow, including in the five areas discussed in the following.[17]

The 2013 NDPG builds on innovative concepts initially set out under the 2010 NDPG; continuity is more evident than change. This continuity underscores the cross-party agreement over security evident in Japan today at the conceptual level (though, obviously, not always at the practical level—as seen in the frequent contentious Diet debates and street demonstrations during Abe's second term). The 2013 NDPG seeks to move the branches of the JSDF and the JCG not just to more effective jointness—institutionalized by the creation of the Joint Staff Office, among other innovations of the 2010 NDPG—but also to truly seamless coordination, including in government institutions (as facilitated by the NSC) and in the US-Japan alliance (as set out in the subsequent 2015 US-Japan Guidelines for Defense Cooperation). The 2013 NDPG also builds on the 2010 concepts of dynamic defense and gray-zone defenses to build what is thought to be a more effective deterrent based both on the quantity and on the quality of assets under the expanded concept of a dynamic joint defense force.[18]

Beyond concepts, the 2013 NDPG and companion MTDP set out to further expand JSDF capabilities through the acquisition of six additional destroyers beyond the 2010 NDPG and the continued plan to acquire six more submarines (which had been the as yet unrealized goal from the 2010 NDPG). (See table 5.1 for a comparison of the major acquisitions set out in the 2004, 2010, and 2013 NDPGs.) Moreover, the additional destroyers will be of the new destroyer type that includes anti-mine capabilities and a towed array sonar system. The shift of JSDF deployment to the southwest deepens in the new NDPG. The JGSDF sees three fewer regionally deployed JGSDF divisions and six fewer

TABLE 5.1
NDPG comparison: Personnel and major equipment

	2004	2010	2013
Total JSDF personnel authorized	155,000	154,000	159,000
JGSDF Regionally deployed units	8 divisions; 6 brigades	8 divisions; 6 brigades	5 divisions; 2 brigades
Tanks	600	400	(not listed)
JMSDF			
Destroyers	47	48	54
Submarines	16	22	22
Combat aircraft	150	150	170
JASDF			
Air warning groups	8	4	0
Squadrons	20	24	28
Combat aircraft	350	340	360
Fighters[a]	260	260	280

Source: Adapted from Ministry of Defense, Defense of Japan 2014, 151–52.
Note: Some of the values are listed as approximate in Defense of Japan 2014.
[a]Subset of combat aircraft.

regionally deployed brigades, in favor of additional "rapid deployment divisions and brigades" as well as the creation three new types of brigades, one each for airborne, helicopter, and "amphibious rapid deployment." The number of combat aircraft also has been increased under the higher defense budget, with an additional squadron of F-15 fighter aircraft positioned at the Naha Air Base in Okinawa. *Defense of Japan 2014* outlines a number of other additional capability enhancements set out in the NDPG and MTDP,[19] some of which are possible via shifting resources (as seen over the past decade of capability enhancements) and others possible only because of the increasing defense budget.

Finally, the 2013 NDPG links these conceptual and capabilities developments by seeking to further streamline defense institutions and practices to provide for the truly seamless operating posture envisioned in the 2013 national security strategy.[20]

Additional Security-Related Legislation

Beyond these core defense policy innovations of Abe's first year in office, the Abe government implemented a series of other policy changes to long-standing practices related to national security in an effort to effect a more "proactive pacifism"—in particular, relaxation of arms export restrictions beyond that implemented by the DPJ government in 2011, new guiding legislation on the use of outer space for defensive purposes beyond relaxations implemented in 2009 at the end of the last LDP-led government, and a new charter to guide Japan's ODA policy to allow for more seamless coordination of Japan's development assistance and security capacity building. Each of these adaptations to past practice helps to implement the broader strategy set out in the national security strategy and illustrates the renaissance in contemporary Japanese security practice.

Contrary to the shorthand often seen in the media, Japan still very much has strict arms export restrictions, though they are framed in a more proactive way as "Three Principles on Transfer of Defense Equipment and Technology."[21] The first principle casts a wide net of areas where weapons and technology may *not* be exported—including to countries currently involved in a conflict that the United Nations is involved in addressing and countries under sanctions. The second principle, "overseas transfer of defense equipment and technology may be permitted in such cases as the transfer contributes to active promotion of peace and international cooperation," may seem counterintuitive to those not used to long-standing Japanese discourse on security[22]—in other words, Japanese firms should export weapons only to promote peace. This second principle adds that such exports should also promote Japan's national interests, another high bar for a private firm. Japan is unlikely to become a major arms exporter because of such remaining restrictions as well as of the internal nature of the defense industry in Japan, which is highly diffuse across companies that focus on nondefense business and which currently lacks a competitive cost structure and international marketing savvy.[23] Similarly, in outer space policy the changes made to past restrictions do allow for some increased defensive use of outer space for activities like satellite surveillance at military-grade resolution, but Japan remains bound by the Outer Space Treaty of 1967—and its own antimilitarist attitudes—which prohibits space-based weapons.[24]

Japan's new ODA charter, adopted in February 2015, also continues to stress long-standing practices, which include an expressed belief in the connection between peace and development.[25] In the latest iteration, this connection is made more explicit and allows for some development assistance that contributes to capacity building that may also have a limited military use—such as a civilian airport or seaport also used by military aircraft and vessels. Thus, a greater flexibility of thinking about new approaches is evident.[26] Even Abe's choice of the first new president in years of the JICA, the principal ODA institution in the Japanese government, illustrates this thinking: Akihiko Tanaka is a professor at the University of Tokyo who specializes in Japanese security, not development or ODA policy; his successor, Shin'ichi Kitaoka, also a former professor, was the deputy chairman of Abe's Advisory Panel on the Reconstruction of the Legal Basis for Security. Still, the new ODA charter is quite clear that Japanese ODA may *not* be provided for facilities or equipment solely for military use. The Japanese government has never provided weapons as a part of its ODA, and that prohibition remains.

These many security policy innovations enacted in just three years, from 2013 to 2015, will create a lasting legacy for future Japanese political leadership. The office of the prime minister (*kantei*) in particular now has many more tools at its disposal to execute foreign policy and diplomacy that include a military component. Moreover, it is highly unlikely that any of these policies will be reversed by future governments as each of the policies was the result of significant compromise informed by the legacies of the past. These legacies, however, have ensured that Japan's security renaissance is not at all a reflection of an entirely new Japanese approach to military security: even the one other significant policy innovation enacted in this period, the legislation allowing for CSD, will not result in Japan's prime minister dispatching the JSDF abroad in the normal course of statecraft, as is the purview of Japan's other major power peers, nor acquiring weapons amassed in Japan that could be used to threaten Japan's neighbors to alter their policies.[27]

Renewed Concerns About Japan's Handling Under Abe of Its Militarist Past

The scale of expansion of Japan's security roles, institutions, and capabilities under Abe, plus Abe's return to power itself, has led to increased questioning and activism related to imperial Japan's campaign of brutal expansion across East Asia. Vocal, organized, and divisive activism for Japan to better address and apologize for its past conduct has been apparent throughout the postwar period but has again risen to prominence since Abe resumed power in December 2012.

Causes and Consequences of a Renewed Focus on Japan's Past

What has been the effect of these history issues on Abe's security policy strategies and Japan's new proactive contributions to peace? The broad coverage of the so-called history issues of Japan's past in the Japanese and global media and tense relations between Japan and its immediate neighbors has not halted important developments in Japan's security renaissance. To the contrary—much like during the Koizumi years, where Japan's relations with its immediate neighbors were chilly but the relationship with the United States and countries further afield were strong—Japan's security policy made substantial leaps in capabilities, institutions, and ambitions in the first three years of Abe's second term. Abe himself met a record number of world leaders in the first year of his second term, including heads of state of all ten ASEAN countries (a first for a Japanese prime minister) as well as the heads of state of Australia, India, and dozens of other countries around the world. But, linking to the history-issue question, Abe did not hold bilateral meetings with the heads of state of either South Korea or China in his first year in office, and even by the fall of 2015, he had met these leaders only on the sidelines of other multilateral meetings where both leaders were already scheduled to be present. This stands in great contrast to Abe's choice in his first term as prime minister of meeting China's president Hu Jintao and South Korean president Roh Moo-hyun before meeting the president of the United States.

In the case of China, numerous other issues (number one being the territorial dispute) arguably drive frosty Japan-China relations with the history issues providing only a surface pretext. The differences between Japan and South Korea are more complex and more directly related to disagreements over past history—not just World War II but also back to the beginning of Japanese colonialism on the Korean Peninsula in 1910, and even the circumstances preceding that. The consequences of these problems are also more acute, as Japan and South Korea could, in principle, be working together to address shared security concerns, including in conjunction with their mutual ally, the United States.[28] Instead, South Korea has found common cause with China over history issues, which has pushed Japan further away.

There are numerous, divergent causes of this renewed attention to Japan's early-twentieth-century militarism. Japan's increasingly proactive security policies are certainly one factor: as Japan engages in military-related activities in the region it once sought to conquer, emotions are bound to rise as citizens of the region are exposed to the new Japanese military forces, the JSDF, for the first time. But this explanation alone is inadequate. For example, it cannot explain why the JSDF was welcomed to provide post-typhoon disaster relief assistance in the Philippines—where the Japanese military caused great suffering—but not postearthquake relief assistance in China (and in a region of China where Japanese forces hardly penetrated);[29] nor can it explain why the comfort women issue is a massive political issue with South Korea but not with Taiwan or the Philippines, despite nationals of all three areas having been subjected to this treatment and all being allies of the United States today. Thus, new Japanese military capabilities and activities alone cannot explain the varied reactions of Japan's neighbors to how Japan has atoned for its militarist past.

Three other factors help to explain why the historical legacy of Japan's militarist and colonial past has risen to unusual prominence under the second Abe administration. Each has a divergent influence on Japan's security renaissance. First, Abe himself, and especially members of his cabinet and other supporters, have made numerous inflammatory statements related to Japanese militarism that have called into question the Abe government's commitment to respect previous Japanese government policies related to Japan's militarist past. They have also questioned the way Japan's militarist past is explained in school curricula and government narratives, provoking strong reaction both abroad and in Japan. Second, changes in Japanese domestic politics have empowered minority voices in the ruling LDP and also in the political opposition, an opposition that previously had been dominated by the political left but now also includes parties and strong voices from the right. Third, and of a different character, changes outside Japan—in particular politically motivated action by individuals and groups in China and South Korea—have sought to counter Japan's regional influence or gain domestic political leverage by playing the "history card." This has led to a reaction in Japan, by both the government and activists, to enact new policies or media campaigns to convey Japan's view of history, which in some areas has created a vicious circle—such as the proclamation of Takeshima Day as a holiday to further assert Japan's territorial claim or the back-and-forth over textbook depictions of Japan's past.[30]

Revisionist Views of Abe and His Supporters

Abe's return to power has led to strong criticism from those who believe Japan denies history. Invectives against Abe's "far right" views are widely published not just on interest-group websites but also in mainstream journals and foreign mass media.[31] A group of prominent scholars in Japan, the United States, and elsewhere signed and circulated a joint statement criticizing Japan and other states in the region for politicizing history, in particular over the comfort women issue.[32] The prominent British specialist on Japanese security Christopher Hughes has described the "Abe Doctrine" as a "radical trajectory" for Japan and that "from autumn 2013 onwards, the full guise of Abe's revisionist agenda . . . has become readily apparent."[33] Mainstream media in Japan, however, have been much more cautious to issue such invectives. Instead, mainstream criticism is limited largely to specific issues, such as Abe's "intimidation diplomacy"[34] or decision to visit Yasukuni Shrine in December 2013—a decision criticized even by the editor of the right-of-center *Yomiuri* newspaper.[35]

Abe has consistently sought to thread the needle between upholding past Japanese government statements of apology for Japan's militarist past and calling into question the accuracy or necessity of such apologies. In his first term in office, Abe's revisionist statements about Japan's past conduct led to a highly unusual public rebuke by the US Congress, among other reactions discussed in chapter 4. In his second term as well, Abe made statements in the Diet and to supporters that called into question his commitment to the 1995 Murayama apology and the 1993 Kōnō statement, though his chief cabinet secretary repeatedly reaffirmed the Abe government's adherence to those statements.[36] In a March 2015 interview with the *Washington Post*, Abe again unequivocally stated his support for all Japan's past major statements of reckoning with Japan's wartime past;[37] widespread skepticism nonetheless remains.

In June 2014, the LDP concluded a study of the circumstances leading to the issuing of the Kōnō statement in 1993. The study formally reaffirmed the content of the Kōnō statement while also noting the politicized nature of the drafting process of the time, which included consultation with the South Korean government about the specific language used.[38] Such a political compromise pleased no one—South Korea and others in Japan and elsewhere in the world saw a watering down of the responsibilities Japan admitted in the Kōnō statement by the many qualifications explained in the new report, and a group of Abe's supporters on the far right were unsatisfied that Abe appeared to back away from his earlier stridency on this issue. The circumstances surrounding the findings of the report—in which an *Asahi* newspaper journalist retracted some of his earlier reporting on this issue that had laid the foundation for aspects of the Kōnō statement and was excoriated by the far right in response (to the extent that the reporter was forced to resign from a teaching position and his daughter's life was threatened)—provided further emotional fervor on the issue, despite it being "resolved" in Abe's official public statements.

Abe's compromise policy related to Yasukuni Shrine in his second term also pleased no one and led to lingering concerns on all sides. In Abe's first term as prime minister, he sought to repair the damage done in relations with China during the Koizumi period, damage resulting in no small part from Koizumi's repeated visits to the shrine. Two early examples of Abe's outreach were his decisions to travel to Beijing to meet President Hu Jintao before traveling to Washington, DC, and to promise to refrain from visiting Yasukuni Shrine while prime minister, a promise he kept during his one year in office. (Abe had repeatedly visited the shrine when a Diet member before becoming prime minister.)

At the start of his second term in office, Abe again inherited a tense relationship with China from his predecessor, though this time due primarily to the escalation of the territorial dispute with China over the Senkaku Islands. Unlike in his first term, however, Abe had repeatedly promised his supporters on the campaign trail that he *would* visit Yasukuni Shrine while prime minister, and he refused to renounce this promise when China sought it as a precondition to scheduling a bilateral meeting between Abe and China's new president, Xi Jinping. On December 23, 2013, Abe followed through on his promise to supporters and visited the shrine, leading to widespread criticism from abroad, including, unusually, from the US embassy in Tokyo. In 2014 and 2015 Abe refrained from again visiting the shrine, but he has not pledged that he would not visit again; moreover, in 2014, 2015, and 2016 he sent ceremonial offerings to the shrine to mark seasonal festival rites—again a sort of compromise that seemingly pleased no one.[39]

Abe sought to address lingering concerns about his position regarding Japan's prewar and wartime history in an interview with the US journal *Foreign Affairs*. In response to the question, "Who is the real Abe," he responded, "Let me set the record straight. Throughout my first and current terms as prime minister, I have expressed a number of times the deep remorse that I share for the tremendous damage and suffering Japan caused in the past to the people of many countries, particularly in Asia. I have explicitly said that, yet it made few headlines." Yet on the sensitive issue of whether Japan committed "aggression," he waffles somewhat, responding, "I have never said that Japan has not committed aggression. Yet at the same time, how best, or not, to define 'aggression' is none of my business. That's what historians ought to work on. I have been saying that our work is to discuss what kind of world we should create in the future."[40] Abe also would not commit as to whether or not he would visit Yasukuni Shrine in the future, and, in fact, he did make his first (and, to date, only) visit to the shrine as prime minister later that year.

In the months leading up to the seventieth anniversary of the end of World War II, the media speculated widely about which words Abe would use to mark the occasion. Interest was high because of both long-standing concerns over Abe's views and Abe's appointment of a special Advisory Panel on History to offer suggestions for how he should commemorate the seventieth anniversary, as discussed in chapter 2.[41] In his seventieth anniversary statement, Abe sought a middle ground that led to criticism from both those seeking a more explicit apology for Japan's past actions and those who wanted Abe to toe the line that Japan had apologized enough and that Japan's future should be forward looking. (The full text of the statement is provided in appendix 3.) This approach follows an earlier pattern seen during his time in office in which he seeks to appeal to different constituencies that hold opposing views—sometimes in sequence, and sometimes (as in his seventieth anniversary statement) simultaneously. This further illustrates how the past as well as the future strongly shapes the ultimate nature of Japan's security policy, and its security renaissance more broadly.

Beyond Abe himself, the company Abe keeps in his own cabinet and among political supporters has also led to charges that Abe is an extreme historical revisionist. Abe's minister of education, culture, sports, science and technology—who leads the ministry that approves textbooks available for adoption by schools nationwide—was among those in the cabinet Abe chose after the December 2012 election who attracted special attention for his statements prior to joining the cabinet calling for the revoking of the Kōnō and Murayama apology statements and for his revisionist views of Japan's wartime past.[42] Numerous other cabinet members across the two Abe cabinets appointed in the period December 2012 to 2015 have also been reported to have previously called for revisions of history textbooks, repeal of the Kōnō statement, and other reforms that critics associate with Japan's militarist past.[43]

Many are members of Diet groups strongly associated with such policy platforms, such as the nationalist organization Nippon Kaigi (the Japan Conference, thirteen of nineteen members of the first Abe cabinet), the Japan's Future and Textbook group (eleven of nineteen members of the first Abe cabinet), and the Worshipping at Yasukuni Shrine Together group (fifteen of nineteen members of the first Abe cabinet).[44] As noted in a report by the US Congressional Research Service, "sizeable numbers of LDP lawmakers, including three Cabinet ministers, have periodically visited the Shrine on ceremonial days, including the sensitive day of August 15, the anniversary of Japan's surrender in World War II."[45]

The Apparent Rise of Nationalism and a Shift to the Political Right

The fact that in contemporary Japan there are competing political parties on the right of the political spectrum leads to greater pressure on the LDP and to more media attention to the conservative agenda such as the so-called history issues. This has led to widespread reporting outside Japan that there is a rising militarism, or at least rising nationalism, in present-day Japan. In Japan as well, there has been significant media attention to the concern over a rising nationalism (though not as often rising militarism),[46] a claim that seems evident from the number of events covered in the media—such as group visits to Yasukuni Shrine by elected politicians and activist groups and the apparently growing number of anti-China and anti-Korea demonstrations and hate speech online.

The anecdotal impression of a rising nationalism in Japan is not as clear from more systematic research, however. For example, Japanese Cabinet Office polling on Japanese self-reported levels of "patriotic feeling" shows little variation in the period 2000 to 2013, though 2013 was the peak year for those describing a "strong affection," at 58 percent.[47] Over a third of those surveyed professed no feeling either way, and a small number reported a weak patriotic feeling. Glosserman and Snyder cite comparative studies of nationalist sentiment in Asia that show that "Japanese exhibit the lowest sense of patriotism among Asian nations. According to Asia Barometer, 27 percent of Japanese are 'proud of their nationality,' considerably less than the 46 percent of Chinese,

75 percent of Malays, and 93 percent of Thais. In the World Values Survey, Japan has the lowest percentage of people (24 percent) 'proud of their country' and willing to fight for their country (16 percent) among all countries polled."[48] Yet one could describe Japanese as looking for respect, as Glosserman and Snyder do when noting, "In 2013, 60 percent of Japanese felt that their country should be more respected in the world than it is."[49] Japanese themselves seem concerned about possible rising nationalism, based on the large number of opinion pieces and editorials that have appeared on this issue in major Japanese newspapers, which could be interpreted as a sign that more nationalist sentiment is visible and aired but could equally be seen as a moderate middle pushing back against such actions.

A related but more complex question is whether there has been a broader shift to the right in Japanese politics. As noted earlier, LDP "landslides" in the past two Lower House elections certainly imply such a shift—but a closer look at voting patterns yields a more mixed picture: there have *not* been more votes for parties on the right than in the past. The new opposition parties on the right have not fared well since their emergence, framing, and breakup on a regular basis. They have struggled to attract sustained support. Far right political candidates have not attracted mainstream voter support in the way seen in some European democracies in recent years. For example, in the Tokyo governor election in February 2014, Toshio Tamogami—the darling of the revisionist right who won a national essay contest with an essay espousing revisionist history views and who was ousted from the JSDF as a result—came in fourth of four major candidates, with only 12.4 percent of the vote, despite the media buzz covering the race. Moreover, as with recent national elections, voter turnout dropped sharply in this election from the previous Tokyo governor election, to 46.1 percent from 62.6 percent in the 2012 election, suggesting that voters were not excited about their candidate choices.

On broader issues associated with the conservative right beyond the security issues that are the focus of this book, there is evidence of support of rightist causes—such as xenophobia or anti-immigrant stances—but these issues do not seem to have resonated among the general public as they have in many European democracies, which in part is because of

Japan's very low levels of immigration and lack of a significant refugee population. Dislike of China is high (around 80 per cent—which is a big negative shift over time) and of the two Koreas as well (for which virulent racist diatribes and attitudes are especially evident in online forums and some print media) but not so of other foreign places—there is very high support for the United States and for cooperative approaches to outreach to Japan's Asian neighbors. In a 2013 NHK survey, 70 percent of Japanese responded that "Japan still has much to learn from other countries," belying the idea of widespread xenophobia beyond what has long been seen in the far right.

Overall, it is rather the two *postwar* historical legacies that have more deeply shaped Japan's security policies under the second Abe administration, the legacy of antimilitarism and the legacy of the complex US-Japan security relationship.

The Postwar Legacy of Antimilitarism
and Japan's Security Renaissance

The publication of Japan's first national security strategy marked a culmination of the first stage of a controversial and closely followed process of reformulation of Japan's security policies under a reportedly nationalist and conservative government that has sought to respond to what it has characterized as "severe" security challenges.[50] Yet the strategy adopted by Abe's purportedly hypernationalist cabinet proclaims repeatedly Japan's long-standing "peace-loving" policies and principles. For example, the text begins, "Japan will continue to adhere to the course that it has taken to date as a peace-loving nation, and as a major player in world politics and economy, continue even more proactively in securing peace, stability, and prosperity of the international community, while achieving its own security as well as peace and stability in the Asia-Pacific region as a 'Proactive Contributor to Peace' based on the principle of international cooperation. This is the fundamental principle of national security that Japan should stand to hold."[51]

How can one reconcile this apparent contradiction? Why doesn't a conservative prime minister with high levels of popular support pursue policies more in line with views widely reported to be central to his values and outlook? One answer is the strength of the historical legacy of antimilitarism—a second history issue that challenges the preferred agenda of the Abe government, in addition to the history issues related to Japan's conduct in the years leading to World War II. By adopting a formal national security strategy document that seeks to guide Japan's national security policy "over the next decade," the Abe government itself provides another important illustration of how seventy years of antimilitarist security practices and institutions will continue to structure Japan's security frame for years to come, despite powerful political actors seeking change not just to policy but also to Japan's broader security identity.[52]

The Resilience of Antimilitarist Beliefs

Looking at the scope and scale of change in Japanese security policy in 2013 to 2016, observers might reasonably surmise that Japanese public attitudes about security have transformed in response to a growing number of threats facing Japan. In fact, extensive polling data convincingly demonstrate that Japanese views about how best to provide for Japan's security have *not* been transformed by a more hostile environment.[53] This lack of transformation of public attitudes is one reason why this book discusses a security "renaissance" rather than a more strident framing of a fundamental transformation of Japan's security approaches.

For example, when asked how Japan should deal with the rising military threat from China, arguably the most important and well-covered security issue in the media, by far the most popular polling response—at 50 percent in 2014—was "strengthen relations with other countries in East Asia," while "deal with China on the basis of deterrence provided by the US-Japan alliance" ranked the lowest, at only 5.2 percent in 2014 (down from 12.4 percent in 2010).[54] "Deal with China through Japan's own independent military capabilities" also ranked quite low and was on the decline, from 25 percent in 2012 to 9.5 percent in 2014. Thinking beyond China specifically, when NHK asked in July 2013 how best to guarantee Japan's security, equal numbers of Japanese—about 45 percent each—chose "cooperate with the United Nations to build a global security system" and "have a degree of military power and rely on the US alliance."[55] Fewer than 5 percent of those polled said that Japan should rely exclusively on its own military power, roughly the same percentage as those who chose "have no military power and remain neutral."

The important change in Japan's security policies in the 1990s to contribute the JSDF to UNPKO on a limited basis is consonant with this support for a UN-centric system of global peace reflected in Japanese public opinion polls and is a "pillar" of Japanese foreign policy as long promoted by Japan's Ministry of Foreign Affairs. When the *Asahi* newspaper asked in 2013 and 2014 about acceptable roles for the JSDF overseas, there was near-universal support for helping at a time of a natural disaster (94 and 95 percent, respectively), but in relation to contemporary debates over the exercise of CSD, only a tiny minority supported "fighting on the front lines in combat with the United States (7 and 5 percent, respectively, so a *decline* year on year); only 17 percent of those polled thought it was acceptable for the JSDF to "provide weapons and fuel support to the US military overseas" (down from 20 percent in 2013).[56]

Clearly, despite a "renaissance" in Japan's approach to its security in the past decade, Japanese views on the utility of the military in conflict resolution have not *transformed* by any means—but rather are grudgingly adapting to a new environment and in some cases being dragged into adapting by a determined political leadership. The postwar legacy of antimilitarism remains quite strong, as does ambivalence related to the utility of the US-Japan alliance for all aspects of Japan's security.

This ambivalence—or outright opposition—extends even to policies that were in fact *implemented* under the Abe administration. For example, fewer than 30 percent of Japanese polled in 2013 and 2014 favored relaxing arms export restrictions—which the Abe government implemented in 2014—versus upward of 60 percent against.[57] A poll conducted by Kyodo News in July 2015 showed 62 percent of respondents opposed the package of security legislation introduced into the Diet in June 2015—though it should be noted, the legislation is a complex package, and levels of support varied substantially based on how the polling questions were formulated.[58] Approval for the Abe cabinet slumped by almost ten percentage points in the first month after the legislation was introduced, to 37.7 percent.[59] Similarly high rates of disapproval were seen in response to the initial 2014 cabinet statement reinterpreting the constitution to allow for CSD and to the SDS law—both of which were also accompanied by public protests of, at minimum, tens of thousands of people in front of the Prime Minister's residence and Diet building.

While Japan's security identity has not been replaced by a new set of guiding principles, a new politics of security has been evident in Japan since the Koizumi period (2001–2006) that includes new attitudes about security among elites. Increased public discussion of alternative security policies—including those advocated by powerful political actors—is not the same as acceptance of these policies, however. For example, great media and public attention to the idea of constitutional revision of Article Nine in 2007 did not lead to revision of the constitution; similarly, discussion of Japan's developing preemptive strike capabilities, for example, made headlines but did not result in a decision to pursue the idea.

Looking forward, in the remaining years of the second Abe administration policies rooted in the postwar antimilitarist legacy will no doubt continue to be challenged, both ideationally and institutionally. Moreover, substantial institutional and political constraints stand in the way of a realization of Abe's full policy objectives vis-à-vis Japan's future security practices. Ultimately even the large victory in the Upper House elections in July 2016 to attempt to implement one of his primary objectives of security policy: formal revision of Article Nine of the postwar constitution. Success in this area requires not just a two-thirds affirmative majority vote in both houses of the Diet but also a majority vote in a national referendum. Thus, even though the LDP—in informal coalition with other, smaller parties—was able to secure a two-thirds majority in the Diet that supports the idea of constitutional revision, there is yet another step, a step that seems unlikely to succeed based on extensive polling data on this question and the reaction to new security legislation passed in the Diet in September 2015. In the interim, however, a number of more limited challenges to the postwar antimilitarist legacy can be expected.

Article Nine and CSD

While Article Nine of the constitution—the so-called war-renouncing clause—plays a central role in anchoring Japan's postwar antimilitarist legacy, political actors must interpret and uphold constitutional principles. The constitution has undergone reinterpretation numerous times in the postwar period and was significantly reinterpreted once again in the second year of the second Abe administration, when the Abe cabinet released a statement indicating a plan to reinterpret the constitution to allow for Japan to exercise its sovereign right to engage in CSD activities with other states closely aligned with Japan's interests.[60]

At the start of his first term in office, Prime Minister Abe made clear that he would like the JSDF to engage in activities related to CSD. The Cabinet Legislative Bureau (CLB) interpretation of this issue, however, stood in conflict with Abe's agenda. It reads (italics added), "International law permits a state to have the right of collective self-defense, which is the right to use force to stop an armed attack on a foreign country with which the state has close relations, even if the state itself is not under direct attack. Since Japan is a sovereign state, it naturally has the right of collective self-defense under international law. *Nevertheless, the Japanese government believes that the exercise of the right of collective self-defense exceeds the limit on self-defense authorized under Article 9 of the Constitution and is not permissible.*"[61]

With formal constitutional revision politically unattainable, Abe sought in his second term a reinterpretation of this opinion. The idea of a reinterpretation of a constitutional provision related to national security is not novel, protests from the left notwithstanding. In conjunction with earlier LDP efforts to expand Japan's international security role, the CLB issued an interpretation that allowed for the JSDF to operate in "areas surrounding Japan" outside Japanese territory—with the restriction that the JSDF could *not* operate in the air, land, or sea territory of another state; it has also reconciled the constitutionality of Japan's participation in an integrated missile defense system with the United States (which some saw as an exercise of CSD) and a range of other security-related issues over the years.

The July 1, 2014, cabinet decision that explicitly allows for the JSDF to participate in CSD activities with other states marks a significant change in a long-standing interpretation of appropriate security practices, though not as significant a change as Abe sought nor as is widely thought. The July 2014 cabinet decision that has been widely reported to have overturned Japan's long-standing policy not to exercise its inherent right to CSD directs that such CSD actions would be undertaken in only extremely limited circumstances: only when not acting "threatens Japan's survival" and "when there is no other appropriate means available to repel the attack" and, even then, that the JSDF is permitted "the use of force to the minimum extent necessary . . . in accordance with the basic logic of the Government's view to date."[62] This result is far less than Abe and many of his supporters sought to achieve in this cabinet statement—but their views were overridden by opposition from within the ruling coalition (both in the LDP and especially from Kōmei) as well as influenced by strong public opposition.

Legislation to implement the July 2014 cabinet decision—one bill to amend twenty laws and another to create a legal framework for the JSDF to participate in international peace cooperation activities outside a UNPKO[63]—was introduced in the Diet in June 2015 and passed in September 2015, despite widespread public opposition and political demonstrations. Once again, however, draft legislation created by the Abe cabinet had to undergo several stages of watering down based on concerns expressed by backbenchers in the LDP, by coalition partner Kōmei, and during Diet interpolations—resulting in a set of policies that were far less than Abe originally sought, even after compromise the previous year on the 2014 cabinet statement. In one sense, it is therefore domestic politics and public opinion that played the direct role in limiting Abe's policy ambitions—but it was the long-standing legacy of postwar antimilitarism that provided the framing language, institutional barriers, and that garnered public support to reshape the preferences of a powerful political actor.

The Influence of Antimilitarism in Other New Security Practices

Beyond these constitutional issues, the Abe administration adopted three new government documents related to national security policy in December 2013, each of which illuminates Abe's new approaches to security. The new NDPG and related MTDP continue the policies set out in the last published NDPG of December 2010 but also push further Abe's preference for a more activist security policy for Japan and a Japan that possesses greater military capabilities. However, the increase is fairly limited and clearly framed with the historical legacy of antimilitarist security practices in mind. The Japanese government's first published national security strategy and the creation of the new NSC also rub against the legacy of antimilitarism though at this point have been adapted to not challenge this legacy overtly. It is illuminating of Japan's postwar security identity that Japan has not even had such a formal strategy document in the past seventy years, illustrating how military policy was not seen as a core tool to promote the national interest—though the MOD (and, prior to that, the Japan Defense Agency) had developed military defense guidelines by way of the aforementioned NDPG since 1976, which have become increasingly detailed and strategic as they have been updated over the years, especially the 2004, 2010, and 2013 versions. This new formal national security strategy is crafted by a new institution, the NSC, operating within the Cabinet Secretariat and including representatives from ministries other than the MOD. The prospect of integrating military strategy into broad Japanese national objectives could mark a significant shift in Japan's approach to military security, but whether this is what actually takes place in this new institution and future iterations of this core strategy document remains to be seen; the first attempt does not appear substantially different from earlier NDPGs, though it officially now expresses a more whole-of-government approach as the product of an internal cabinet body. At this point, however, Japanese policy makers certainly have many more tools at their disposal for utilizing military power to achieve broader national objectives, crossing to some degree previous boundaries imposed by the postwar legacy of antimilitarism.

The rise in presence and prominence of JSDF officers in Japan's defense planning is also a notable sign of Japan's security renaissance and one that challenges old taboos. After the July 2014 cabinet statement related to CSD, the JMSDF assigned an officer to work with the US Department of Defense to enhance the operational integration of the US Navy and JMSDF in regional operations.[64] The JASDF had already dispatched such a liaison to Washington the previous year under the Abe government.[65] These examples, together with a general rise in responsibilities of uniformed JSDF officers in defense policy planning in the MOD and the new NSC, mark a significant shift from what was considered politically possible in pre-renaissance Japan. There were certainly precedents in the preceding years—from around the time of the last US-Japan defense guidelines in 1997[66]—but the normalcy of civilian-military interactions in contemporary Japan (between the "uniforms" and the "suits") is what marks the renaissance of the past decade.

New precedents related to civilian-military interaction continue to be set in the Abe second term, such as the first-ever public speeches of Japan's top military officers in Washington, DC—both the chief of the JSDF Joint Staff Office, Admiral Katsutoshi Kawano, and the JMSDF chief of staff, Admiral Tomohisa Takei, delivered public lectures in uniform (and in English) in July 2015.[67] In their lectures they reported an impressive number of high-level meetings with senior US government officials and military commanders and touted the benefits of expanded US-Japan military-to-military cooperation. That such high-level consultations are taking place is itself notable, but that they are being publicly touted is another indication of Japan's security renaissance.

In addition to the aforementioned new NSC, the Abe government envisions an "upgrade" to the institutions underpinning the Japan-US security alliance through implementation of the new US-Japan Guidelines for Defense Cooperation adopted in April 2015. Institutionalized military cooperation with the United States has long been a controversial aspect of security policy in Japan but has grown less so in recent years. Still, the level of cooperation and the sorts of roles that Japan will play within the alliance framework continue to be issues that challenge Japan's postwar antimilitarist legacy. As noted in a recent report by Japan's National Institute for Defense Studies, "the scope to the US-Japan alliance has expanded from the 'defense of Japan' to 'the Asia-Pacific region' and thence to 'global cooperation.'"[68] The last significant expansion of US-Japan cooperation took place under the Koizumi administration with the dispatch of the JSDF abroad to support US combat operations (discussed in chapter 2), a decision that was quite controversial and ultimately very limited in scope.

The Abe government has also crafted, and seeks to expand, institutionalized security cooperation with other states in the region, building on recent developments with Australia in particular.[69] Whether the Abe administration, or a future Japanese administration, will be able to routinize and expand such out-of-area cooperation—or development of "dynamic defense cooperation" during ordinary times and not only in emergencies—remains to be seen. The package of new security legislation passed in the Diet in September 2015 sets very narrow limits for JSDF cooperation with other states in the area of CSD, limiting such actions to cases that "threaten Japan's survival,"[70] an early concession to substantial opposition to the legislation that emerged early on. This legislation came into effect only in March 2016, after government bureaucrats devised procedures and new processes to enact the changes legislated to twenty existing laws. Some aspects of the legislation may not be acted upon until much later, however—depending on domestic politics and the evolving international situation. The core aspect of the legislation, regarding JSDF participation in CSD activity, would not actually take place unless Japan was gravely threatened. However, an important aspect of the passage of the new security legislation is that it enables Japan's defense establishment to legally plan for possible security contingencies that would involve CSD and to develop bilateral and multilateral exercises to train for this possibility—something that has not previously been possible.

Other areas of greater cooperation, by contrast, though new, are easily reconciled with the past antimilitarist practices—such as increased cooperation in regional HADR and in addressing threats in cyberspace: both areas scheduled for deepened cooperation under the new US-Japan guidelines and new security legislation. The extent to which the JSDF can cooperate with countries other than the United States is also an important question raised in Japan's new national security strategy, and in the 2010 and 2013 NDPGs. Such cooperation need not conflict with past antimilitarist security practices, but it could depending on how it is framed—particularly in areas related to CSD. An expansion of defense cooperation with other states would be a new development—and certainly would present a new image for Japan overseas—but security cooperation with states other than the United States in itself would not be an indication of identity shift; it would depend on the nature of that cooperation.

The Abe government also seeks to increase the capabilities of the JSDF—as evidenced in the 2013 NDPG and MTDP documents. The question of what capabilities the JSDF should have has been controversial since its creation in 1954 and has historically been rooted in the concept of "minimum force necessary for the defense of Japan." What was considered minimally necessary is, of course, related to perceptions of threat and to evolving military technologies. For example, some technologies once considered solely military but that now have widespread civilian uses have become uncontroversial in use by the JSDF: satellite communications and surveillance satellites are examples. In addition, as international cooperation was a core mission of the MOD at the time it was established as a ministry, new capabilities needed for this mission also have become uncontroversial—such as heavy-lift air transport capabilities, which were once imagined as a threatening means to transport soldiers and weapons abroad are now seen as a way to deliver humanitarian assistance.

Other aspects of enhanced JSDF capabilities remain controversial in relation to the legacy of antimilitarism—such as overt strike capability. Such a capacity is reportedly desired by Prime Minister Abe but, notably, has not been directly requested in policy documents to date, suggesting a continued resilience of the antimilitarist legacy even in changed domestic and international political circumstances. Recent Cabinet Office polling similarly lends support to the idea that the Abe government must be cautious in this area. While longitudinal public opinion surveys conducted by the Cabinet Office show the number of Japanese who believe that JSDF capabilities "should be increased" has jumped significantly from 14.1 percent in January 2009 to 24.8 percent in January 2012[71] and to 29.9 percent in 2015,[72] it is nonetheless notable that fewer than one-third of Japanese express this view.

The prioritizing of incremental change to security policies that can be articulated within the discourse of postwar practices rooted in antimilitarist rhetoric confirms the continued resilience of this historical legacy. Other, overlapping explanations for security policy continuity can be offered beyond the antimilitarist legacy—but the effect of the postwar antimilitarist legacy remains strong even in contemporary Japan under Prime Minister Abe and even in the midst of a security renaissance.

Recrafting the Legacy of the US-Japan Security Relationship for a New Era

Let the two of us, America and Japan, join our hands together and do our best to make the world a better, a much better, place to live. . . . Together, we can make a difference.

—PRIME MINISTER SHINZŌ ABE, ADDRESS TO A JOINT MEETING OF THE US CONGRESS, APRIL 29, 2015

Japan's expanded security relationship with the United States is an integral part of Japan's security renaissance. Much of the JSDF's increased capabilities and missions are either assisted by the United States (in terms of sharing weapons technology, training, or equipment) or taking place within the framework of the US-Japan alliance. Of what remains, much is discussed between the United States and Japan and serves to benefit shared security objectives—such as Japan's provision of capacity building to Philippine and Vietnamese coastal defenses, assistance in anti-piracy efforts in the area around the South China Sea and the Gulf of Aden, and deepened security cooperation with fellow US alliance partner Australia. There are some areas where US and Japanese interests diverge (such as over Russia) or where strategic priorities have diverged (such as at times over North Korea), but overall any difficulties in the alliance relationship today are no longer related to strong Japanese voices for greater autonomy or neutrality but rather to long-standing complications pertaining to the unequal nature of the alliance.

Several prominent politicians who led calls for greater Japanese defense autonomy in the 1990s and early in the following decade were relegated to marginal roles by the time of negotiation of the new US-Japan Guidelines for Defense Cooperation in 2013 to 2015.[73] On the other end of the spectrum, political platforms calling for the end of the US-Japan military alliance virtually disappeared; only the JCP included this item in its political manifesto in the December 2014 Lower House election. However, the strong legacy of antimilitarism also continues to limit US-Japan joint military action, as seen in the many compromises the Abe administration had to make to pass new security legislation related to CSD in the Diet in 2015.

Japan's security relationship with the United States has never been more broadly supported among the Japanese public and Japanese elected officials than in the past decade, with 83 percent public support in January 2015, according to one national poll.[74] There has been some fluctuation around the record-high levels of support after US assistance to Japan after the March 2011 triple disaster, including some expressions of concern about further alliance deepening after the release of the 2015 US-Japan Guidelines for Defense Cooperation, but overall support for the US-Japan security alliance is very high—and transcends party lines. In the past, it was taboo for certain constituencies on the left and on the far right to support the maintenance of the alliance. Today, outright opposition to the alliance in any form is rare.[75] Even the JCP does not stress that aspect of its political manifesto in its campaign. Such reticence to criticize the alliance makes political sense in contemporary Japan since, as noted in the previous section, fewer than 5 percent of Japanese replied in NHK polling that they would prefer for Japan to rely solely on its own military capabilities or to have no military power and remain neutral. The postwar legacy of the complex security relationship with the United States continues on many fronts—from broad concerns over abandonment and entrapment to practical concerns about the concentration of US military forces in Okinawa—but the discourse over the alliance has transformed and at the elite level has moved much more to the aim of operational coordination than a decade ago.

A New Dimension of Entrapment Versus Abandonment Concerns

Historically the Japanese view of the alliance has fluctuated between concerns of "entrapment" in US conflicts in the region or globally and those of "abandonment" by the United States at a time of need of the security commitment rooted in the 1960 US-Japan Security Treaty. While both concerns continue to be visible for different reasons, abandonment concerns are most visible in the second Abe administration, while entrapment concerns still resonate strongly with the general public. Concerns about abandonment are visible in public and private discussions of most of the major security contingencies Japan faces. Most visible is the fear that the United States will not come to Japan's assistance in the event of a Chinese attempt to forcibly "reclaim" the Senkaku Islands. The United States has sought to assuage this worry by actions on many levels, from public reaffirmation that Article Five of the security treaty unambiguously applies to the Senkaku Islands by senior administration officials, including President Obama himself, to new levels of joint training between the US military and the JSDF on island defenses. In a sign of Japan's security renaissance visible in the United States, the *New York Times* printed a color picture of members of the JSDF in camouflage on an island off the coast of California, in a story about the JSDF working together with the US military to thwart a simulated island attack.[76] While the postwar legacies of antimilitarism and of sensitivity in the US-Japan security relationship remain—in addition to concerns related to World War II—that the JSDF allowed such a photo to be taken shows new attitudes about what is acceptable to portray of Japan's military in contemporary Japan.

Beyond the Senkaku issue specifically, many Japanese question more broadly whether the United States will remain committed to Japan's defense as China's rise reaches even higher levels. Japanese watch with concern the discourse in Australia—led by strategic thinkers such as Hugh White[77]—arguing for the need to accommodate a rising China and fear a spread of such discourse to US-Japan relations. Japanese government officials and media carefully parse US public statements about official documents related to China strategy, at times expressing concerted opposition to specific language, such as the apparent US acceptance of the Chinese call for "a new model of great power relations" in a 2014 speech by US national security advisor Susan Rice.[78] Abandonment concerns reach beyond China, however. As North Korea's nuclear program marches forward, and missile capabilities also increase, many Japanese question whether the United States would really sacrifice Los Angeles for Tokyo, as the model of extended deterrence in the alliance posits.

Meanwhile, the Japanese public in particular simultaneously expresses concern about entrapment in the alliance. This concern was especially evident in the heated debates over CSD in the summer of 2015 and the preceding year and in plans outlined in the 2015 US-Japan guidelines, discussed in the following section. These guidelines set out multiple areas of alliance deepening that evoke possible entrapment scenarios—such as Japan being pulled into a war with China in the midst of a conflict over Taiwan or with North Korea over an outbreak of hostilities on the Korean Peninsula—because of US bases in Japan being used by

US forces in those conflict scenarios or the JSDF's being deployed as part of newly authorized CSD operations.

Progress and Challenges in the New US-Japan Guidelines for Defense Cooperation

The Japanese government has taken several important steps to secure the resilience of the alliance commitment for the coming years, including via negotiations to update the formal US-Japan Guidelines for Defense Cooperation for the first time in nearly twenty years. Abe's ability to forge a four-year bond with President Obama has also contributed to alliance deepening, in contrast to the five prime ministers who served in the five years before Abe's return to power in December 2012. This personal bond is not as deep as that forged between President Bush and Prime Minister Koizumi but was cemented by the US agreement to Prime Minister Abe's goal of becoming the first Japanese prime minister to address a joint session of the US Congress during a state visit to Washington in April 2015.

Abe's speech to Congress was notable for its explicit reflection on the complexity of the postwar legacy of the US-Japan security relationship. Abe started the speech by evoking his grandfather, Prime Minister Kishi, who had delivered a speech in the same venue nearly sixty years prior. Abe also included in his delegation a cabinet member whose grandfather had fought in the protracted Battle of Iwo Jima and mentioned this in his speech.

Within Abe's conservative support base, there is a long thread of calls for greater autonomy from the United States.[79] Such thinking is now less visible, likely given the new international environment Japan faces and the relative decline of Japan in the region and globally. It does not mean, however, that such concerns have disappeared in the minds of political conservatives in Japan. In the shifting security environment Japan faces, it would appear that some of the conservative pushes for "autonomy" on history questions can be interpreted as an offset for lack of actual military autonomy in this new era. In the US-Japan joint vision statement released by the two governments during the April 2015 Abe visit to Washington, both countries expressed that "the experiences of the past should inform but not constrain the possibilities of the future."[80]

The next steps in alliance deepening in the now seventy-year-old postwar security relationship between the United States and Japan are set out in the new US-Japan Guidelines for Defense Cooperation released in April 2015.[81] These new guidelines were envisioned in part as a response to the dramatically changed security environment in East Asia compared with 1997, when the guidelines were last revised. They set out new formalized cooperation in areas not prominent (or even in existence) at the time of the last revision, including cyber warfare, cooperation in outer space, and ballistic missile defense—plus further operationalization of defense cooperation around the concept of gray-zone defense.

In another indication of Japan's security renaissance, the proposal to initiate the discussion to revise the guidelines came from Japan, under the DPJ leadership of Prime Minister Kan. The frequent leadership turnover in Japan hindered progress, however. Even under the Abe government, domestic politics delayed formal conclusion of the guidelines by at least six months while the LDP negotiated with its coalition partner, Kōmei, about some of the legislation that would be necessary to implement the new plans, particularly related to CSD. The LDP agreed to delay until after the nationwide local elections in April 2015, reflecting the continued concerns over some of the more controversial security policy decisions by the Abe government.

As described in the "US-Japan Joint Vision Statement" released the day after the text of the guidelines, "The new Guidelines for US-Japan Defense Cooperation will transform the Alliance, reinforce deterrence, and ensure that we can address security challenges, new and old, for the long term. The new Guidelines will update our respective roles and missions within the Alliance and enable Japan to expand its contributions to regional and global security."[82] Four aspects of the new guidelines illustrate Japan's security renaissance of the past decade and, likely, the coming years.

First, the new guidelines seek more flexibility in US-Japan military cooperation as a regularized activity—not just after a contingency in a "situation in areas surrounding Japan" is evoked as under the old guidelines.[83] US military forces and the JSDF now plan for a whole new level of regularized interaction in peacetime through what the guidelines call the Alliance Coordination Mechanism "to ensure seamless and effective whole-of-government Alliance coordination that includes all relevant agencies."[84]

Second, the new guidelines seek to address the gray-zone arena and allow US-Japan military cooperation absent a full declaration of war— a change not unique to US-Japan relations but seen also in US–South Korea concerns about "low-level provocation."

Third, the new guidelines seek to support trilateral and multilateral cooperation, including with South Korea, Australia, India, and others. The document states, "In an increasingly interconnected world, Japan and the United States will take a leading role in cooperation with partners to provide a foundation for peace, security, stability, and economic prosperity in the Asia-Pacific region and beyond."[85]

Finally, and most controversially in Japan, the guidelines set out "actions in response to an armed attack against a country other than Japan"—that is, a CSD role for Japan in one of five specified contingencies.

Beyond these four broad themes, the twenty-three-page document sets out new forms of cooperation in cyberspace and outer space, HADR, intelligence collection, and a number of other areas—illustrating how broadly alliance cooperation has evolved in over fifty-five years of cooperation under the current security treaty and the scale of Japan's security renaissance of the past decade.

The Continuing Challenge of Historical Legacies to the US-Japan Security Relationship

The two previously discussed historical legacies pose contrasting challenges to the US-Japan security relationship—historical revisionism as one barrier to deepening with the United States and staunch antimilitarism as another. As framed in a recent report by the nonpartisan US Congressional Research Service, "On the one hand, Abe is a popular leader with an ambitious agenda that in many ways supports US policy goals. On the other hand, a pattern of activities by Tokyo that re-open historical wounds has hampered Japan's ability to develop constructive relations with South Korea and to manage potentially explosive issues with China, thereby jeopardizing US interests in East Asia."[86]

The Obama administration has expressed support for Abe's domestic agenda, including CSD. Beyond the military-security agenda, Abe's early support for Japan to enter the TPP trade negotiations was also welcomed by the United States, as are a wide range of other aggressive economic policy initiatives to foster growth in the world's third-largest economy. Although the United States has in general strongly and publicly supported Abe's moves to increase Japanese military capabilities and military-related activities in the region and globally, there have been some instances of past history issues interfering with this strong message—such as the US embassy expression of "disappointment" over Abe's visit to Yasukuni Shrine in December 2013[87] and the decision by Secretary of State John Kerry and Secretary of Defense Chuck Hagel to pay respects for Japan's war dead at the Chidorigafuchi National Cemetery—what many critics of Yasukuni Shrine visits see as an alternative site for official visits—during the first Tokyo-based meeting of the Security Consultative Committee (aka "2+2 talks") held in October 2013.

Strong opposition in Okinawa to the alliance-deepening plans agreed to over a decade ago in the 2006 roadmap discussed in chapter 2 and to aspects of the new US-Japan defense guidelines exposes the resilience and continued impact of all three historical legacies—from Japan's wartime conduct (which led to an unconscionable number of civilian deaths in Okinawa) to the postwar legacies of antimilitarist activism strongly apparent in Okinawa to the complex political bargains struck between Tokyo and Washington over the years (beginning with the "original sin" of Tokyo's agreeing to continued US administration of Okinawa until 1972 while the military occupation of the rest of Japan ended in 1952). Prime Minister Abe expended some political capital to move forward the long-delayed plan for relocation of the US Marine Corps air station at Futenma in his first years back in office, successfully convincing Okinawa Governor Hirokazu Nakaima to approve construction of an offshore landfill necessary for rebuilding the replacement facility at Henoko Bay in Nago City in the less-populated, northern part of the island. But since the December 2014 Lower House election, in which all LDP candidates were defeated in the Okinawan constituencies, and, in a different election in November 2014, an anti-base governor was elected to replace Governor Nakaima, the Abe administration has not been able to sustain the momentum. This issue illustrates in microcosm the interplay of politics and history still evident in contemporary Japanese security policies and planning.

Japan's security renaissance has presented new possibilities for US-Japan security coordination within the US-Japan alliance framework and more broadly. It has not erased the complex legacy of the past, however—and many challenges remain. Beyond the narrower subjects of security contingencies in the region, the United States and Japan struggle to coordinate global security strategies, where the United States and Japanese national interests diverge at least to some degree—such as related to Japan's extreme energy dependence and thus higher sensitivity to conflict in the Middle East and in connection with Iran or Japanese relations with Russia. In this latter area, Prime Minister Abe has exerted great effort to build a solid relationship with Russian president Vladimir Putin in the hopes of reaching a resolution over the long-standing dispute over the Northern Territories and fully concluding a peace treaty more than seventy years after the end of World War II. These efforts have been greatly complicated by Russia's actions in Crimea and Ukraine and the US- and EU-backed sanctions against Russia that Japan has grudgingly agreed to respect. Thus, though a new thinking about and approach to military security is evident in contemporary Japan and the US-Japan relationship is quite strong, the US-Japan security relationship will surely continue to be complex and challenging in the coming years and under a post-Abe political leadership.

In the first three years of Abe's second term as prime minister, Japan's security renaissance has become more apparent and more institutionalized. A wide range of once-taboo subjects have been debated, and many constraints of the past have been overridden or reframed. Japan's avowed policy of "proactive contributions to peace"—a phrase coined in the period of DPJ rule but institutionalized under Abe—has sought to rebrand Japan's increased international security roles and increased military capabilities. Despite some opposition, including some very strident voices domestically and internationally, however, the pace of change in Japan's security policies under the second Abe administration is remarkable.

Japan's parliamentary system does not impose fixed terms for prime ministers, and so it is uncertain how much longer Abe will be able to make further strides to institutionalize and to push forward Japan's security renaissance. Abe secured a second three-year term as president of the LDP in September 2015 but under current LDP rules is limited that second term. He is slated to lead his party into the next scheduled national elections for the Lower House of the Diet. These elections are not required before December 2018, though they are likely to take place earlier if the LDP—or Abe himself—sees a political advantage in doing so. Abe became only the sixth prime minister in postwar Japan to enter his fifth year in office in December 2015 and would be the longest-serving prime minister in Japanese history if he remains in office until August 2018. Regardless, his legacy on postwar Japan will surely be far beyond just reaching this milestone.

Apart from the question of the remaining amount of time Abe has in office, his ability to continue to push forward Japan's security renaissance will also be affected by his success in addressing a wide range of other domestic political issues that also vie for his attention—such as fiscal and demographic issues as well as broader issues of economic policy, in addition to the highly contentious issue of restarting Japan's nuclear power reactors, among others. Surely it was a lesson from the first Abe administration (which lost the Upper House election after only ten months in power) that voters demand attention to many areas simultaneously and also expect an ability to manage the country effectively. In addition, the LDP must continue to maintain a healthy working relationship with its coalition partner, Kōmei—in the aftermath of the controversial security legislation passed in September 2015 after a contentious summer of Diet deliberations.

It is too early to tell what major domestic issues will frame the next national election in the Lower House. As with past elections since the burst of the asset bubble in the early 1990s and Japan's entry into an extended period of deflation and economic stagnation, however, it is clear that the extent to which Abe and the LDP-Kōmei coalition government are able to achieve sustained economic growth, a modest level of inflation, and a healthier fiscal balance sheet will be primary measures by which the coalition government is evaluated in the upcoming elections. The state of the political opposition, currently deeply fractured and without any single party garnering even sustained double-digit support, will also be a crucial factor in the upcoming elections.

A wide range of unknowable future security contingencies and crises may also affect the popularity of the Abe government in the time leading up to the nationwide elections—for better or for worse. The leading up to the nationwide elections—for better or for worse. The widespread perception of Prime Minister Hatoyama's mishandling of the US-Japan relationship was clearly linked to the sinking popularity of his administration and to his ultimate resignation in advance of an important Upper House election. Similarly, the DPJ government's role in the escalation of tensions with China over the "nationalization" of the Senkaku Islands under Prime Minister Noda in the summer of 2012 also contributed to the premature resignation of Noda and the call for early Lower House elections.

Looking beyond the Abe government, however long it may last, Japan faces a wide range of security challenges rooted both in widely known domestic challenges such as fiscal health and demographic shifts and in an uncertain regional and global security environment. The concluding chapter considers these challenges in the context of likely next steps in Japan's security renaissance and discusses the implications of Japan's security renaissance for Japan as well as for the United States, the Asian region, and global security cooperation.

Conclusion

Implications and Next Steps in
Japan's Security Renaissance

Just as the influence of the European Renaissance of the distant past extended far beyond its birthplace, Japan's security renaissance also has reached far beyond Tokyo to include Japan's neighbors and its longtime alliance partner, the United States. These effects of Japan's more practical discussion of its security needs and the need for new institutions and practices to manage them have already been widely seen: JSDF capabilities have grown, procedures streamlined, and roles and missions expanded to include a number of activities beyond Japanese territory; ruling coalitions led by the DPJ and the LDP alike have supported these developments and contributed to their developments—often leading to rising tensions with Japan's close neighbors; JSDF officers now routinely participate in high-level government planning meetings in Tokyo and liaise with counterparts around the world. Even further influences are certain to emerge in the near term as new security legislation is implemented and after national elections in July 2016, but in what manner is not yet clear.

Still, many constraints on the JSDF and on Japan's political leadership to utilize Japan's military power remain firmly in place, and public opposition to some aspects of Japan's security renaissance continues. Also like the European Renaissance, the past continues to deeply inform Japan's security future—and to limit Japan's strategic options. Nostalgia for the past—both for the patriotism and willingness to sacrifice for the nation ascribed to Japan's imperial era by some and for the purported pacifism of Japan's economic boom years recalled by many—coexists with and also challenges new thinking about security that seeks to transcend old taboos. Steps toward a new security approach, as well as the many continued constraints, have important ramifications for Japan, the United States, and the region.

For the United States, Japan is likely to be an even more valuable partner to counterbalance China's military rise but could also draw the United States into a military conflict with China: fears of entrapment are now a two-way street between the United States and Japan. Japan's increasing security-related activity around the South China Sea could provide another voice for stability or contribute further to escalating military tensions and spending in the region. The prime minister's new authority to dispatch the JSDF to participate in CSD operations outside Japan could lead to a new round of global security contributions by Japan in either peacetime or during one of many possible military crises that are feared in Japan's close neighborhood, or the prime minister's decision *not* to exercise this power could cause a major rift in the US-Japan alliance or with Japan's other new security partners.

The mythology of "pacifist Japan"—or the related variant, "buck-passing Japan"—remains deeply engrained in many quarters around the world. However, the implications of Japan's security renaissance should not be underestimated: Japan is playing a greater role in the US-Japan alliance and assisting new security partners outside Japan in important ways not widely understood outside elite circles. Japan still boasts the world's third-largest economy—giving it economic power to back new military roles despite its relative economic decline and the accumulation of staggering public debt. And, as detailed in this book, Japan's military forces are among the most capable in the world, are training for a range of new combat-related missions, and are increasingly led by political leadership that has expressed an interest in using these forces not only for the core defense of Japan but also for broader "international contributions" to regional and global peace and security. Japan's domestic political debates about its military capabilities and roles beyond Japan continue to arouse heated emotions, however. Japan's future security contributions—in either peacetime or during a military crisis regionally or globally—are far from certain.

Implications of Japan's Security Renaissance

Japan's security renaissance has important implications for the United States, the Asian region, and global security—and for Japan itself. Japan's present and future security contributions—its "proactive contributions to peace"—stand poised to transform the way both Japanese themselves and the world around them view Japan's military forces and Japan's contributions to global peace and prosperity.

Implications for Japan

Four implications of Japan's security renaissance for Japan itself deserve special attention.

First, Japan is now better prepared to handle possible security contingencies. Moreover, its improved capabilities and practices for managing these assets improve its deterrence posture, ideally preventing a security contingency from occurring in the first place. Japan is more secure due to the efforts of Japan's political leadership across parties and dedicated security-related bureaucrats and JSDF personnel.

Second, despite cross-party support and leadership to improve Japan's military roles and capabilities in recent years, organized opposition to many of the new security practices implemented by the Abe government in 2013 to 2016 shows continued disagreement about important choices in Japan's security future. Japan's security renaissance does not represent a break from the past but rather a new framing of the present in relation to the past. The entire postwar period of Japanese politics has been characterized by protracted, deep disagreements among important political actors regarding the appropriate military security posture for Japan. These disagreements have not been erased in the past decade and will continue to shape Japan's security future—and Japan's domestic politics as well.

Third, seventy years after the conclusion of World War II, Japan must still make progress toward addressing the first historical legacy of

Japan's past: its colonial-era and wartime conduct and policies. The Abe government's 2015 Advisory Panel on History report makes positive and useful suggestions for some next steps that the Japanese government should pursue to better address the legacies of this period,[1] including introducing a course on contemporary Japanese history (which, astonishingly, does not yet exist) into the national high school curriculum and support of further expert-level study of the history of the twentieth century in Asia from a cross-national perspective—but political leaders must play a leading role in reshaping the discourse on Japan's past beyond well-vetted anniversary statements. If Prime Minister Abe and his successors truly wish to create a Japan where future generations are not "predestined to apologize"—as Abe called for in his cabinet statement marking the seventieth anniversary of the end of World War II—they must more fully convey in *this* generation an appreciation for the harm that Japan caused in that period of its history and the active responsibility Japanese at the time had in causing that harm. This is not only a moral responsibility. In terms of implications for Japan's contemporary security renaissance, these history issues limit Japan's strategic choices (such as working more closely with South Korea) and make other actions more politically or diplomatically costly than they need be. That said, Japanese leaders need willing counterparts in neighboring states to make true progress on reconciliation, partners shown to be in short supply of late.

Fourth, Japan's relationship with the United States has deepened, reinforcing an important counterweight to China's rise in the region and ensuring Japan's access to some of the most advanced technology and practices for enhancing its security—such as improved missile defense, the most comprehensive surveillance satellite network in the world, and important tools to prepare for new security domains of cyberspace and outer space. This strengthening of the US-Japan military relationship has an important implication for Japan, though it is not without continued problems—from broad concerns about both entrapment and abandonment to practical ones over the sustainability of the concentrated military presence in Okinawa. Some of these issues are discussed in the section on Japan's security future later in this chapter.

Implications for the United States

Japan's security renaissance of the past decade and deepening of its security relationship with the United States in years prior have made Japan a more reliable security partner and contributed to a more stable and peaceful East Asia. The government-to-government relationship between the United States and Japan is improved by Japan's growing engagement with security concerns and challenges the United States perceives in the region and globally; the relationship between the two governments is the strongest it has ever been, despite disagreements across a range of policy issues from nuclear weapons to currency intervention and other areas where agreement is present but implementation is lacking. Japan's new security posture and attitudes have also posed some drawbacks for the United States, however, and there are still numerous areas where the long-standing US view that Japan is not doing enough in terms of a security contribution remains.

In contrast to the many years that the US-Japan security relationship could be described as one where Japan has feared to varying degrees entrapment in US conflicts, this is one area where the alliance has truly become more equal in recent years—with the United States now concerned about entrapment in several areas as well. The possibility of being pulled into a war with China over "uninhabited rocks" between Japan and China is one concern that is new to the US-Japan relationship and likely to continue for the foreseeable future. This is not to imply that Japan's actions precipitated this possibility but rather that increased combat readiness and new deployment patterns of the JSDF to manage such a contingency—such as the shift of forces to the southwest in Japan and more seamless coordination among the branches of the JSDF—make this worst-case scenario more imaginable than it had been at earlier stages of Japan's military readiness. The United States has sought to address this concern through private discussions with Japanese leaders to mitigate unnecessary military escalation. The United States has also sought to bolster deterrence of military action by China through more frequent rhetorical support for the US commitment to defend all territory administered by Japan—despite not taking a formal position on the sovereignty of the disputed territory between Japan and China. Moreover, expanded training with the JSDF for such operations both in Japan and by hosting JSDF forces in the United States seeks to limit the potential for an unfavorable escalation of military tensions between Japan and China.

The war of words between Japan and China and between Japan and South Korea over history issues also generates some negative effects on the United States. While these history issues are not a new aspect of Japan's postwar security development, they take on a new importance as the United States seeks to deepen partnerships with multiple states in the region as part of its rebalancing strategy. Japan's frosty relations with South Korea—which persisted during the period of DPJ governance and intensified under the Abe administration—complicate US security planning for the region and inhibit synergies that would otherwise be possible between the two "spokes" of strong US alliances with the two countries.[2] Moreover, the troubled Japan–South Korea relationship also has spillover effects in US domestic politics, as a growing number of local constituencies in the United States wade into the complicated politics of the comfort women, the formal designation of the Sea of Japan, and Takeshima territory issues by seeking to erect memorial statues and revise US school textbook maps and descriptions.[3]

Japan's new security practices and explanation of them in the region also have the potential to disrupt the US-China relationship beyond the Senkaku entrapment issue. Japan hands (and US government officials dealing with Japan) often repeat the famous phrase by former US senator and ambassador to Japan Mike Mansfield that the US-Japan relationship is the most important bilateral relationship in the world "bar none"—and arguably this is still true. But the most consequential bilateral relationship is that between the United States and China,[4] despite not being nearly as cooperative or multifaceted as the US-Japan relationship. China historically has tended to view the US-Japan security alliance with suspicion and sometimes derision but also as a useful "cork in the bottle" on resurgent Japanese militarism.[5] As JSDF capabilities have increased in the past several decades—beginning with the controversial issue of missile defense in the late 1990s—China has become more critical of US support for Japan's "remilitarization" (as China often labels it). Japan's new security relationships with other states in the region—which China views as being encouraged by the United States—can intensify Chinese perceptions of "containment" or "encirclement" by the US military and its allies. Japan's support of other states with territorial disputes with China[6]—like the Philippines and Vietnam in the South China Sea—could potentially complicate the delicate balance the United States seeks in its relationship with China.

Managed properly, though, the limited downsides of Japan's security renaissance for the United States are more than offset by the contributions Japan's expanded security role in its own self-defense as well as regionally and globally makes to US strategic objectives. Such expanded roles help US defense planners to manage a period of declining defense budgets in the United States and offer new possibilities for synergies using Japan's advanced technologies and manufacturing prowess as well as regional expertise. The core implication of Japan's security renaissance for the United States is of a more reliable US ally and enhanced long-term strategic partner in the region and globally, despite continuing vocal opposition in Japan—and in Okinawa in particular—to some aspects of a deepened US-Japan alliance.

Implications for the Asian Region

Japan has gradually expanded its security presence in the Asian region over the past two decades, but it has initiated bilateral military cooperation with other states in the region only in recent years. Japan is now a core contributor in numerous multilateral security institutions in the region, frequent participant in multilateral military training exercises, provider of security-related technical and training assistance—and, more recently, military equipment—to numerous states, and the JSDF and JCG are frequent providers of security in the region (albeit to date generally still in limited roles). The implications of this increased Japanese military engagement with the region depend on one's perspective or, more often, one's nationality.

The states of Southeast Asia generally welcome Japan's expanded security role in the region, despite its wartime invasion and often brutal conduct in those places. For all states in the region, Japan represents another *option* for security cooperation, beyond the United States and China. More choice is better, seems to be the mantra of the ASEAN states—even those more closely aligned with China, such as Cambodia and Myanmar.

Japan's new security partnerships in the region have been pursued to the deepest level with Australia, to the degree that some have begun to refer to the Japan-Australia connection as a quasi alliance.[7] Although a lively debate is taking place in Australia today about the best way to accommodate China's rise, the benefit of having an additional security partner in Japan is not among the contentious points. Australia and India, which also has increased military-to-military ties and joint exercises with Japan, are both currently pursuing new opportunities to purchase Japanese military technology and equipment under the relaxation of Japan's arms export restrictions that took place in 2014. Although a recent proposal for Australia to acquire Japanese-made diesel submarines to enhance Australian capabilities around the South China Sea and to deepen military ties with Japan was not realized, that this was even on a possible agenda illustrates the significant change that has taken place in Japan's security policies in the past decade.

In the 1990s, before Japan began direct military-to-military operations in the region, the JCG (with some indirect support from the JMSDF) played an important role in combating piracy in the region, contributing to the reduction in the number of incidents from hundreds a year to virtually none in the past several years. Building on the experience of working with coast guards of several states in the region, the JCG and now JMSDF have begun to work as well with the naval forces of some states on improving capacity and capabilities for self-defense. This self-defense-only mandate is important to stress, both in terms of implications for the region and in understanding continuing redlines in Japanese military policy despite the renaissance in thinking about best practices for the twenty-first century. The view of those states benefiting from such assistance (including the Philippines and Vietnam most extensively), of the United States, and, of course, of the Japanese themselves is that capacity building for territorial defense is a stabilizing measure for the region and promotes the continued peaceful interaction of states in the region.

To China, a rival claimant to territories in the South China Sea, Japan's provision of security assistance to other states to enhance their capacity to counter China's growing capabilities is destabilizing and unwelcome. Moreover, the Chinese resist the linkage Japan has made of China's claim to Japan's territory in the East China Sea and China's claims in the South China Sea. In addition, as previously discussed in the context of the US-Japan alliance, China is increasingly critical of enhanced capabilities of the JSDF and JCG as Japan expands its roles and missions within the US-Japan alliance as well as on its own. From Japan's perspective, its growing military capabilities vis-à-vis China are purely defensive, and the enhanced deterrent effect of Japan's greater capabilities should lead to a more stable region and make a military conflict between China and Japan (in particular over the Senkaku Islands) less likely.

Deeper security cooperation between Japan and South Korea is stymied by history at present, as it was in earlier periods, though to a lesser —and less emotional—degree. As Japan's capabilities and engagement with the region and globally continue to increase, and if South Korea continues to seek to expand its regional and global role, increased security cooperation between these two natural allies is inevitable, even if years away.[8] One implication of Japan's expanded regional role for South Korea is the opportunities this provides, even modestly, for the two states to work together away from the sensitive area around Korean territory itself, where a physical Japanese military presence is still anathema to the general public.

Implications for Global Security

Japan's gradual security awakening has led to a marked increase in Japan's contribution to cooperative international security activities, such as UNPKO and more ad hoc joint security efforts, and it offers the potential for further such increases as outlined in Japan's 2013 national security strategy, which calls for greater proactive contributions to peace globally. Scholars such as Bhubhindar Singh and Lindsay Black have documented Japan's increased international contributions of the recent past,[9] and new security legislation recently passed in the Diet authorizes further contributions in a number of areas. The 2015 US-Japan Guidelines for Defense Cooperation also tout plans for an expanded global security contribution by Japan.

However, Japan's power relative to other states in the region and worldwide is shrinking, its resources are severely strained by interest on huge government debt and a troubling demographic future, and the security challenges it faces close to home are increasing in orders of magnitude. These realities suggest that despite a new willingness to consider international security contributions and new capabilities and institutions for effectively making such contributions, in fact such new commitments are not likely to be substantially larger in the coming years than the notable increases in the past decade.

That said, one lesson gleaned from careful examination of Japan's post–Cold War security transformation is that significant improvements in Japanese capabilities and contributions are possible without significantly more spending—through improved efficiencies in procurement, better institutional management, and more effective and targeted strategies and practices. Japan's defense budget was more or less unchanged from 2003 to 2012, yet both its capabilities and operations improved substantially. Moreover, Japan's underlying regional and global strategy of proactive contributions to peace is not limited to the activities of the JSDF. Japan has long linked its ODA policy to contributions to global peace and stability, for example, but under the new 2015 ODA charter, it has even more closely connected the importance of economic development and social stability to the long-term achievement of peace.[10]

While Japan's ODA budget is much less than at its peak in the 1980s and is not set to increase in the near term, institutional innovations and greater cooperative efforts across government arguably will lead to greater impact. It should not be forgotten that Japan was, apart from the United States, by far the largest donor to the reconstruction of Afghanistan in the first decade of the present century—illustrating in practice the linkage between military security and ODA.[11] More recently, Japan's innovative ODA financing via low-interest yen loans for Syrian refugee assistance to Jordan and to Turkey shows how new institutional practices can create better outcomes at virtually no cost.[12] Japan's 2014 relaxation of arms export restrictions is another area where Japanese technology and manufacturing prowess may constitute a global security contribution at no direct additional cost to Japan's budget (and, indeed, perhaps in the medium term potentially at a *savings* to Japan's own weapons development and manufacture through cooperative partners and efficiencies of scale). In sum, the global implications of Japan's security renaissance have already been visible to those affected and will likely become more widely visible in the coming years.

Next Steps and Wild Cards in Japan's Security Future

Japan faces a number of challenges domestically and internationally in the coming decade. Domestically the return of the Japanese economy to a period of steady growth is the most important challenge, as this is inextricably linked to Japan's fiscal and budgetary health as well as Prime Minister Abe's political ability to implement further security policy innovation. In the medium term, however, Japan's rapidly aging and gradually shrinking population also poses significant security challenges for Japan. Internationally, China's continued (if slowed) rise economically and militarily together with increased global economic competition and global security cooperation will also push Japan to further internationalize its approach to military security. In response, Japan will need to consider expanded regional security cooperation and perhaps even revision of its long-standing "peace constitution." The next national elections—in the Lower House, by December 2018—will offer political parties new opportunities to further illustrate the renaissance in Japan's security approaches to coming challenges and voters an opportunity to influence the next steps of Japan's security future. Japan's regional security environment is constantly evolving, however, with many uncertainties. Japan's future security path will be determined in part by these uncertainties and by political decisions made in other states in response to such change.

A Changing Japan

Japan's domestic politics have been in flux since the early 1990s and still have not reached a new equilibrium despite several major political realignments via shifting political party composition.[13] Prime Minister Abe's leadership has greatly shaped Japan's security renaissance and will provide a lasting legacy for Japan's security future. At the time of this writing—after the September 2015 reelection of Abe as president of the LDP for a second three-year term and with his popularity far above any political rival after the July 2016 Upper House election—it seems likely that he will lead his party into national elections in the Lower House again, which must be held sometime before December 2018.

The fractured state of Japan's political opposition—which has greatly benefited Abe's political agenda—will not continue indefinitely, however. Forces opposing Abe's agenda—both outside and inside the LDP—may coalesce to present a true challenge in a future election, different from the unsuccessful attempt in advance of the Upper House elections in July 2016. One aspect of this opposition may coalesce around the contentious security politics that were strongly in evidence in 2015—though, as before, the primary concerns of voters will continue to be about the state of Japan's economy and the prosperity of Japanese citizens. Here Japan faces many challenges that will greatly, if indirectly, affect its security future.

Japan's continuing demographic evolution into uncharted territory will play a major role in its economic and security future. It is very difficult to revive an economy with staggering public and private debt and a shrinking and super-aging population. Politicians naturally lean toward quick and dramatic fixes. These problems, however, demand sustained attention on multiple levels. They also require addressing problems that Japan has faced for decades. Japan's birthrate slipped below replacement levels in 1974. The bubble economy burst in 1990. Women have never had equal opportunity in the workplace. Japan's previous limited experiments with even low levels of immigration generated a wide variety of problems in a country where 98.5 percent of the residents are ethnically Japanese. More effectively addressing each of these long-standing challenges will be necessary, however, to boost Japan's long stagnating economy and to keep the country from falling even further behind relative to its neighbors.

In the area of military security, Japan's shrinking working-age population will have real consequences. As noted by Toshi Yoshihara, "The cost of fielding troops for combat will rise as manpower availability dwindles"—and dwindle it will. "By 2030," Yoshihara continues, "SDF-eligible males will fall to less than 5 million"—from a peak of nine million in 1994 and six million in 2015.[14] Japan's advanced technology will go only so far to protect Japan—and, in any case, *someone* has to pay for it.

Beyond demographics and the concomitant drain on government finance, Japan faces countless other economic challenges. Its experience in the past two decades does not instill confidence that new political leadership will emerge to implement the sort of bold solutions that economists suggest are necessary to fundamentally transform the Japanese economy in the twenty-first century back to global competitiveness across many sectors. The TPP idea holds some promise for helping Abe and perhaps his successor to implement some of the structural reform to the economy attached to his "third arrow"—but implementation of TPP remains stalled, and even these reforms would mark only a down payment to the sort of structural reforms that are widely seen as necessary for the Japanese economy to reach the growth rates of its neighbors.

Without robust growth, Japan not only cannot pay for its more ambitious defense outlays and other proactive contributions to peace such as capacity building of the defenses of other states and generous ODA to promote peace but also loses regional and global stature. Japan's soft power has been strong for half a century—but its essence has shifted in the past several decades away from being a beacon of democracy and high-growth economic prosperity to the "cool Japan" of excellent cuisine and cutting-edge fashion and design.[15] This is not enough to balance China's growing soft power, which is still linked to its economic success and ability to lift the poor out of poverty through jobs—jobs created by Chinese economic growth; nor will Japan's calls for respect of the rule of law and international institutions be as strong without Japan itself being seen as a beacon for future success.

Japanese society also has transformed in response to the many challenges Japan has faced throughout decades of economic stagnation in ways that also affect its security future.[16] Political conservatives' efforts to encourage women to bear more children and to reintroduce "patriotic education" into public schools notwithstanding, R. Taggart Murphy seems on track about the societal limitations of Japan's security future when he writes, "In the era of the *gyaru* [trendy women reluctant to marry], the herbivore male, and the *otaku* [nerd culture]—not to mention a rapidly aging society—there is no going back to the 1930s and millions of young men thirsting to die for the emperor."[17] This is a good thing, but concerns of many social conservatives in Japan about the low level of patriotic feeling in Japan also deserve attention—though not necessarily in the ways many social conservatives suggest.

Japan's topsy-turvy domestic politics of the past two decades have both frustrated and alienated many voters. Political movements and political parties rise and fall, party affiliation has weakened to a point that "unaffiliated" is now the majority political affiliation, and voter turn-out has declined markedly in the past four national elections, to only 52.7 percent in the December 2014 Lower House election (down from nearly 70 percent in 2009). True solutions to Japan's long-term economic stagnation and ballooning government debt remain elusive.[18] Despite this challenging political environment, however, real discussions and debate over Japan's proper level of security preparedness and contribu-tions have been taking place, with notable implementation of a consis-tent medium-term plan across political parties and political leadership.

This is not to say that there is a consensus about Japan's recent moves or need for future innovation. In particular, the hugely divisive issue of possible formal revision of the postwar constitution—for the first time since its adoption in 1947—remains deeply contested, whether over the revered Article Nine or other elements of the constitution. Mass public demonstrations, acrimonious debates in the Diet, and scathing opin-ion pieces in the media from multiple angles show that Japan's security policies remain a divisive political issue, with a potential to shift in new ways in response to a security shock or dramatically shifting regional tectonics.

A Changing Region

There are many regional wild cards in Japan's security future. De-spite decades of stability that has undergirded the region's remarkable economic growth, the region has faced—and will continue to face—numerous possible catastrophic security threats: renewed war on the Ko-rean Peninsula or, worse, a nuclear provocation by North Korea; a war between China and Taiwan that draws in the United States and Japan; a miscalculation in the daily close operations of Japanese, Chinese, and US military and coast guard forces around the Senkaku Islands escalat-ing into a major military conflict. Such massive escalations seem unlikely because of careful planning and calculated actions by the states involved but cannot be dismissed—and will continue to be a primary factor in Japanese defense planning, as they will in the defense planning of other states.

Even a lower-level security incident could spark a new stage of Japa-nese security engagement with the region, or movement to spend more on defense or to develop even greater military capabilities—as the North Korean Taepodong missile overflight of Japan in 1998 led to the development of long-opposed missile defense cooperation with the United States and development of indigenous surveillance satellites. Note that Japan's ally, the United States, more than doubled its military spending after the September 11, 2001, terrorist attacks on its territory, despite the huge deficit spending this required. Japan's more recent concern with gray-zone conflict, particularly related to the Senkaku Islands, could also evolve into an actual limited fighting conflict, shaping the next steps of Japan's security renaissance.

China will continue to be a major driver of Japan's evolving security strategy, and, as with Japan's economic challenges, the future of the Chinese economy is a major wild card in Japan's security future. China's economic slowdown in 2015 and devaluation of the yuan could have positive implications for Japan's security future by slowing the growth of Chinese military spending and potentially leading to more positive outreach to Japan by Chinese leaders seeking to promote more Japanese investment and trade with China. Alternatively, however, a broader economic slowdown in China could lead to further scapegoating of Japan for China's problems. Either way, China's future will play an outsized role in Japan's future.[19]

The broader dynamics of this changing region will also affect the next steps in Japan's security renaissance. For several decades now a contest for regional leadership has been under way. The latest stage of this contest is no longer for outright leadership by any one player—whether Japan, China, or the United States—but a complex multipolar courting of support via many different means, including economic, soft power, and military cooperation. An important aspect of Japan's security renaissance is Japan's foray into the military cooperation arena. How deeply Japan develops further military partnerships in the region will depend on other regional actors as well as domestic politics in Japan.

The Continuing Legacies of Militarism and Antimilitarism

Events and coverage surrounding Japan's commemoration in 2015 of the end of World War II starkly illustrate that Japanese leaders will continue to struggle with the legacies of Japan's colonialist and militarist past for the foreseeable future. One of the implications of Japan's security renaissance is that Japan needs to more effectively address this primary history issue in order to more smoothly proceed with planning for the security challenges of the mid-twenty-first century. Whether or not this will happen, however, remains a wild card in Japan's security future. Skeptics of Prime Minister Abe's efforts to address the issue question whether he possesses the resolve to address it, but even putting this question aside, it is clear that the compromises evident in his 2015 statements about Japan's wartime past reflect the political agenda of important constituencies in the conservative coalition in contemporary Japanese politics. If the LDP is to remain in power, as looks likely for the foreseeable future, future prime ministers will also be constrained by such influential political actors on the right and far right.

The sustained, organized opposition to much of the Abe government's security agenda—and especially the 2015 security legislation related to CSD—strongly suggests that Japan's postwar antimilitarist legacy will also continue to critically shape Japan's security future. Contrary to what some expected, younger generations of Japanese have not shown markedly different attitudes about Japan's security posture than older generations; in some areas, in fact, older generations are *more* hawkish in their views related to some security issues, despite the purportedly stronger pacifism of the early postwar years.[20] Thus, although the political parties that have most represented the views of the more dovish elements of Japanese society have been on the decline for quite some time, public attitudes continue to reflect these preferences, and the LDP risks a serious backlash if it fails to heed these views. The long history of the LDP over more than half a century shows that it has been willing to sacrifice first-choice policies in favor of staying in power, sacrifice it has repeatedly made in the area of security policy preferences over the years.[21] The multiple compromises to the package of security legislation passed in the Diet in September 2015 show that the LDP remains adept at advancing its agenda even in stages.

A reversal of the past several years of security-related legislation and practices under a new government seems very unlikely given that when the DPJ was in power it advocated for many of the same sorts of policies and that the security policy innovation of recent years has also been the result of political compromise. Thus, the more pertinent wild card is whether the influence of Japan's antimilitarist political forces will further decline in the coming decades to allow for a much more muscular Japan than seen to date. One can imagine future "shock" scenarios that could lead to such a major political transformation, but absent such a shock, a wholesale abandonment of this antimilitarist legacy of the past seems quite unlikely.

The United States and Japan: Toward Implementing the 2015 Defense Guidelines

This book has focused on a decade that began at a high point in US-Japan relations at the end of the Koizumi period, weathered the turbulence of the early DPJ governance years, and has emerged post–March 11 and under Prime Minister Abe's return at a peak in US-Japan security cooperation. Few question the resilience of the alliance today even despite obvious obstacles ahead related to the inability to proceed with long-standing agreements related to Okinawa and continued challenges to coordinating policy vis-à-vis China. Nor do many expect any future path other than the broadening and deepening of the security relationship between the United States and Japan in the coming years—though the pace of this broadening and deepening continues to be a question. Still, there are challenges to implementation of current plans and always the potential for a crisis, whether caused by one of the long-standing possible regional security contingencies outlined in the preceding pages (which the guidelines are meant to mitigate against) or by an individual incident like the rape of a twelve-year-old girl by three US servicemen that sparked widespread anti-base protests in Okinawa in 1995 or an accident that harms or threatens the local population around a US base in Okinawa or elsewhere in Japan.

Despite new US-Japan Guidelines for Defense Cooperation in 2015 that seek to develop more advance planning for security contingencies, it is not clear how a crisis would unfold vis-à-vis the US-Japan alliance. The new security legislation passed in September 2015 allows for more advance planning of such coordinated action and is expected to lead to more multilateral exercises in the coming years as the legislation is implemented. Still, there remains no unified US-Japan combined military command and little prospect of one given all three historical legacies that continue to affect Japan's security planning. Coordination and preparation of joint action will continue to require concerted effort.

Japan's recent moves to more operational capabilities and a regional role for the JSDF, as well as more realistic discussions of Japan's security challenges, allow for deeper coordination between the United States and Japan not just to address Japan's own security—which, after all, is the core function of the alliance from Japan's perspective—but also to work together more closely on ensuring peace and security in the Asian region as a whole, which is the primary purpose of the alliance from the US perspective and now also a "core mission" of the MOD.[22] Both states benefit from the latest round of alliance deepening: Japan can feel more secure in its ability to address or deter new security contingencies it fears, and the United States has a new partner for a number of important regional and global security challenges it perceives as well as more burden sharing in the possible defense of Japan. Such win-win dynamics have created unprecedented levels of public support for the alliance in both countries, which should help with weathering a crisis that might appear. Both states—together and individually—will continue to recruit new partners to help address the rising challenges of the mid-twenty-first century, but no other state in the region can offer the range of capabilities and history of cooperation as the United States and Japan do for each other.

While long-standing voices in Japan calling for more autonomy for Japan's military forces have been unusually silent in recent years, we should not assume that they will remain so indefinitely—particularly as conservative voices vie for power in the post-Abe political order that is to come. Moreover, there continue to be regular expressions of concern about abandonment of Japan at a time of crisis, requiring regular reassurance by the United States. These long-standing aspects of the complex postwar US-Japan relationship will remain possible disruptors of the alliance in the medium term.

The concentration of US forces in Okinawa presents the greatest challenge for alliance managers and for Japanese politicians. Despite Prime Minister Abe's progress on many areas of the common alliance agenda in his first three years back in office since December 2012, the controversial relocation of Futenma Air Station continues to face serious local political opposition—fully two decades after the events that

led to the plan to relocate the base in the first place. Organized local political activism against the long-term presence of US forces in Okinawa
at current levels is only intensifying. At the same time, China's rapid rise
of offensive military capabilities poses new threats to the concentration
of US and Japanese military forces in any one place, which has already
led to the removal of some US forces from Okinawa beyond what was
envisioned after the last comprehensive review of US force distribution
in the Defense Policy Review Initiative (DPRI) conducted from 2002 to
2006. Given the escalating cost estimates of relocation of US forces to
Guam, however, and continued reluctance of both alliance managers
and local communities on the Japanese main islands to host US forces,
it is difficult to see innovative solutions to this challenge emerging in
the near term; in the medium term, a greater regional distribution of
US forces seems likely given growing Chinese military capabilities, but
this alone will not address the conundrum of US force concentration in
Japan—and, in particular, base concentration—in the short term.

Thus, while the alliance is on a positive trajectory, the complex historical legacy of the now seventy years of a shared security agenda
between Japan and the United States under greatly disproportionate
American power will continue to challenge alliance managers and Japan's elected officials, despite the renaissance in Japan's approaches to
its security seen these early years of the twenty-first century. Threaded
together with new responses to the continued historical legacies of both
militarism and antimilitarism in Japan's past, the United States and
Japan seem destined to continue forging joint solutions to regional and
global security challenges in an era in which the relative power resources
of both states are in decline.

Japan's future security choices will be informed by its past, but Japan
will not return to its past—neither a militarist past nor a purely antimilitarist one. Japanese security politics and policies have entered a new
stage from which there is no return. In the coming decade, the JSDF
will increase its presence overseas in training with friendly states, providing disaster relief, and engaging in at least limited joint operations
to promote regional and global security. JSDF officers, together with
their MOD colleagues, will become even more visible in world capitals
and in multilateral institutions as they represent Japan to create a safer

security environment. At home, political debates will continue to rage—including new public protests—about the degree to which Japan should expand its contributions to regional and global security and the sort of capabilities the JSDF should develop. These debates will continue to become more grounded in awareness of the physical threats Japan faces and the dynamics of military cooperation overseas but will also reflect peculiarities and limitations based on the legacies of Japan's distant and more recent past.

The next steps of Japan's security renaissance will depend on a number of choices made by the Japanese people and political leadership—and the peoples and political leaderships of a number of different states. This interactive dynamic between the international environment and Japan's domestic politics will shape both Japan's security future and the future security environment in East Asia and beyond.

APPENDIX 1

Japanese Prime Ministers and Party Affiliations, 2000 to 2016

NAME	PARTY	DATES IN OFFICE
Shinzō Abe	LDP	12/26/2012–
Yoshihiko Noda	DPJ	9/2/2011–12/26/2012
Naoto Kan	DPJ	6/8/2010–9/2/2011
Yukio Hatoyama	DPJ	9/16/2009–6/8/2010
Tarō Asō	LDP	9/24/2008–9/16/2009
Yasuo Fukuda	LDP	9/26/2007–9/24/2008
Shinzō Abe	LDP	9/26/2006–9/26/2007
Jun'ichirō Koizumi	LDP	4/26/2001–9/26/2006
Yoshirō Mori	LDP	4/5/2000–4/26/2001
Keizō Obuchi	LDP	7/30/1998–4/5/2000

Source: http://www.kantei.go.jp/jp/rekidainaikaku/index.html.

APPENDIX 2

Percentage of Party Vote and Seats in National Elections, 2005 to 2016

TABLE A2.1
Lower House elections (including dates and voter turnout percentages)

Party	2014 12/14/2014 [52.7]			2012 12/16/2012 [59.3]			2009 8/30/2009 [69.3]			2005 9/11/2005 [67.5]		
	Seats[a]	SMD[b]	PR[c]	Seats	SMD	PR	Seats	SMD	PR	Seats	SMD	PR
LDP[d]	61.26	48.1	33.11	61.25	43.01	27.62	24.79	38.68	26.73	61.67	47.77	38.18
KP[e]	7.37	1.45	13.71	6.46	1.49	11.83	4.38	1.11	11.45	6.46	1.44	13.25
DPJ[f]	15.37	22.51	18.33	11.88	22.81	16.00	64.17	47.43	42.41	23.54	36.44	31.02
JCP[g]	4.42	13.3	11.37	1.67	7.88	6.13	1.88	4.22	7.03	1.88	7.25	7.25
SDP[h]	0.42	0.79	2.46	0.42	0.76	2.36	1.46	1.95	4.27	1.46	1.46	5.49
JRP[i]	8.63	8.16	15.72	11.25	11.64	20.38	n/a	n/a	n/a	n/a	n/a	n/a
YP[i]	n/a	n/a	n/a	3.75	4.71	8.72	1.04	0.87	4.27	n/a	n/a	n/a
Other	2.52	5.69	5.3	3.33	7.72	6.97	2.29	5.74	3.84	5.00	5.62	4.80

TABLE A2.2

Upper House elections (including dates and voter turnout percentages)

Party	2016 7/10/2016 [54.7]			2013 7/21/2013 [52.6]			2010 7/11/2010 [59.7]			2007 7/29/2007 [58.6]		
	Seats	SMD	PR	Seats[a]	SMD[b]	PR[c]	Seats	SMD	PR	Seats	SMD	PR
LDP[d]	46.28	39.94	35.91	53.72	42.74	34.68	42.15	33.38	24.07	30.58	31.35	28.08
NKP[e]	11.57	7.54	13.52	9.09	5.13	14.22	7.44	3.88	13.07	7.44	5.96	13.18
DPJ[f]	26.45	7.26	10.74	14.05	16.29	13.40	36.36	38.97	31.56	49.59	40.45	39.48
JCP[g]	0.83	0.51	2.74	6.61	10.64	9.68	2.48	7.29	6.10	2.48	8.70	7.48
SDP[h]	5.79	5.84	9.2	0.83	0.51	2.36	1.65	1.03	3.84	1.65	2.28	4.47
JRP[i]	4.12	14.85	8.31	6.61	7.25	11.94	n/a	n/a	n/a	n/a	n/a	n/a
YP[j]	–		–	6.61	7.84	8.93	8.26	10.24	13.59	n/a	n/a	n/a
Other				2.48	9.60	4.78	1.65	5.22	7.77	8.26	11.27	7.30

Source: Ministry of Internal Affairs and Communications; compiled by Naoko Funatsu, East-West Center, Washington, DC, http://www.soumu.go.jp/senkyo/senkyo_s/data/index.html#chapter1.

[a] Percentage of seats of those contested: 480 in Lower House (475 in 2014); 121 in Upper House

[b] Percentage of vote in SMD: small member/prefectural districts in Upper House

[c] Percentage of vote in PR district[s]

[d] Liberal Democratic Party

[e] [New] Kōmeitō Party

[f] Democratic Party [of Japan]

[g] Japan Communist Party

[h] Social Democratic Party

[i] Japan Restoration Party (Japan Innovation Party in 2014 and One Osaka in 2016)

[j] Your Party

APPENDIX 3

Selected Historical Apology Statements by Japanese Officials, 1993 to 2015

1. Chief Cabinet Secretary Yōhei Kōno on the result of the study on the issue of comfort women, August 4, 1993
2. Prime Minister Tomiichi Murayama on the occasion of the fiftieth anniversary of the war's end, August 15, 1995
3. House of Representatives, National Diet of Japan, Resolution to Renew the Determination for Peace on the Basis of Lessons Learned from History, June 9, 1995
4. Prime Minister Jun'ichirō Koizumi on the occasion of the sixtieth anniversary of the end of World War II, August 15, 2005
5. Prime Minister Naoto Kan on the occasion of the one hundredth anniversary of the Japan-Korea Annexation Treaty, August 10, 2010
6. Prime Minister Shinzō Abe on the occasion of the seventieth anniversary of the end of World War II, August 15, 2015 (cabinet statement)

1. Statement by Chief Cabinet Secretary Yōhei Kōno on the Result of the Study on the Issue of Comfort Women, August 4, 1993

The Government of Japan has been conducting a study on the issue of wartime "comfort women" since December 1991. I wish to announce the findings as a result of that study.

As a result of the study which indicates that comfort stations were operated in extensive areas for long periods, it is apparent that there existed a great number of comfort women. Comfort stations were operated in response to the request of the military authorities of the day. The then Japanese military was, directly or indirectly, involved in the establishment and management of the comfort stations and the transfer of comfort women. The recruitment of the comfort women was conducted mainly by private recruiters who acted in response to the request of the military. The Government study has revealed that in many cases they were recruited against their own will, through coaxing, coercion, etc., and that, at times, administrative/military personnel directly took part in the recruitments. They lived in misery at comfort stations under a coercive atmosphere.

As to the origin of those comfort women who were transferred to the war areas, excluding those from Japan, those from the Korean Peninsula accounted for a large part. The Korean Peninsula was under Japanese rule in those days, and their recruitment, transfer, control, etc., were conducted generally against their will, through coaxing, coercion, etc.

Undeniably, this was an act, with the involvement of the military authorities of the day, that severely injured the honor and dignity of many women. The Government of Japan would like to take this opportunity once again to extend its sincere apologies and remorse to all those, irrespective of place of origin, who suffered immeasurable pain and incurable physical and psychological wounds as comfort women.

It is incumbent upon us, the Government of Japan, to continue to consider seriously, while listening to the views of learned circles, how best we can express this sentiment.

We shall face squarely the historical facts as described above instead of evading them, and take them to heart as lessons of history. We hereby reiterate our firm determination never to repeat the same mistake by forever engraving such issues in our memories through the study and teaching of history.

As actions have been brought to court in Japan and interests have been shown in this issue outside Japan, the Government of Japan shall continue to pay full attention to this matter, including private researched [sic] related thereto (Ministry of Foreign Affairs, http://www.mofa.go.jp/policy/women/fund/state9308.html).

2. Statement by Prime Minister Tomiichi Murayama on the Occasion of the Fiftieth Anniversary of the War's End, August 15, 1995

The world has seen fifty years elapse since the war came to an end. Now, when I remember the many people both at home and abroad who fell victim to war, my heart is overwhelmed by a flood of emotions.

The peace and prosperity of today were built as Japan overcame great difficulty to arise from a devastated land after defeat in the war. That achievement
is something of which we are proud, and let me herein express my heartfelt
admiration for the wisdom and untiring effort of each and every one of our
citizens. Let me also express once again my profound gratitude for the indispensable support and assistance extended to Japan by the countries of the
world, beginning with the United States of America. I am also delighted that
we have been able to build the friendly relations which we enjoy today with
the neighboring countries of the Asia-Pacific region, the United States and the
countries of Europe.

Now that Japan has come to enjoy peace and abundance, we tend to over-
look the pricelessness and blessings of peace. Our task is to convey to younger
generations the horrors of war, so that we never repeat the errors in our history. I believe that, as we join hands, especially with the peoples of neighboring countries, to ensure true peace in the Asia-Pacific region—indeed, in the
entire world—it is necessary, more than anything else, that we foster relations
with all countries based on deep understanding and trust. Guided by this
conviction, the Government has launched the Peace, Friendship and Exchange
Initiative, which consists of two parts promoting: support for historical research into relations in the modern era between Japan and the neighboring
countries of Asia and elsewhere; and rapid expansion of exchanges with
those countries. Furthermore, I will continue in all sincerity to do my utmost
in efforts being made on the issues arisen from the war, in order to further
strengthen the relations of trust between Japan and those countries.

Now, upon this historic occasion of the 50th anniversary of the war's end,
we should bear in mind that we must look into the past to learn from the
lessons of history, and ensure that we do not stray from the path to the peace
and prosperity of human society in the future.

During a certain period in the not too distant past, Japan, following a
mistaken national policy, advanced along the road to war, only to ensnare the
Japanese people in a fateful crisis, and, through its colonial rule and aggression, caused tremendous damage and suffering to the people of many countries, particularly to those of Asian nations. In the hope that no such mistake
be made in the future, I regard, in a spirit of humility, these irrefutable facts of
history, and express here once again my feelings of deep remorse and state my
heartfelt apology. Allow me also to express my feelings of profound mourning
for all victims, both at home and abroad, of that history.

Building from our deep remorse on this occasion of the 50th anniversary
of the end of the war, Japan must eliminate self-righteous nationalism, promote international coordination as a responsible member of the international
community and, thereby, advance the principles of peace and democracy. At
the same time, as the only country to have experienced the devastation of

atomic bombing, Japan, with a view to the ultimate elimination of nuclear weapons, must actively strive to further global disarmament in areas such as the strengthening of the nuclear non-proliferation regime. It is my conviction that in this way alone can Japan atone for its past and lay to rest the spirits of those who perished.

It is said that one can rely on good faith. And so, at this time of remembrance, I declare to the people of Japan and abroad my intention to make good faith the foundation of our Government policy, and this is my vow (Ministry of Foreign Affairs, http://www.mofa.go.jp/announce/press/pm/mura yama/9508.html).

3. House of Representatives, National Diet of Japan, Resolution to Renew the Determination for Peace on the Basis of Lessons Learned from History, June 9, 1995

The House of Representatives resolves as follows:

On the occasion of the 50th anniversary of the end of World War II, this House offers its sincere condolences to those who fell in action and victims of wars and similar actions all over the world.

Solemnly reflecting upon many instances of colonial rule and acts of aggression in the modern history of the world, and recognizing that Japan carried out those acts in the past, inflicting pain and suffering upon the peoples of other countries, especially in Asia, the Members of this House express a sense of deep remorse.

We must transcend the differences over historical views of the past war and learn humbly the lessons of history so as to build a peaceful international society.

This House expresses its resolve, under the banner of eternal peace enshrined in the Constitution of Japan, to join hands with other nations of the world and to pave the way to a future that allows all human beings to live together (Ministry of Foreign Affairs, http://www.mofa.go.jp/announce/press/pm/murayama/address9506.html).

4. Statement by Prime Minister Jun'ichirō Koizumi on the Occasion of the Sixtieth Anniversary of the End of World War II, August 15, 2005

On the 60th anniversary of the end of the war, I reaffirm my determination that Japan must never again take the path to war, reflecting that the peace and prosperity we enjoy today are founded on the ultimate sacrifices of those who lost their lives for the war against their will.

More than three million compatriots died in the war—in the battle field thinking about their homeland and worrying about their families, while others perished amidst the destruction of war, or after the war in remote foreign countries.

In the past, Japan, through its colonial rule and aggression, caused tremendous damage and suffering to the people of many countries, particularly to those of Asian nations. Sincerely facing these facts of history, I once again express my feelings of deep remorse and heartfelt apology, and also express the feelings of mourning for all victims, both at home and abroad, in the war. I am determined not to allow the lessons of that horrible war to erode, and to contribute to the peace and prosperity of the world without ever again waging a war.

After the war, Japan rebuilt itself from a devastated land owing to the ceaseless efforts of its people and the assistance extended by many countries, and accepted the San Francisco Peace Treaty, being the first step of its reversion to the international community. Japan has resolutely maintained its principle of resolving all matters by peaceful means and not by force, and proactively extended material and personnel assistance for the sake of the peace and prosperity of the world through official development assistance (ODA) and United Nations peace keeping operations.

Japan's post war history has indeed been six decades of manifesting its remorse on the war through actions.

The post war generations now exceed 70% of Japan's population. Each and every Japanese, through his or her own experience and peace-oriented education, sincerely seeks international peace. Today, many Japanese are actively engaged in activities for peace and humanitarian assistance around the world, through such organizations as the Japan Overseas Cooperation Volunteers, and have been receiving much trust and high appreciation from the local people. Exchange with Asian countries in a wide variety of areas, such as economy and culture, has also increased on an unprecedented scale. I believe it is necessary to work hand in hand with other Asian countries, especially with China and the Republic of Korea, which are Japan's neighboring countries separated only by a strip of water, to maintain peace and pursue the development of the region. Through squarely facing the past and rightly recognizing the history, I intend to build a future-oriented cooperative relationship based on mutual understanding and trust with Asian countries.

The international community is now faced with more complex and difficult challenges than ever imagined before: progress of the developing counties, alleviation of poverty, conservation of the global environment, nonproliferation of weapons of mass destruction, and the prevention and eradication of terrorism. In order to contribute to world peace, Japan will proactively fulfill its role as a responsible member of the international community, upholding its pledge not to engage in war and based on its experience as the only nation to have suffered from the atomic bombings and the path it has followed over the 60 years after war.

On this occasion marking the 60th anniversary of the war's end, Japan, as a peace-loving nation, expresses here again that it will work to achieve peace and prosperity of all humankind with all its resources, together with all the nations of shared aspiration (Ministry of Foreign Affairs, http://www.mofa .go.jp/announce/announce/2005/8/0815.html).

5. Statement by Prime Minister Naoto Kan on the Occasion of the One Hundredth Anniversary of the Japan-Korea Annexation Treaty, August 10, 2010

This year marks a significant juncture for the Japan–Republic of Korea relationship. In August precisely one hundred years ago, the Japan-Korea Annexation Treaty was concluded, making the beginning of the colonial rule of thirty six years. As demonstrated by strong resistance such as the *Samil* independence movement, the Korean people of that time was [*sic*] deprived of their country and culture, and their ethnic pride was deeply scarred by the colonial rule which was imposed against their will under the political and military circumstances.

I would like to face history with sincerity. I would like to have courage to squarely confront the facts of history and humility to accept them, as well as to be honest to reflect upon the errors of our own. Those who render pain tend to forget it while those who suffered cannot forget it easily. To the tremendous damage and sufferings that this colonial rule caused, I express here once again my feelings of deep remorse and my heartfelt apology.

Guided by such understanding, I will build a future-oriented Japan–Republic of Korea relationship by placing the next one hundred years to come in my prospect. I will continue in all sincerity conducting such humanitarian cooperation as the assistance to ethnic Koreans left in Sakhalin and the assistance in returning remains of the people from the Korean Peninsula. Moreover, in response to the expectations of the Korean people, I will transfer precious archives originated from the Korean Peninsula that were brought to Japan during the period of Japan's rule through the Governor-General of Korea and the Government of Japan possesses, such as the Royal Protocols of the Joseon Dynasty.

Japan and the Republic of Korea, through active exchanges of cultures and peoples for over two thousand years, deeply share wonderful culture and tradition that are renowned to the world. In addition, the exchange between our two nations today is remarkably multi-layered and wide-ranging, as well as the affinity and friendship which the peoples of our two nations mutually embrace are stronger than ever. Furthermore, the scale of economic relations and people-to-people exchanges between our two nations has dramatically expanded since our relationship was normalized, and our ties have become extremely solid while both sides have been improving together by friendly rivalry.

Japan and the Republic of Korea have become the most important and closest neighboring nations now in this twenty-first century, sharing such values as democracy, freedom, and market economy. Our relationship is not confined to our bilateral relations, but rather it is a partnership where we cooperate and exercise leadership for the peace and prosperity of the region and the world by encompassing a broad spectrum of agenda: the peace and stability of this region envisioning, among others, the future establishment of an East Asia community, the growth and development of the world's economy, as well as issues of global scale such as nuclear disarmament, climate change, poverty and peace-building.

At this significant juncture of history, I strongly hope that our bond will become even more profound and solid between Japan and the Republic of Korea, and I declare my determination to make every ceaseless effort to open the future between our two nations (Cabinet Office, http://japan.kantei.go.jp/kan/statement/201008/10danwa_e.html).

6. Statement by Prime Minister Shinzō Abe on the Occasion of the Seventieth Anniversary of the End of World War II, August 15, 2015 (Cabinet Statement)

On the 70th anniversary of the end of the war, we must calmly reflect upon the road to war, the path we have taken since it ended, and the era of the 20th century. We must learn from the lessons of history the wisdom for our future.

More than one hundred years ago, vast colonies possessed mainly by the Western powers stretched out across the world. With their overwhelming supremacy in technology, waves of colonial rule surged toward Asia in the 19th century. There is no doubt that the resultant sense of crisis drove Japan forward to achieve modernization. Japan built a constitutional government earlier than any other nation in Asia. The country preserved its independence throughout. The Japan-Russia War gave encouragement to many people under colonial rule from Asia to Africa.

After World War I, which embroiled the world, the movement for self-determination gained momentum and put brakes on colonization that had been underway. It was a horrible war that claimed as many as ten million lives. With a strong desire for peace stirred in them, people founded the League of Nations and brought forth the General Treaty for Renunciation of War. There emerged in the international community a new tide of outlawing war itself.

At the beginning, Japan, too, kept steps with other nations. However, with the Great Depression setting in and the Western countries launching economic blocs by involving colonial economies, Japan's economy suffered a major blow. In such circumstances, Japan's sense of isolation deepened and it attempted to overcome its diplomatic and economic deadlock through the use of force. Its domestic political system could not serve as a brake to stop such attempts. In this way, Japan lost sight of the overall trends in the world.

With the Manchurian Incident, followed by the withdrawal from the League of Nations, Japan gradually transformed itself into a challenger to the new international order that the international community sought to establish after tremendous sacrifices. Japan took the wrong course and advanced along the road to war.

And, seventy years ago, Japan was defeated.

On the 70th anniversary of the end of the war, I bow my head deeply before the souls of all those who perished both at home and abroad. I express my feelings of profound grief and my eternal, sincere condolences.

More than three million of our compatriots lost their lives during the war: on the battlefields worrying about the future of their homeland and wishing for the happiness of their families; in remote foreign countries after the war, in extreme cold or heat, suffering from starvation and disease. The atomic bombings of Hiroshima and Nagasaki, the air raids on Tokyo and other cities, and the ground battles in Okinawa, among others, took a heavy toll among ordinary citizens without mercy.

Also in countries that fought against Japan, countless lives were lost among young people with promising futures. In China, Southeast Asia, the Pacific islands and elsewhere that became the battlefields, numerous innocent citizens suffered and fell victim to battles as well as hardships such as severe deprivation of food. We must never forget that there were women behind the battlefields whose honour and dignity were severely injured.

Upon the innocent people did our country inflict immeasurable damage and suffering. History is harsh. What is done cannot be undone. Each and every one of them had his or her life, dream, and beloved family. When I squarely contemplate this obvious fact, even now, I find myself speechless and my heart is rent with the utmost grief.

The peace we enjoy today exists only upon such precious sacrifices. And therein lies the origin of postwar Japan.

We must never again repeat the devastation of war.

Incident, aggression, war—we shall never again resort to any form of the threat or use of force as a means of settling international disputes. We shall abandon colonial rule forever and respect the right of self-determination of all peoples throughout the world.

With deep repentance for the war, Japan made that pledge. Upon it, we have created a free and democratic country, abided by the rule of law, and consistently upheld that pledge never to wage a war again. While taking silent pride in the path we have walked as a peace-loving nation for as long as seventy years, we remain determined never to deviate from this steadfast course.

Japan has repeatedly expressed the feelings of deep remorse and heartfelt apology for its actions during the war. In order to manifest such feelings through concrete actions, we have engraved in our hearts the histories of suffering of the people in Asia as our neighbours: those in Southeast Asian countries such as Indonesia and the Philippines, and Taiwan, the Republic of Korea and China, among others; and we have consistently devoted ourselves to the peace and prosperity of the region since the end of the war.

Such position articulated by the previous cabinets will remain unshakable into the future.

However, no matter what kind of efforts we may make, the sorrows of those who lost their family members and the painful memories of those who underwent immense sufferings by the destruction of war will never be healed.

Thus, we must take to heart the following.

The fact that more than six million Japanese repatriates managed to come home safely after the war from various parts of the Asia-Pacific and became the driving force behind Japan's postwar reconstruction; the fact that nearly three thousand Japanese children left behind in China were able to grow up there and set foot on the soil of their homeland again; and the fact that former POWs of the United States, the United Kingdom, the Netherlands, Australia and other nations have visited Japan for many years to continue praying for the souls of the war dead on both sides.

How much emotional struggle must have existed and what great efforts must have been necessary for the Chinese people who underwent all the sufferings of the war and for the former POWs who experienced unbearable sufferings caused by the Japanese military in order for them to be so tolerant nevertheless?

That is what we must turn our thoughts to reflect upon.

Thanks to such manifestation of tolerance, Japan was able to return to the international community in the postwar era. Taking this opportunity of the 70th anniversary of the end of the war, Japan would like to express its heartfelt gratitude to all the nations and all the people who made every effort for reconciliation.

In Japan, the postwar generations now exceed eighty per cent of its population. We must not let our children, grandchildren, and even further generations to come, who have nothing to do with that war, be predestined to apologize. Still, even so, we Japanese, across generations, must squarely face the history of the past. We have the responsibility to inherit the past, in all humbleness, and pass it on to the future.

Our parents' and grandparents' generations were able to survive in a devastated land in sheer poverty after the war. The future they brought about is the one our current generation inherited and the one we will hand down to the next generation. Together with the tireless efforts of our predecessors, this has only been possible through the goodwill and assistance extended to us that transcended hatred by a truly large number of countries, such as the United States, Australia, and European nations, which Japan had fiercely fought against as enemies.

We must pass this down from generation to generation into the future. We have the great responsibility to take the lessons of history deeply into our hearts, to carve out a better future, and to make all possible efforts for the peace and prosperity of Asia and the world.

We will engrave in our hearts the past, when Japan attempted to break its deadlock with force. Upon this reflection, Japan will continue to firmly uphold the principle that any disputes must be settled peacefully and diplomatically based on the respect for the rule of law and not through the use of force, and to reach out to other countries in the world to do the same. As the only country to have ever suffered the devastation of atomic bombings during war, Japan will fulfil its responsibility in the international community, aiming at the non-proliferation and ultimate abolition of nuclear weapons.

We will engrave in our hearts the past, when the dignity and honour of many women were severely injured during wars in the 20th century. Upon this reflection, Japan wishes to be a country always at the side of such women's injured hearts. Japan will lead the world in making the 21st century an era in which women's human rights are not infringed upon.

We will engrave in our hearts the past, when forming economic blocs made the seeds of conflict thrive. Upon this reflection, Japan will continue to develop a free, fair and open international economic system that will not be influenced by the arbitrary intentions of any nation. We will strengthen assistance for developing countries, and lead the world toward further prosperity. Prosperity is the very foundation for peace. Japan will make even greater efforts to fight against poverty, which also serves as a hotbed of violence, and to provide opportunities for medical services, education, and self-reliance to all the people in the world.

We will engrave in our hearts the past, when Japan ended up becoming a challenger to the international order. Upon this reflection, Japan will firmly uphold basic values such as freedom, democracy, and human rights as un-yielding values and, by working hand in hand with countries that share such values, hoist the flag of "Proactive Contribution to Peace," and contribute to the peace and prosperity of the world more than ever before.

Heading toward the 80th, the 90th and the centennial anniversary of the end of the war, we are determined to create such a Japan together with the Japanese people (Cabinet Office, http://japan.kantei.go.jp/97_abe/statement/201508/0814statement.html).

Notes

1. Japan's Twenty-First-Century Security Renaissance

1. The DPJ merged with the Japan Innovation Party and "Vision of Reform" to form the Democratic Party (minshintō) on March 27, 2016. This book maintains the DPJ abbreviation, while recognizing that in the later half of 2016 the party had taken on a new identity.

2. The complete text of Article Nine reads as follows: "1. Aspiring sincerely to an international peace based on justice and order, the Japanese people forever renounce war as a sovereign right of the nation and the threat or use of force as a means of settling international disputes. 2. In order to accomplish the aim of the preceding paragraph, land, sea, and air forces, as well as other war potential, will never be maintained. The right of belligerency of the state will not be recognized."

3. "Sebuntīnzu de kangaeyō sengo nanajūnen" [Let's think about the seventy years of the postwar period at the age of seventeen], *Sebuntīn*, September 2015; "Anpo hōsei mada kutsugaeseru" [We can still overturn the security bill], *Shūkan pureibōi*, August 3, 2015; "Ikura heiwashugi o tanaetemo, Nihon wa Isuramukoku ni nerawareru" [Chanting pacifism will not make Japan immune from the Islamic State's threats], *Sapio*, April 2015. Other examples would include "Okāsan koso kaiken no maeni chiken" [We mothers need to know about the constitution before the constitution changes], *VERY*, March 2014, and "Anpo hōsei dewa heiwa ni naranai" [The security bill will not make peace], *SPA!*, September 15, 2015.

4. Takashi Umehara et al., *Kenpō kyūjō wa watashitachi no anzen soshō desu* [Our security rests on Article Nine] (Tokyo: Iwanami shoten, 2015); Aritsune Toyota, *Kokubō onchi ga kuni o horobosu* ["Defense tone deafness" will destroy our nation] (Tokyo: Shōdensha, 2015). Examples of more middle-of-the-road attempts to discuss the merits of security reform would include Akira Ikegami, *Sekai kara sensō ga nakunaranai hontō no riyū* [True reasons why war will not disappear from the world] (Tokyo: Shōdensha, 2015), and Yōji Kōda, *Sansei, hantai o iumae no shūdan jieiken nyūmon* [Introduction to collective self-defense, before deciding yes or no] (Tokyo: Gentōsha, 2014).

5. Stockholm International Peace Research Institute, Military Expenditure Database, 1988–2014, http://milexdata.sipri.org/files.

6. International Institute for Strategic Studies, *The Military Balance 2012* (London: Routledge, 2012).

7. The ten members of ASEAN are Brunei, Cambodia, Indonesia, Laos, Malaysia, Myanmar, the Philippines, Singapore, Thailand, and Vietnam.

8. Andrew L. Oros, *Normalizing Japan: Politics, Identity, and the Evolution of Security Practice* (Stanford, Calif.: Stanford University Press, 2008), develops the latter argument in depth, that Japan's Cold War military policies evolved in important ways in response to an evolving domestic and international environment, and that Japan contributed to Cold War–era global military strategy in many ways that were downplayed to the Japanese public during this period. Yasuhiro Izumikawa, "Explaining Japanese Antimilitarism: Normative and Realist Constraints on Japan's Security Policy," *International Security* 35, no. 2 (fall 2010): 123–60, and Paul Midford, *Rethinking Japanese Public Opinion and Security* (Stanford, Calif.: Stanford University Press, 2011), also argue that Japan's antimilitarist past has been overstated. I return to this subject in chapter 2.

9. Daily protests in front of the prime minister's official residence in June 2014 over the reported plan by Prime Minister Abe to reinterpret Article Nine of Japan's constitution to allow the JSDF to participate in CSD activities with other militaries and a reprisal of such protests when enabling legislation was introduced into the Diet in June 2015 are two recent examples, discussed in chapters 5 and 6.

10. Daisuke Tsuda et al., *Abe seiken no netto senryaku* [The Abe government's "net" strategy] (Tokyo: Tsukuru shuppan, 2013), demonstrates Abe's skillful use of Facebook and other social media to mobilize the so-called *net uyoku* (right-wing netizens) in support of his policies. On the broader transformation of Japanese politics as a result of new media, see Iwao Ōsaka, "Sōsharu media ga kaeru seiji to sono genkai" [Politics in the era of social media: Its impact and limits], *Voters*, February 2012, 10–12.

11. Kenneth B. Pyle, *Japan Rising: The Resurgence of Japanese Power and Purpose* (New York: PublicAffairs, 2007). Other recent books predicting Japan's growing military power include Michael Green, *Japan's Reluctant Realism: Foreign Policy Challenges in an Era of Uncertain Power* (New York: Palgrave, 2001); Richard Samuels, *Securing Japan: Tokyo's Grand Strategy and the Future of East Asia* (Ithaca, New York: Cornell University Press, 2007); and Christopher W. Hughes, *Japan's Remilitarisation* (London: International Institute for Strategic Studies, 2009). Dennis Yasutomo has argued that Japan "crossed the Rubicon" with its limited dispatch of the JSDF to Iraq in 2003: *Japan's Civil-Military Diplomacy: The Banks of the Rubicon* (New York: Routledge, 2014).

12. The Kōmei Party changed its English-language name from New Kōmei Party in 2014; in this book I use the direct translation of the long-standing Japanese Kōmeitō, or Kōmei Party, for both before and after 2014.

13. In addition to my previous argument of this position in *Normalizing Japan*, see Linus Hagström, "The 'Abnormal' State: Identity, Norm/Exception and Japan," *European Journal of International Relations* 20, no. 2 (2014): 1–24, for another caution over the unreflective use of this term.

14. Political heavyweight Ichirō Ozawa is generally credited with popularizing the discourse on normalization in Japanese with his call for Japan to become a *futsū no kuni* (normal nation) in his 1994 book *Blueprint for a New Japan: The Rethinking of a Nation*, trans. Louisa Rubinfien (Tokyo: Kodansha International, 1994), but many others in Japan have characterized Japan's behavior in the realm of military security as "abnormal," dating back to the early postwar years and the predecessors of Shinzō Abe, such as discourse under the political reign of Abe's grandfather, Nobusuke Kishi (1957–1960), in the context of efforts to revise the initial Mutual Defense Treaty between Japan and the United States.

15. The term "normal" is used in this book generally without quotation marks to reflect the conventions in discourse regarding this concept in writings both inside and outside Japan.

16. Ministry of Land, Infrastructure, Transport, and Tourism, *White Paper on Land, Infrastructure, Transport and Tourism, 2013*, http://www.mlit.go.jp/common/001063075.pdf.

17. Citing Ministry of Land, Infrastructure, Transport, and Tourism, *White Paper on Land, Infrastructure, Transport and Tourism, 2010*, Smith writes, "96 percent of Japan's energy supply and 60 percent of its food supply come from overseas" (*Intimate Rivals: Japanese Domestic Politics and a Rising China* [New York: Columbia University Press, 2015], 196).

18. Walter LeFeber, *The Clash: U.S.-Japanese Relations throughout History* (New York: Norton, 1997), and Odd Arne Westad, *Restless Empire: China*

and the World Since 1750 (New York: Basic Books, 2012), offer two very readable narratives of this early modern period of Japan's history in relation to the United States and China. Prime Minister Abe's Advisory Panel on the History of the Twentieth Century and on Japan's Role and the World Order in the Twenty-First Century offers a contemporary Japanese narrative of the period that exposes the continuing disagreement among states in the region about the origins of World War II in Asia. The panel's report was issued on August 6, 2015, and is available at http://www.kantei .go.jp/jp/singi/21c_koso/pdf/report_en.pdf.

19. The complete text of this document is available at http://www.cas.go.jp/jp/ siryou/131217anzenhoshou/nss-e.pdf.

20. Oros, *Normalizing Japan*, discusses these debates over the extent of postwar rearmament in chapter 2. Green, *Japan's Reluctant Realism*, explains these debates in terms of the Yoshida Doctrine developed by Prime Minister Shigeru Yoshida in the early postwar period; Samuels, *Securing Japan*, explains these developments under the mantra of "baking the pacifist loaf" (chapter 2).

21. Amy Catalinac convincingly demonstrates the effect of the changed electoral system in *Electoral Reform and National Security: From Pork to Foreign Policy* (Cambridge: Cambridge University Press, 2016); Tomohito Shinoda discusses the effect of institutional reform in the prime minister's office (*kantei*) on foreign policy, in *Koizumi Diplomacy: Japan's Kantei Approach to Foreign and Defense Affairs* (Seattle: University of Washington Press, 2007), and in his later work *Contemporary Japanese Politics: Institutional Changes and Power Shifts* (New York: Columbia University Press, 2013).

22. The LDP did briefly lose its grip on power for nine months in 1993–1994 due to a split in the LDP that led some party members to bolt and to join a coalition of opposition parties in what proved to be an unwieldy coalition. The LDP returned to power in 1994 in a coalition with its former archrivals, the JSP, which had the result of accelerating the decline of the JSP.

23. Cabinet Secretariat, *National Security Strategy: December 17, 2013*. Note that the literal translation of what the Japanese government calls in English "proactive contributions to peace" (*sekkyokuteki heiwashugi*) is "proactive pacifism." Arguably the alternative translation more accurately conveys the spirit of the phrase to an English-speaking audience.

24. Michael Green, in *Japan's Reluctant Realism*, published in 2001, was prescient in his prediction of such a shift.

25. Smith, *Intimate Rivals*, develops the argument that China's rise has deeply influenced Japan's domestic politics but does not examine in depth the implications for Japan's security policies. Numerous contributors to a recent special issue of *Pacific Review* argue that the scholarly approach

of "relational constructivism" explains well this interactive dynamic between international and domestic political change; for an overview, see Linus Hagström and Karl Gustafsson, "Japan and Identity Change: Why It Matters in International Relations," *Pacific Review* 28, no. 1 (March 2015): 1–22.

26. The scholarly literature explaining this predominant theory and seeking to adapt it to address perceived flaws in the core theory is vast. One variant, called postclassical realism, has been applied by numerous scholars to the case of Japan. See Gideon Rose, "Neoclassical Realism and Theories of Foreign Policy," *World Politics* 51, no. 1 (October 1998): 144–72, for an explanation of this and other variants, and Tsuyoshi Kawasaki, "Postclassical Realism and Japanese Security Policy," *Pacific Review* 14, no. 2 (June 2001): 221–40, for one of several applications of an adapted realist paradigm to Japan.

27. Oros, *Normalizing Japan*, chapter 14, among other works, develops this argument.

28. Ibid., 9.

29. Recent inquiry along these lines related to Japan includes several contributors to a special issue of *Pacific Review*, introduced by Hagström and Gustafsson, "Japan and Identity Change."

30. On the concept of a security dilemma, see Robert Jervis, "Cooperation Under the Security Dilemma," *World Politics* 30, no. 2 (January 1978): 167–214. For a post–Cold War application of this concept to East Asia, see Richard K. Betts, "Wealth, Power, and Instability: East Asia and the United States after the Cold War," *International Security* 18, no. 3 (winter 1993–1994): 34–77.

31. Two intriguing examinations of the latter phenomenon, the diffusion of power in the system, are Joseph S. Nye, Jr., *The Future of Power* (New York: PublicAffairs, 2011), and Moisés Naím, *The End of Power: From Boardrooms to Battlefields and Churches to States, Why Being in Charge Isn't What It Used to Be* (New York: Basic Books, 2013).

32. These documents are available in English at http://www.mod.go.jp/j/approach/agenda/guideline/2014/pdf/20131217_e2.pdf, and http://www.cas.go.jp/jp/siryou/131217anzenhoshou/nss-e.pdf.

33. Jing Sun, *Japan and China as Charm Rivals: Soft Power in Regional Diplomacy* (Ann Arbor: University of Michigan Press, 2012), and Claude Meyer, *China or Japan: Which Will Lead Asia?* (New York: Columbia University Press, 2011), examine this broader competition beyond military power.

34. China's direct military threat to Japan is focused on the Senkaku Islands, which China and Taiwan both claim but which Japan administers. The United States does not take a position on the sovereignty of the islands but

has pledged, under Article 5 of the US-Japan Security Treaty, to protect any territory Japan administers, which thus includes these islands.

35. Ellis S. Krauss and Robert J. Pekkanen, *The Rise and Fall of Japan's LDP: Political Party Organizations as Historical Institutions* (Ithaca, N.Y.: Cornell University Press, 2011). provides a comprehensive overview of the LDP's evolution from its creation in 1955 to its fall from power to the DPJ in 2009.

36. Gerald L. Curtis, *The Japanese Way of Politics* (New York: Columbia University Press, 1988), explains the electoral logic of the old system, and *The Logic of Japanese Politics* (New York: Columbia University Press, 1999), also by Curtis, elucidates the early dynamics under the new electoral system. Tomohito Shinoda offers an updated overview and analysis in *Contemporary Japanese Politics: Institutional Changes and Power Shifts* (New York: Columbia University Press, 2013).

37. The generational-shift aspect of this changeover, from the former LDP leaders who had some direct experience with World War II to what is known as the postwar generation of Prime Minister Abe, is discussed in Atsutoshi Yamada, "Sensō o shiranai Abe seiken no bōsō o ureru riberaru-ha no chōrōtachi" [Liberal elders lament the runaway Abe administration ignorant of war], *Keizaikai*, August 5, 2014. One English-language description of this factional shift is Kazuhiko Togo, "The Assertive Conservative Right in Japan: Their Formation and Perspective," *SAIS Review of International Affairs* 30, no. 1 (winter–spring 2010): 77–89. Samuels, *Securing Japan*, discusses the beginning of this shift in the broader context of security policy through 2007.

38. "Iro aseta 'hoshu honryū'" [The fading conservative mainstream], *Sankei shimbun*, June 17, 2014, and "Hoshu honryū wa dareno te ni" [Who will inherit the conservative mainstream?], *Asahi shimbun*, February 9, 2014, both develop this theme.

39. These two documents are examined in chapters 4 and 5, respectively.

40. It should be noted, however, that Noda's move to nationalize the islands was driven in large part by the policy activism of the far right, led by then governor of Tokyo Shintarō Ishihara.

41. Abe Shinzō, "Japan Is Back: A Conversation with Shinzo Abe," *Foreign Affairs* (July/August 2013), https://www.foreignaffairs.com/interviews/2013-05-16/japan-back.

42. There is an extensive scholarly literature on these earlier historical disjunctures. Pyle, *Japan Rising*, offers a strong introduction to the topic with many citations to other scholarly work.

43. Jennifer Lind, *Sorry States: Apologies in International Politics* (Ithaca, N.Y.: Cornell University Press, 2008), aptly notes that expressing contri-

tion does not always lead to acceptance by the aggrieved party and can also cause domestic political backlash.

44. Thomas U. Berger, *War, Guilt, and World Politics after World War II* (Cambridge: Cambridge University Press, 2012), chapter 4, provides an excellent summary of this narrative.

45. Thomas U. Berger, *Cultures of Antimilitarism: National Security in Germany and Japan* (Baltimore: Johns Hopkins University Press, 1998), popularized the term "antimilitarism" over the also commonly used term "pacifism." Green, *Japan's Reluctant Realism*, among others, argues that postwar Japanese security policy is better described as rooted in the Yoshida Doctrine, of which antimilitarist or pacifist security policies are one facet.

46. Oros, *Normalizing Japan*, among others, develops this argument, rooted in the concept of security identity. Bhubhindar Singh, *Japan's Security Identity: From a Peace State to an International State* (London: Routledge, 2013), applies this framework to Japanese security policy through 2012.

47. Chapter 2 discusses earlier battles to adapt Japan's antimilitarist security identity, particularly precursors to Japan's security renaissance under the rule of Prime Minister Koizumi, 2001–2006.

48. John Dower, *Embracing Defeat: Japan in the Wake of World War II* (New York: Norton, 1999), reproduces this photograph and offers many other striking visual portrayals of the occupation, together with a masterful, Pulitzer Prize-winning cultural and historical narrative that was a best seller in its two-volume Japanese translation—itself an indicator of Japanese interest and attention to this period of their history.

49. George R. Packard, *Protest in Tokyo: The Security Treaty Crisis of 1960* (Princeton, N.J.: Princeton University Press, 1966), provides a compelling narrative of the period soon after the events; John Swenson-Wright, *Unequal Allies? United States Security and Alliance Policy Toward Japan, 1945–1960* (Stanford, Calif.: Stanford University Press, 2005), provides new insights on this period using expanded documentary evidence.

50. Emma Chanlett-Avery et al., *Japan-U.S. Relations: Issues for Congress*, CRS Report 7-5700, September 29, 2015 (Washington, DC: Congressional Research Service).

51. Ibid., 20. Details about the funding mechanisms for the Japanese government portion are provided in this source.

52. Ibid., 22.

53. Lindsay Black, *Japan's Maritime Security Strategy: The Japan Coast Guard and Maritime Outlaws* (New York: Palgrave Macmillan, 2014).

54. The authoritative study of this deployment in English is Yasutomo, *Japan's Civil-Military Diplomacy*.

55. Cabinet Office polling has indicated Japanese "affinity" toward the United States at over 80 percent since 2011.
56. Chanlett-Avery et al., *Japan-US Relations*, i.
57. Two contrasting studies of the broader US-Japan relationship are Kent Calder, *The Pacific Alliance: Reviving U.S.-Japan Relations* (New Haven, Conn.: Yale University Press, 2009), and Gavan McCormack, *Client State: Japan in the American Embrace* (New York: Verso, 2007).

2. The Gradual Awakening

1. Yasuhiro Izumikawa, "Explaining Japanese Antimilitarism: Normative and Realist Constraints on Japan's Security Policy," *International Security* 35, no. 2 (fall 2010): 123–60, provides a good summary of different viewpoints on this debate circa 2010.
2. Nicholas Eberstadt, "Demography and Japan's Future," in *Reimagining Japan: The Quest for a Future That Works*, edited by McKinsey and Company, 82–87 (San Francisco: VIZ Media, 2011). Japan's demographic challenges are discussed further in chapter 3.
3. Andrew L. Oros, *Normalizing Japan: Politics, Identity, and the Evolution of Security Practice* (Stanford, Calif.: Stanford University Press, 2008). My work was intended to build on important work in this area by Thomas U. Berger, *Cultures of Antimilitarism: National Security in Germany and Japan*. Baltimore: Johns Hopkins University Press, 1998), and Peter Katzenstein, *Cultural Norms and National Security: Police and Military in Postwar Japan* (Ithaca, N.Y.: Cornell University Press, 1996); others have further built on this framework, including Bhubhindar Singh, *Japan's Security Identity: From a Peace State to an International State* (London: Routledge, 2013).
4. Two recent English-language works in this area, which both cite extensive literature in English and in Japanese, are Thomas U. Berger, *War, Guilt, and World Politics after World War II* (Cambridge: Cambridge University Press, 2012), and Jennifer Lind, *Sorry States: Apologies in International Politics* (Ithaca, N.Y.: Cornell University Press, 2008).
5. Two important English-language works in this area that both cite extensive literature in English and in Japanese and present quite different perspectives are Kent Calder, *The Pacific Alliance: Reviving U.S.-Japan Relations* (New Haven, Conn.: Yale University Press, 2009), and Gavin McCormack, *Client State: Japan in the American Embrace* (New York: Verso, 2007). Two more recent and policy-focused studies are Sheila A. Smith, *Japan's New Politics and the U.S.-Japan Alliance* (Washington, DC: Council on Foreign Relations Press, July 2014), and Michael Green and Zack Coo-

per, eds., *Strategic Japan: New Approaches to Foreign Policy and the US-Japan Alliance* (Washington, DC: Center for Strategic and International Studies, 2015).

6. A lively debate informed by excellent scholarly research has populated major journals on this subject in the past decade. See Jennifer Lind, "Pacifism or Passing the Buck? Testing Theories of Japanese Security Policy," *International Security* 29, no. 1 (summer 2004): 92–121; Izumikawa, "Explaining Japanese Antimilitarism"; Akitoshi Miyashita, "Where Do Norms Come From? Foundations of Japan's Postwar Pacifism," *International Relations of the Asia-Pacific* 7, no. 1 (January 2007): 99–120; Paul Midford, "The Logic of Reassurance and Japan's Grand Strategy," *Security Studies* 11, no. 3 (spring 2002): 1–43; and Christopher P. Twomey, "Japan, a Circumscribed Balancer: Building on Defensive Realism to Make Predictions about East Asian Security," *Security Studies* 9, no. 4 (summer 2000): 167–205.

7. Three that cover the full postwar period are Kenneth B. Pyle, *Japan Rising: The Resurgence of Japanese Power and Purpose* (New York: PublicAffairs, 2007); Richard Samuels, *Securing Japan: Tokyo's Grand Strategy and the Future of East Asia* (Ithaca, N.Y.: Cornell University Press, 2007); Kazuhiko Togo, *Japan's Foreign Policy 1945–2003: The Quest for Proactive Policy* (Leiden: Brill, 2005).

8. Indirectly, however, political actors in Japan from the left and the right were concerned by the threat posed to Japan by the deepened American influence, the long-term plan for a US military presence in Japan that would result, and Japan's dependence on this one ally for military security—the third historical legacy discussed in this book.

9. However, as critics often note, Japan possesses one of the largest plutonium stockpiles in the world, and though carefully monitored by the International Atomic Energy Agency, Japan has the technology to make a nuclear weapon fairly quickly. Moreover, Japan enjoys extended deterrence under the US nuclear umbrella, so whether it truly would prefer a world without nuclear weapons remains an open question.

10. The "Basic Policy for National Defense" is included annually in *Defense of Japan*—for example, Ministry of Defense, *Defense of Japan 2007* (Tokyo: Inter Group, 2007), 462. The policy also commits Japan to support of the UN system and roots Japanese security in the US-Japan alliance.

11. Until Japan's first formal national security strategy was crafted in 2013, the NDPG served effectively in that role, while the MTDP that followed soon after each NDPG would set out numerical targets and operationalization of the NDPG. Annual defense white papers, published since 1975, have been a third major official source on Japanese defense planning—until the fourth, the national security strategy, was developed in 2013.

12. James Auer, "Japan's Military Capability in 2015," SAIS Policy Forum Series, no. 5 (Washington, DC: Johns Hopkins University, December 1998), 5.

13. Ron Matthews and Keisuke Matsuyama, *Japan's Military Renaissance?* (New York: St. Martin's Press, 1993), 11.

14. Ibid.

15. Ibid., 12.

16. James Auer and Robyn Lim, "The Maritime Basis of American Security in East Asia," *Naval War College Review* 54, no. 1 (2001): 48.

17. Christopher W. Hughes, "Japan's Military Modernization: In Search of a 'Normal' Security Role," in *Strategic Asia 2005–06: Military Modernization in an Era of Uncertainty*, edited by Ashley J. Tellis and Michael Wills, 105–36 (Seattle: National Bureau of Asian Research, 2005).

18. The full document is reproduced in the annual *Defense of Japan* volumes and also posted in both English and Japanese at http://www.mod.go.jp.

19. Japan's first non-LDP prime minister in almost forty years, Morihiro Hosokawa, caused alarm in Washington, DC, and among Japanese defense elites when he published an article after the end of his term as prime minister in the influential US journal *Foreign Affairs*, asking in his provocative title, "Are U.S. Troops in Japan Needed?" (July/August 1998:2–5).

20. Oros, *Normalizing Japan*, includes two tables that summarize twenty-two important security-related developments from 1998 to 2007 (such as North Korea's nuclear and missile tests and China's foray into manned space flight) and fifteen important Japanese security decisions in response in table 10 (p. 177) and table 11 (p. 179), respectively. Annual *Defense of Japan* volumes also include a detailed chronology of major events affecting Japan's security and Japan's major security policy decisions.

21. Oros, *Normalizing Japan*, discusses the decision to develop surveillance satellites and missile defense in chapters 5 and 6.

22. Thomas J. Christensen, "China, the U.S.-Japan Alliance, and the Security Dilemma in East Asia," *International Security* 23, no. 4 (spring 1999): 49–80.

23. Lindsay Black, *Japan's Maritime Security Strategy: The Japan Coast Guard and Maritime Outlaws* (New York: Palgrave Macmillan, 2014).

24. For a useful chart of total numbers of piracy incidents in Southeast Asia, around Somalia, and worldwide, 1991–2012, see ibid., 175.

25. Ibid., 118.

26. Jeffrey Hornung interviewed several of these decision makers and argues that this event was a critical turning point in Japan's security policy evolution ("Learning How to Sweat: Explaining the Dispatch of Japan's Self-Defense Forces in the Gulf War and Iraq War" [PhD diss., George Washington University, 2009]).

27. The full document is reproduced in the annual *Defense of Japan* volumes and also posted in both English and Japanese at http://www.mod.go.jp.
28. Dennis T. Yasutomo, *Japan's Civil-Military Diplomacy: The Banks of the Rubicon* (New York: Routledge, 2014), provides the authoritative account to date of the JSDF role in Iraq.
29. *Japan Today*, May 28, 2015.
30. The count of fourteen consists of two "special measures deployments" (to the Indian Ocean and to Iraq), eight instances of International Peace Co-operation Activities (Cambodia, Mozambique, Rwanda, Golan Heights, twice to East Timor, Afghanistan, and Iraq), and six instances of International Disaster Relief Activities (Honduras, Turkey, India, Iran, Thailand, and Indonesia). East Timor and Iraq are counted only once each, and the Indian Ocean as a single region, to reach a total of fourteen. The MOD itself lists a higher count of JSDF deployments as a result of multiple missions within many of the mentioned cases—for example, JASDF activities in Kuwait, JGSDF activities in Samawah, and JMSDF activities in the Persian Gulf are counted as three instances (and areas) of overseas deployment despite all being coordinated as assistance to the US-led coalition in Iraq. Further information about these deployments is provided in *Defense of Japan 2007*, 577–79.
31. Singh, *Japan's Security Identity*.
32. SIPRI data shows peak Japanese spending to date as the 2003 calendar year, in constant 2011 US dollars. In unadjusted yen terms, the peak was in 2000 according to SIPRI data. (According to the MOD, the peak was in 2002, but spending was more or less constant from 1997 to 2003—see *Defense of Japan 2007*, 488.) As discussed in chapters 3 and 5, Japanese defense spending has been more or less stagnant since 2002, with a modest rise in yen terms in 2014 and 2015 after over a decade of modest decline or flat budgets (though in US dollars the decline continues because of the declining value of the yen); Stockholm International Peace Research Institute, SIPRI Military Expenditure Database, 1988–2014, http://www.sipri.org/research/armaments/milex/.
33. See, for example, Christopher W. Hughes, *Japan's Re-emergence as a "Normal" Military Power* (New York: Oxford University Press, 2004).
34. Christopher Hughes describes this operation as follows: "This flotilla carried five GSDF helicopters and twenty GSDF trucks, and acted as a 'floating camp' for joint MSDF and GSDF operations" ("Japan's Military Modernization: In Search of a 'Normal' Security Role," in *Strategic Asia 2005–06: Military Modernization in an Era of Uncertainty*, ed. Ashley J. Tellis and Michael Wills [Seattle: National Bureau of Asian Research, 2005], 114).

35. Writing in 2013, Swaine et al. argue that "the development of the JMSDF's air-capable ships is a noteworthy twenty-five-year saga of Japan's sea service overcoming political, legal, financial, and bureaucratic obstacles with single-minded purpose and a consistent operational vision" (*China's Military and the U.S.-Japan Alliance in 2030: A Strategic Net Assessment* [Washington, DC: Carnegie Endowment for International Peace, 2013], 345n66). This source continues with one-paragraph descriptions of Ōsumi-, Hyūga-, and "improved" Hyūga-class ship features.
36. Hughes, "Japan's Military Modernization," summarizes these major developments, drawing on multiple years of *Defense of Japan* white papers. Swaine et al., *China's Military*, 131–33, also provides a useful summary of Japan's emerging capabilities.
37. Swaine et al., *China's Military*, 133.
38. Further description of this new joint operations posture is provided in *Defense of Japan 2007*, 218–20, and in later volumes.
39. Swaine et al., *China's Military* 3, 124. Beyond the JSDF itself, Prime Minister Abe's recent Advisory Panel on the History of the Twentieth Century also stresses the continuing constraints on Japan's international contributions to date, writing, "Looking back on the Japanese actions since the first half of the 1990s, it cannot be denied that they have been a half step behind the actual needs. . . . It cannot be said that Japan has been able to properly contribute in a manner that fully responds to the demands of the international community" ("Report of the Advisory Panel on the History of the Twentieth Century and on Japan's Role and the World Order in the Twenty-First Century," August 6, 2015, http://www.kantei.go.jp/jp/singi/21c_koso/pdf/report_en.pdf).
40. Hughes, "Japan's Military Modernization," 122–23. On the budget issue in particular, see also David Fouse, "Japan's FY 2005 National Defense Program Outline: New Concepts, Old Compromises," *Asia-Pacific Security Studies* 4, no. 3 (March 2005): 2–8.
41. As Hughes writes in "Japan's Military Modernization," "Following five years of deliberation, the National Diet's House of Representatives and House of Councilors [*sic*] released separate reports on constitutional revision in April 2005. . . . The House of Councilors [*sic*] failed to agree on revisions to Article 9, and neither of the houses was able to reach a consensus on revisions relating to the exercise of the right of collective self-defense—although they both agreed that Japan should engage more actively in international security cooperation" (115–16).
42. Japan's territorial dispute with the Soviet Union was the most strategic in terms of the Cold War since the Soviet naval fleet could have been more effectively blocked had Japan controlled the Northern Territories (where

the Soviets garrisoned troops). It is also the only one of the three territorial disputes that involves inhabited islands. Moreover, while the Northern Territories are small in relation to Japan's main islands, they are larger than the southern outlying islands of Okinawa, which support a population of over one million Japanese and the majority of US forces based in Japan.

43. John Dower has described the controversy over the Smithsonian Institution's plan to provide a broader historical narrative related to its display of the *Enola Gay*, the plane that dropped the atomic bomb on Hiroshima, at the time of the fiftieth anniversary of the end of World War II and the dropping of the bomb ("How a Genuine Democracy Should Celebrate Its Past," in *Ways of Forgetting, Ways of Remembering: Japan in the Modern World*, 176–84 [New York: New Press, 2012]). This volume includes a chapter on Japanese narratives of the atomic bombings: "The Bombed: Hiroshimas and Nagasakis in Japanese Memory."

44. Berger, *War, Guilt, and World Politics*, 12.

45. Dower discusses the successes and shortcomings of these proceedings in *Embracing Defeat: Japan in the Wake of World War II* (New York: Norton, 1999), chapter 4.

46. Berger, *War, Guilt, and World Politics*, 152–53.

47. Mitsubishi Materials senior chief executive Hikaru Kimura apologized on behalf of its predecessor firm, Mitsubishi Mining, to an audience in Los Angeles that included a surviving American forced laborer POW. The firm was reported to have operated four sites in Japan that at the time of liberation in 1945 held about 876 American POWs; 27 Americans died in those camps (http://www.theguardian.com/world/2015/jul/20/mitsubishi-materials-apologizes-for-using-us-prisoners-of-war-as-slave-labor).

48. According to Berger, *War, Guilt, and World Politics*, article 2 of the agreement on settlement of wartime claims obligated Japan to provide "economic cooperation assistance" worth $500 million in exchange for the statement that wartime claims between the two countries "is settled completely and finally" (27). Since that time, he writes, well over $4 billion of additional assistance has been provided.

49. Details on the Korean case are provided in Lind, *Sorry States*, chapter 2. In the 1972 joint communiqué between Japan and China that led the way to resumption of diplomatic relations, the Chinese stated, "In the interest of the friendship between the Chinese and the Japanese peoples, it renounced its demand for war reparation from Japan" (http://www.mofa .go.jp/region/asia-paci/china/joint72.html). For details on Japan's reconciliation with China, see Yinan He, *The Search for Reconciliation: Sino-Japanese and German-Polish Relations since World War II* (Cambridge: Cambridge University Press, 2009).

50. Lind, *Sorry States*, 168.
51. "Report of the Advisory Panel on the History of the Twentieth Century," 8. Beyond such "heart-to-heart diplomacy," however, the report also argues that "war reparations from Japan and its subsequent economic cooperation were of extremely huge significance and played a major part in reconciliation between Japan and Southeast Asia" (31) and that the "efforts of Japanese companies, together with ODA, bore fruit in a big way in improving the image of Japan in Asia" (8).
52. One collection of memories from former imperial soldiers and sailors from this period is provided in Takeo Okuno, *Taiheiyō sensō: Heishi to shimin no kiroku* [The Pacific War: A record of soldiers and citizens] (Tokyo: Sōgōsha, 1995).
53. Tatsuzō Ishikawa, *Nankin kōryakusen rupo* [Reportage on the Nanking invasion war] (Tokyo: Bungei shunjū, 1999).
54. According to Naoko Kumagai, 60 Korean women accepted atonement money from the Asia Women's Fund, of a total of 285 across South Korea, Taiwan, and the Philippines ("Asia Women's Fund Revisited," *Asia-Pacific Review* 21, no. 2 [2014]: 118, 121).
55. Berger, *War, Guilt, and World Politics*, 183.
56. The proportion of those who said yes was 53.1percent, while 24.8 percent said no (a roughly equal percentage to those who said "don't know"); conducted by the *Yomiuri shimbun*, October 5, 1993, as reported in Dower, *Ways of Forgetting*, 110.
57. The text of this speech is available at http://www.mofa.go.jp/region/n-america/us/fmv0109/010908.html.
58. Berger, *War, Guilt, and World Politics*, 124.
59. "Report of the Advisory Panel on the History of the Twentieth Century," 19.
60. Lind, *Sorry States*.
61. Brad Glosserman and Scott A. Snyder, *The Japan–South Korea Identity Clash: East Asian Security and the United States* (New York: Columbia University Press, 2015).
62. Berger, *Cultures of Antimilitarism*, and Katzenstein, *Cultural Norms*, explain the effect of these concerns on Japan's Cold War–era security policies, drawing on extensive Japanese-language scholarship of this period. Oros, *Normalizing Japan*, and Singh, *Japan's Security Identity*, continue the narrative into the post–Cold War period.
63. "Report of the Advisory Panel on the History of the Twentieth Century," 4.
64. This point is developed further in Oros, *Normalizing Japan*, 4. For a more recent theoretical explication of this concept in relation to recent innovations in international relations theories, see Andrew L. Oros, "International and Domestic Challenges to Japan's Postwar Security Identity:

'Norm Constructivism' and Japan's New 'Proactive Pacifism,'" *Pacific Review* 28, no. 1 (March 2015): 139–60.

65. Oros, *Normalizing Japan*, chapter 2, describes the establishment and evolution of this security identity over the course of the early postwar and Cold War periods.

66. A more detailed discussion of the party politics of Japan's Cold War–era security identity is provided ibid.

67. Ibid., chapter 7, argues that the hegemonic security identity of domestic antimilitarism continued to set the boundaries and to shape political debate even in the 1998 to 2007 period, when, others have argued, Japan's security identity, or strategic culture, had shifted (e.g., Samuels, *Securing Japan*, and Christopher W. Hughes, *Japan's Remilitarisation* [London: International Institute for Strategic Studies, 2009]).

68. Oros, *Normalizing Japan*, 17.

69. Michael J. Green, *Arming Japan: Defense Production, Alliance Politics, and the Postwar Search for Autonomy* (New York: Columbia University Press, 1995), provides one such narrative.

70. Scholars have devoted substantial attention to the complexity of the relationship, however, from many angles beyond just the US-Japan military alliance. Dower, *Embracing Defeat*, discusses the complexity from the "original sin" of the occupation period, and Michael Schaller, *Altered States: The United States and Japan since the Occupation* (New York: Oxford University Press, 1997), continues the story into the postwar period; other works, such as Naoko Shibusawa, *America's Geisha Ally: Reimagining the Japanese Enemy* (Cambridge, Mass.: Harvard University Press, 2010), and Michael Auslin, *Pacific Cosmopolitans: A Cultural History of U.S.-Japan Relations* (Cambridge, Mass.: Harvard University Press, 2011), convey the social concerns related to the US influence, while such work as McCormack, *Client State*, take up US imperialism. An extensive Japanese-language literature covers similar themes.

71. The JSDF to this day has not lost a single member to a force-related casualty, though there have been numerous deaths and injuries related to training exercises, accidents, and suicide. Japan's de facto cap on military spending as 1 percent of GDP, instituted in the mid-1960s, is far below the limit of the United States or most NATO allies during the Cold War period.

72. Tim Weiner wrote an extended article on this subject quoting numerous sources ("C.I.A. Spent Millions to Support Japanese Right in 50's and 60's," *New York Times*, October 9, 1994); subsequently, many more documents and interviews have revealed further details, though a full accounting has never been provided by the US government, despite the timing well beyond the standard release of such information.

73. Dower, *Embracing Defeat*, explains the "reverse course" policies; George R. Packard, *Protest in Tokyo: The Security Treaty Crisis of 1960* (Princeton, N.J.: Princeton University Press, 1966), explains the events of 1959 to 1960 and Kishi's actions related to the passage of the security treaty.

74. Mike Mochizuki maps out these different schools of conservative thought in *Japan: Domestic Change and Foreign Policy* (Santa Monica, Calif.: RAND, 1995); Samuels, *Securing Japan*, develops a similar typology and updates it for the later post–Cold War period. On the issue of "interoperability" and weapons autonomy in particular, see Green, *Arming Japan*, and Richard J. Samuels, *"Rich Nation, Strong Army": National Security and the Technological Transformation of Japan* (Ithaca, N.Y.: Cornell University Press, 1994).

75. An English translation is available at https://www.jimin.jp/english/. For a critical overview of the draft, see Lawrence Repeta, "Japan's Democracy at Risk: The LDP's Ten Most Dangerous Proposals for Constitutional Change," *Asia Pacific Journal* 11, no. 28 (July 15, 2013), http://www.japanfocus.org/-lawrence-repeta/3969/article.html.

76. "Report of the Advisory Panel on the History of the Twentieth Century," 16.

77. These dual concerns are the subject of countless scholarly articles on the dynamics of the US-Japan alliance and indeed of scholarship on alliances in general. See, for example, Izumikawa, "Explaining Japanese Antimilitarism," and Midford, "Logic of Reassurance."

78. The full text of the treaty, formally called the Treaty of Mutual Cooperation and Security between Japan and the United States of America, is available at http://www.mofa.go.jp/region/n-america/us/q&a/ref/1.html.

79. As the 2015 Advisory Panel on the History of the Twentieth Century states, "The United States began seeing Japan, which had become a major economic power by then, as a rival" (16).

80. Under the latest five-year agreement for the period 2011 to 2016, Japan pays for most of the salaries of about twenty-five thousand Japanese employees at US military installations, at a cost of about ¥188 billion annually (about $1.6 billion at ¥120 to US$1). The Japanese government also pays a large portion of utility costs at US facilities, which was agreed to shrink to 72 percent over this five-year period; Emma Chanlett-Avery et al., *Japan-U.S. Relations: Issues for Congress*, CRS Report 7-5700, September 29, 2015 (Washington, DC: Congressional Research Service), 14.

81. Whether this "areas surrounding Japan" included the area around Taiwan was a principal concern of opponents of the new guidelines given the Taiwan Strait crisis that had unfolded around the time of the guidelines revision process.

82. Michael Green and Patrick Cronin, eds., *The U.S.-Japan Alliance: Past, Present, and Future* (New York: Council on Foreign Relations Press, 1999),

and Yoichi Funabashi, *Alliance Adrift* (New York: Council on Foreign Relations Press, 1999), provide two detailed accounts of issues leading to the 1997 guidelines and the challenges of implementing them after they were adopted.

83. Two important studies of this period are Akikazu Hashimoto, Mike Mochizuki, and Kurayoshi Takara, eds., *The Okinawa Question and the U.S.-Japan Alliance* (Washington, DC: George Washington University, Sigur Center for Asian Studies, 2005), and Laura Elizabeth Hein and Mark Selden, eds., *Islands of Discontent: Okinawan Responses to Japanese and American Power* (Lanham, Md.: Rowman and Littlefield, 2003).

84. Yasutomo, *Japan's Civil-Military Diplomacy*, provides a detailed account of the JGSDF operations in Iraq and some discussion of the prior deployment of the JGSDF and JASDF to the area.

85. Paul Midford, *Rethinking Japanese Public Opinion and Security* (Stanford, Calif.: Stanford University Press, 2011), provides comprehensive time-series polling data related to the overseas dispatch of the JSDF.

86. Oros, *Normalizing Japan*, chapter 7, develops this argument in greater depth.

3. Japan's Relative Decline and New Security Challenges in a Multipolar Asia

1. International Institute for Strategic Studies, *The Military Balance 2012* (London: Routledge, 2012), as quoted in David Shambaugh, "International Relations in East Asia: A Multidimensional Analysis," in *International Relations of Asia*, ed. David Shambaugh and Michael Yahuda, 2nd ed. (Lanham, Md.: Rowman and Littlefield, 2014), 8.

2. "Trends in World Military Expenditure, 2014," SIPRI Fact Sheet, April 2015, 3, http://books.sipri.org/files/FS/SIPRIFS1504.pdf.

3. This three-tiered approach is set out in the 2013 national security strategy.

4. World Bank database, http://data.worldbank.org/indicator/NY.GDP.MKTP.KD.ZG.

5. David Shambaugh, "International Relations in East Asia: A Multidimensional Analysis," in *International Relations of Asia*, ed. David Shambaugh and Michael Yahuda, 2nd ed. (Lanham, Md.: Rowman and Littlefield, 2014), 8.

6. Figure 3.5 shows US military spending in relation to Asian states; the vastly larger scale of US spending somewhat obscures the spending by smaller, Asian states.

7. This data is presented in chart form in *The Foreign Policy and Security Implications of Global Aging for the Future of Japan-U.S. Relations: Report of the Sixth Annual Japan-U.S. Joint Public Policy Forum* (Washington, DC: Wilson Center; Tokyo: Sasakawa Peace Foundation, October 9,

2014), https://www.wilsoncenter.org/sites/default/files/asia_150128_global_aging_report_0310.pdf.

8. Brigitte Miksa, "The Future Is Gray for the Developed World," *Japan Times*, September 1, 2015.

9. David Chiavacci explains the complex nexus of practical needs and political realities related to immigration in Japan in "Indispensable Future Workforce or Internal Security Threat? Securing Japan's Future and Immigration," in *Governing Insecurity in Japan: The Domestic Discourse and Policy Response*, ed. Wilhelm Vosse, Reinhard Drifte, and Verena Blechinger-Talcott, 116–40 (New York: Routledge, 2014).

10. Miksa, "Future Is Gray."

11. Ibid.

12. Data for this estimate is from Jack A. Goldstone, "Global Population Megatrends and Japan's Demographic Crisis: Devastating Threat or Manageable Challenge?" (paper presented at the Sixth Annual Japan-U.S. Joint Public Policy Forum, Tokyo, October 9, 2014).

13. Michael Swaine et al., *China's Military and the U.S.-Japan Alliance in 2030: A Strategic Net Assessment* (Washington, DC: Carnegie Endowment for International Peace, 2013), 74–78, discusses different aspects of China's demographic challenges.

14. http://www.globalfirepower.com/, accessed July 24, 2015. The site explains the methodology for its overall calculations as follows: "The GFP ranking is based on a formula utilizing over fifty different factors, compiled and measured against each nation. Bonuses (ex: low oil consumption) and penalties (ex: high oil consumption) are applied to further refine the list. The finalized GFP value is recognized as the 'Power Index' (PwrIndx) which supplies a nation its respective positioning in the rankings."

15. Jeffrey W. Hornung and Mike M. Mochizuki usefully compare Japan's "power-projection capabilities" with those of seven other "middle powers" in "Japan: Still an Exceptional Ally," *Washington Quarterly* 39, no. 1 (spring 2016): 95–116. While the article does not directly address possible combat scenarios in East Asia, it does underscore that Japanese military forces have numerous strengths beyond what many would expect from a state that stresses in public diplomacy its limited military power.

16. International Institute for Strategic Studies, *The Military Balance 2012* (London: Routledge, 2012).

17. Ministry of Defense, *Defense of Japan 2014*, shows a steadily increasing number of scrambles related to the Russian military, up from 124 in 2003 to 359 in 2013. The peak number of scrambles during the Cold War was 944, not substantially higher than the 810 in 2013, though in 2012 and 2013 the largest number of scrambles was related to China, not Russia. (see figure III-1-1-3, p. 183.)

18. Robert Kaplan, *Asia's Cauldron: The South China Sea and the End of a Stable Pacific* (New York: Random House, 2014), 5.
19. Alessio Patalano, *Post-war Japan as a Sea Power: Imperial Legacy, Wartime Experience and the Making of a Navy* (London: Bloomsbury Academic, 2015).
20. Richard Samuels, " 'New Fighting Power!' Japan's Growing Maritime Capabilities and East Asian Security," *International Security* 32, no. 3 (winter 2007/2008): 84–112.
21. Denny Roy, *Return of the Dragon: Rising China and Regional Security* (New York: Columbia University Press, 2013), 75.
22. There is a large body of scholarly literature that examines Japan-China relations in a number of different areas. One recent book that stresses the interactions between China and Japan as both sought to modernize is Odd Arne Westad, *Restless Empire: China and the World Since 1750* (New York: Basic Books, 2012). A short book on the contemporary period is Michael Yahuda, *Sino-Japanese Relations after the Cold War: Two Tigers Sharing a Mountain* (New York: Routledge, 2013). On recent interactions between the two states from a Japanese perspective, see Akio Takahara and Ryūji Hattori, eds., *Nitchū kankeishi, 1972–2012* [A history of Japan-China relations, 1972–2012] (Tokyo: University of Tokyo Press, 2012). For a longer historical narrative, see Ming Wan, *Sino-Japanese Relations: Interaction, Logic, and Transformation* (Stanford, Calif.: Stanford University Press, 2006).
23. Sheila Smith, *Intimate Rivals: Japanese Domestic Politics and a Rising China* (New York: Columbia University Press, 2015), 9.
24. Japan Center for Economic Research, "The 37th Middle-Term Economic Forecast (2010–2020)," February 2011. Full text available at https://www.jcer.or.jp/eng/pdf/m37_summary.pdf.
25. Smith, *Intimate Rivals*, 9.
26. Ibid., 258.
27. Still, as Kenneth Pyle writes in *Japan Rising: The Resurgence of Japanese Power and Purpose* (New York: PublicAffairs, 2007), 35–36, China's rise in the seventh century spurred the Japanese state to act even back then.
28. Speech by Premier Wen Jiabao of the State Council of the People's Republic of China at the Japanese Diet, Tokyo, April 12, 2007; full text available at http://manchester.china-consulate.org/eng/xwdt/t311107.htm.
29. Smith, *Intimate Rivals*, xi.
30. Roy, *Return of the Dragon*, 3.
31. Reported on China View, the English-language site of the Xinhua News Agency: http://news.xinhuanet.com/english/2006-10/08/content_5177334.htm.
32. Wen's speech included the following: "Since the normalization of diplomatic ties between China and Japan, the Japanese Government and lead-

ers have on many occasions stated their position on the historical issue, admitted that Japan had committed aggression and expressed deep remorse and apology to the victimized countries. The Chinese Government and people appreciate the position they have taken" (http://manchester .china-consulate.org/eng/xwdt/t311107.htm).

33. Japan External Trade Organization, "2008 Jetro White Paper on 'International Trade and Foreign Direct Investment'": http://www.jetro.go.jp/en/ reports/white_paper/trade_invest_2008.pdf

34. The full text is available at http://www.fmprc.gov.cn/mfa_eng/wjdt_665385 /2649_665393/t458431.shtml.

35. The exact sequence of events is disputed and the subject of considerable media coverage and debate. Smith, *Intimate Rivals*, chapter 6, and James Manicom, *Bridging Troubled Waters: China, Japan, and Maritime Order in the East China Sea* (Washington, DC: Georgetown University Press, 2014), chapter 2, among others, offer details on the origins and unfolding of this incident.

36. Japan's official position is explained in a pamphlet distributed by the MOFA: http://www.mofa.go.jp/region/asia-paci/senkaku/pdfs/senkaku_pamphlet .pdf.

37. As computed in constant 2011 US dollars by SIPRI: http://www.sipri.org/ research/armaments/milex/.

38. Roy, *Return of the Dragon*, 63–64. Richard A. Bitzinger, "China's Double-Digit Defense Growth: What It Means for a Peaceful Rise," *Foreign Affairs*, March 19, 2015, https://www.foreignaffairs.com/articles/ china/2015-03-19/chinas-double-digit-defense-growth, states that China's official defense spending is widely considered to be underreported and that China is able to acquire more for what it spends than other major military spenders because of lower costs of acquisition and labor in China.

39. Bjørn Elias Mikalsen Grønning, "Japan's Shifting Military Priorities: Counterbalancing China's Rise," *Asian Security* 10, no. 1 (2014): 15.

40. Jeffrey Hornung, "Japan's Growing Hard Hedge Against China," *Asian Security* 10, no. 2 (2014): 97. This article includes numerous useful references to other recent articles that track Japan's growing military response to China's rise.

41. Roy, *Return of the Dragon*, 70.

42. Brad Glosserman and Scott A. Snyder, *The Japan–South Korea Identity Clash: East Asian Security and the United States* (New York: Columbia University Press, 2015), 43.

43. Details can be found in Roy, *Return of the Dragon*, 60–62.

44. Ibid., chapter 7, offers five "mitigating factors" for why the security relationship with China may not deteriorate as much as some fear: (1) US-China relations appear stable and there are efforts on both sides to keep

that the case, (2) the system works for China too, (3) China itself does not seem to want to be a global superpower with all the responsibilities that entails, (4) other actors are balancing against China's military rise, (5) China itself argues that it seeks to achieve a "peaceful rise." And yet Roy sees a persistent risk of conflict because of factors such as that "aggression is in the eye of the beholder" and that many Chinese are acting in a way that seeks to legitimate a "Chinese sphere of influence" in East Asia.

45. Numerous contributors to a recent special issue of the *Pacific Review* argue this point in relation to Japan's perception of change in the Asian region; for an overview, see Linus Hagström and Karl Gustafsson, "Japan and Identity Change: Why It Matters in International Relations," *Pacific Review* 28, no. 1 (March 2015): 1–22

46. Smith, *Intimate Rivals*, argues convincingly that Japanese leaders and the Japanese public alike perceive a growing threat from China across the board: "Most Japanese citizens did not see China's rise as a distant phenomenon but as a recurring stream of incidents and crises that could affect their daily lives" (237). The end result, it concludes, is a substantial effect on Japan's internal governing practices, in particular: (1) voices in the debate over appropriate policies toward China have diversified beyond the previous dominance of business leaders and diplomats and (2) issues related to China have been integral to debates over the need for broader governance reform in Japan (238–39).

47. As noted earlier, however, the figures look more balanced between the United States and China if figures are computed using PPP.

48. "Trends in World Military Expenditure," 2.

49. US Department of Defense, *Quadrennial Defense Review Report* (Washington, DC, 2006), http://archive.defense.gov/pubs/pdfs/QDR20060203.pdf.

50. Smith, *Intimate Rivals*, 259.

51. Ibid., 260.

52. T. J. Pempel, "Japan's Search for the 'Sweet Spot': International Cooperation and Regional Security in Northeast Asia," *Orbis* 55, no. 2 (spring 2011): 273.

53. Corey J. Wallace, "Japan's Strategic Pivot South: Diversifying the Dual Hedge," *International Relations of the Asia-Pacific*, 2013, 484.

54. Bhubhindar Singh, *Japan's Security Identity: From a Peace State to an International State* (London: Routledge, 2013), provides additional details on these cases.

55. Annual *Defense of Japan* white papers list such bilateral defense-related meetings.

56. Wallace, "Japan's Strategic Pivot South," 490.

57. Jing Sun, *Japan and China as Charm Rivals: Soft Power in Regional Diplomacy* (Ann Arbor: University of Michigan Press, 2012), provides an overview of both aspects.

58. Swaine et al., *China's Military.*

59. Smith, *Intimate Rivals*, 260, develops this point further.

4. Domestic Power Transitions and Japan's Evolving Strategic Posture, 2006 to 2012

1. The LDP briefly lost power to a rival coalition for nine months after the 1993 Lower House election, but the LDP had won the largest number of seats of any party in that election.

2. Major scholarly works by Kenneth Pyle, Richard Samuels, and Christopher Hughes predict a more or less continuous "normalization" of Japan through this domestic power transition.

3. The House of Councillors was created by the postwar constitution from the previous House of Peers and is generally is a coequal house in Japan's bicameral parliament—with the exceptions that the House of Representatives can pass legislation not passed or voted on in the House of Councillors with a two-thirds majority vote and that prime ministers tend to be drawn from the members of the House of Representatives.

4. The complete text of these guidelines is available at http://www.mod .go.jp/e/d_act/d_policy/pdf/guidelinesFY2011.pdf.

5. The early post–Cold War period also saw a dramatically altered international environment, but not the same sense of immediate threat. The North Korea missile and nuclear threat created a first-round shock in the late 1990s (and early 1990s for defense watchers in the Japan Defense Agency). Domestic crises—in particular the Great Hanshin earthquake and sarin gas attack on a Tokyo subway, both in 1995—also had created impetus for institutional change to better address crisis management. Tomohito Shinoda, *Koizumi Diplomacy: Japan's Kantei Approach to Foreign and Defense Affairs* (Seattle: University of Washington Press, 2007), traces the evolution toward more centralization of power in the prime minister's office—a trend that intensified throughout the period examined in this book.

6. Twenty-seven Lower House elections were conducted between 1946 and 2015, a span of sixty-nine years.

7. Thirty-three prime ministers have served in the seventy years from August 1945 to August 2015.

8. Richard Samuels, *Machiavelli's Children: Leaders and Their Legacies in Italy and Japan.* Ithaca, N.Y.: Cornell University Press, 2005, chapter 8, explains Yoshida's pivotal role.

9. The Constitutional Revision in Japan Research Project at the Reischauer Institute of Japanese Studies at Harvard University maintains an archive of the numerous specific proposals that have been advanced by a number

of different political actors in Japan, including the 1994 and 2005 drafts mentioned here; see http://wax.lib.harvard.edu/collections/collection.do?coll=101.

10. It is frequently noted that Abe is the grandson of former prime minister Nobusuke Kishi, who served in the wartime Tōjō cabinet as minister of munitions and thus shared responsibility for Japan's wartime conduct, but, as noted by Japanese historian Kenichi Matsumoto, it is rarely noted in media reporting that Kishi later opposed the Tōjō cabinet and was jailed for his opposition; nor that Abe's other grandfather, Kan Abe, actively resisted the network of political parties led by Tōjō, the so-called Taisei Yokusankai. See Kenichi Matsumoto, "(Right Tilt?): Is 'Japan Moves to Right' True? Second Abe Administration Faces Test of Realism," Discuss Japan: Japan Foreign Policy Forum, nos. 13–15 (March 5, 2013), http://www.japanpolicyforum.jp.

11. Among the voluminous writings on Abe's background, see Muneo Narusawa, "Abe Shinzo: Japan's New Prime Minister a Far-Right Denier of History," Asia-Pacific Journal / Japan Focus 11, no. 1 (January 14, 2013), http://apjjf.org/2013/11/1/Narusawa-Muneo/3879/article.html, and Mike M. Mochizuki and Samuel Parkinson Porter, "Japan under Abe: Toward Moderation or Nationalism?" Washington Quarterly 36, no. 4 (2013): 25–41.

12. R. Taggart Murphy takes a more strident stand on Abe, writing, "For no sooner was Abe in office than he set out to enact what Koizumi had only hinted at: replacement of the postwar constitution; a robust, unapologetic military; an affirmation of the central place of the Imperial House in the sovereign edifice of the Japanese state; and the promotion of an understanding of the events of the 1930s that would portray them as a legitimate response to Western colonialism and the threats of alien ideologies" (Japan and the Shackles of the Past: What Everyone Needs to Know [Oxford: Oxford University Press, 2014], 311). See also Kenneth B. Pyle, "Abe Shinzo and Japan's Change of Course," NBR Analysis, October 2006, http://nbr.org/publications/issue.aspx?id=97.

13. See, for example, an address by Abe's foreign minister Tarō Asō, "On the 'Arc of Freedom and Prosperity,'" March 12, 2007, http://www.mofa.go.jp/policy/pillar/address0703.html. Weston S. Konishi offers critical analysis of this strategy in "Will Japan Be Out of Tune with a Concert of Democracies?" Asia Pacific Bulletin, no. 19 (June 27, 2008), http://www.eastwestcenter.org/publications/will-japan-be-out-tune-concert-democracies.

14. Daniel Sneider, "The New Asianism: Japanese Foreign Policy under the Democratic Party of Japan," in Japan under the DPJ: The Politics of Transition and Governance, ed. Kenji E. Kushida and Phillip Y. Lipscy (Stanford, Calif.: Walter H. Shorenstein Asia-Pacific Research Center, 2013), 386.

15. An overview of the DPJ founding period is offered in Kenji E. Kushida and Phillip Y. Lipscy, "The Rise and Fall of the Democratic Party of Japan," in Kushida and Lipscy, *Japan under the DPJ*. The short summary in this paragraph draws from this extended history.

16. The issue of candidate backgrounds for DPJ candidates from the creation of the party through the 2012 Lower House election is examined in detail in Daniel M. Smith, Robert J. Pekkanen, and Ellis S. Krauss, "Building a Party: Candidate Recruitment in the Democratic Party of Japan, 1996–2012," in Kushida and Lipscy, *Japan under the DPJ*.

17. James Manicom, *Bridging Troubled Waters: China, Japan, and Maritime Order in the East China Sea* (Washington, DC: Georgetown University Press, 2014), chapter 5, discusses this agreement.

18. Most prominent among such reports was the so-called Second Armitage-Nye report (Richard L. Armitage, Joseph S. Nye, "The U.S.-Japan Alliance: Getting Asia Right through 2020," CSIS Report, 2007, http://csis.org/files/media/csis/pubs/070216_asia2020.pdf). Later, the "Unmet Expectations" report was also widely circulated (Michael Finnegan, *Managing Unmet Expectations in the US-Japan Alliance*, NBR Special Report, no. 17 [Seattle: National Bureau of Asian Research, November 2009], http://nbr.org/publications/issue.aspx?id=188).

19. The expert panel report and the official government report are both available, in Japanese, at http://www.mofa.go.jp/mofaj/gaiko/ mitsuyaku/ kekka .html. For an English-language overview, see Jeffrey Lewis, "More on US-Japan 'Secret Agreements,'" http://lewis.armscontrolwonk.com/archive/2660/more-on-us-japan-secret-agreements.

20. Steven R. Reed, "The Survival of 'Third Parties' in Japan's Mixed-Member Electoral System," in Kushida and Lipscy, *Japan under the DPJ*, 113.

21. Ibid., 118.

22. Kushida and Lipscy, "Rise and Fall," 8.

23. Smith, Pekkanen, and Krauss, "Building a Party," 179.

24. They made up only 3 percent of Noda's appointees, which was more on a par with their overall percentage in the Diet. See Christopher Hughes, "The Democratic Party of Japan's New (but Failing) Grand Security Strategy: From 'Reluctant Realism' to 'Resentful Realism'?" In Kushida and Lipscy, *Japan under the DPJ*, 179–80.

25. Weston S. Konishi, *From Rhetoric to Reality: Foreign-Policy Making under the Democratic Party of Japan* (Boston: Institute for Foreign Policy Analysis, 2012), v–vi and 15–22, where Konishi expands on these schools.

26. Konishi makes a similar argument, writing, "The 'big change' in Japanese foreign policy following the DPJ's takeover in 2009 did not transpire according to some expectations. On the contrary, the DPJ's foreign policy

increasingly resembles the status quo—emphasizing the centrality of the US-Japan alliance" (ibid., v).

27. See Bhubhindar Singh, *Japan's Security Identity: From a Peace State to an International State* (London: Routledge, 2013), for examples and references to a wider literature.

28. Konishi, *From Rhetoric to Reality*, v.

29. Ibid., 23.

30. Kushida and Lipscy, "Rise and Fall," use this term to describe the governing style between Hatoyama and Ozawa.

31. Under Ozawa's leadership, the DPJ won a significant victory in the Upper House elections in 2007, setting the stage for the 2009 victory in the Lower House. An Ozawa premiership may have even further cemented the transformation of Japan's security posture during the DPJ years without the difficulties in US-Japan relations suffered under Hatoyama. As Sneider writes in "The New Asianism," "Ozawa had a reputation as a conservative nationalist, even as an advocate of Japanese military buildup. . . . As an LDP leader, Ozawa had advocated support for the Gulf War in 1991 based on the formation of a UN-sanctioned international coalition. After failing in an earlier attempt, Ozawa was instrumental in pushing through the 1992 law authorizing Japanese forces to participate in peacekeeping operations (PKO)." Even more recently, Sneider continues, "this stance was visible when the DPJ— albeit with some dissenters from among the ex-Socialists—backed the post-9/11 decision to dispatch Japanese naval forces in a noncombat, logistical role in support of Afghanistan operations in 2002" (377).

32. Hughes, "Democratic Party," 359.

33. Sneider, "New Asianism," 395.

34. Matteo Dian, *The Evolution of the US-Japan Alliance: The Eagle and the Chrysanthemum* (Oxford: Chandos, 2014), 174, also emphasizes the historical legacy argument in his explanation for why deepened security cooperation with external partners progressed faster with India and Australia than with South Korea.

35. Ichiro Ozawa, *Blueprint for a New Japan: The Rethinking of a Nation*, trans. Louisa Rubinfien (Tokyo: Kodansha International, 1994).

36. Ministry of Defense, *Defense of Japan 2010*, introduction by Defense Minister Kitazawa.

37. According to research conducted by Kushida and Lipscy, only about 40 percent of proposed legislation passed during the regular Diet session of 2010, and, even more surprising, the rate was only 55 percent for cabinet-submitted legislation ("Rise and Fall," 20).

38. *Defense of Japan 2012* provides polling data—in both areas exceeding 80 percent.

39. Kushida and Lipscy, "Rise and Fall," 14, includes a useful table of approval and disapproval ratings of both the DPJ and the LDP from 1998 to 2012.

40. Konishi, *From Rhetoric to Reality*, offers a useful chart aggregating support rates of the three DPJ governments as measured by both *Asahi shimbun* and Y*omiuri shimbun* polls, permitting a comparison of poll results from the left of center and right of center, respectively. It is notable, if predictable, that the most right-leaning DPJ prime minister also shows higher support rates in the *Yomiuri* poll.

41. Sneider, "New Asianism," 370–71.

42. Smith, Pekkanen, and Krauss, "Building a Party," 167.

43. Additional discussion of this pivotal election follows in chapter 5.

44. Sneider, "New Asianism," 371.

45. Ibid.

46. Ibid., 396.

47. Ibid., 398.

48. On the international politics–public opinion nexus, see, for example, Paul Midford, *Rethinking Japanese Public Opinion and Security* (Stanford, Calif.: Stanford University Press, 2011), and, on the domestic politics–international politics interaction, see Linus Hagström, "The 'Abnormal' State: Identity, Norm/Exception and Japan," *European Journal of International Relations* 20, no. 2 (2014): 1–24.

49. Hughes, "Democratic Party," 335.

50. See Shogo Suzuki, "The Rise of the Chinese 'Other' in Japan's Construction of Identity: Is China a Focal Point of Japanese Nationalism?" *Pacific Review* 28, no. 1 (March 2015): 95–116, and Alexander Bukh, "Shimane Prefecture, Tokyo, and the Territorial Dispute over Dokdo/Takeshima: Regional and National Identities in Japan," *Pacific Review* 28, no. 1 (March 2015): 47–70.

5. The New Conservative Mainstream and New Security Policies Under Prime Minister Shinzō Abe, 2012 to 2016

1. As with public protests in other democracies, discerning an accurate head count is both difficult and highly politicized. Organizations supporting the demonstrations have claimed turnouts of well over one hundred thousand, while the mainstream media has generally reported participation at around half that figure.

2. *Japan Times*, July 29, 2015.

3. The SIPRI database shows 2014 spending at about $45.8 billion, which is a modest drop from the previous year in US dollars despite being a rise of about 2 percent in yen terms—the largest rise in defense spending in Japan in three years and, before that, since 1998. The Abe government claims to be the first to increase defense spending in over a decade, because some

costs that SIPRI considers defense related are not included in Japan's official defense budget. In addition, SIPRI provides data by calendar year rather than the fiscal year used by the Japanese government. Using SIPRI data, once again Japan's security renaissance can be traced back to the years of DPJ rule. In constant 2011 US dollars, Japan spent about the same on defense in 1999 as it did in 2014, with a peak in 2003 and a roughly annual modest decline since that time.

4. This argument is further developed in Andrew L. Oros, "Does Abe's Rightward Shift Threaten His Legacy?" *PacNet*, no. 2 (January 7, 2014), http://csis .org/publication/pacnet-2-does-abes-rightward-shift-threaten-his-legacy.

5. See George Ehrhardt et al., eds., *Kōmeitō: Politics and Religion in Japan* (Berkeley: Institute of East Asian Studies, University of California, 2014), for a broad overview of this pivotal and understudied party in contemporary Japanese politics.

6. This despite the obvious difference that the United States has a treaty obligation to protect the Senkaku Islands but not eastern Ukraine and multiple reassurances by US officials that the United States would protect Japan in such a case.

7. In fact, crisis management continues to be the charge of the deputy cabinet secretary for crisis management, though the NSC helps facilitate meetings. Reportedly this arrangement was the result of a compromise in setting up the NSC to satisfy concerns of the National Police Agency; interview with Cabinet Secretariat staff, Tokyo, June 2014.

8. For an overview of Japan's previous thinking about security, including the idea of comprehensive security from the Cold War era and human security in the post–Cold War era, see Christopher Hughes, *Japan's Security Agenda: Military, Economic, and Environmental Dimensions* (Boulder, Colo.: Rienner, 2004).

9. National Institute for Defense Studies, *East Asian Strategic Review 2014*, 46. For an extended discussion in Japanese of the evolution of the NSC, see Tsuyoshi Sunohara, *Nihonban NSC to wa nani ka* [What is the Japan-style NSC?] (Tokyo: Shinchōsha, 2014). For an English-language summary, including an organizational chart, see Ministry of Defense, *Defense of Japan 2014*, 125–26.

10. *Defense of Japan 2014*, 126.

11. National Institute for Defense Studies, *East Asian Strategic Review 2014*, 43. Other ministers represented in the Nine-Minister Meeting in addition to the six already mentioned are the minister of finance, the minister of public management, home affairs, post and telecommunications, and the chairman of the National Public Safety Commission.

12. In the first Abe administration, the US director of national intelligence Admiral Dennis Blair is quoted as saying that he insisted that the MOD

share US-provided information with other ministries in Japan only with express US permission, given lax information security laws in Japan at the time; *Asahi shimbun*, October 6, 2013.

13. *Defense of Japan 2014*, 127.

14. SEALDs is the name the group uses in Japanese, an English-language acronym for Students Emergency Action for Liberal Democracy. The group's goals and action items are outlined in English at http://sealdseng .strikingly.com/.

15. Nihon Bengoshi Rengōkai [Japan Federation of Bar Associations], "Himitsu hogohō no mondaiten wa?" [What are the problems with the secrets law?], http://www.nichibenren.or.jp/activity/human/secret/problem.html.

16. "Himitsu hogo hōan: Nōberushō gakushara kōgi seimei" [The designated secrets bill: Nobel laureates issue protest statement], *Mainichi shimbun*, November 28, 2013; my translation.

17. For more detailed analysis of the national security strategy and likely next steps, see *East Asia Strategic Review 2014*, 48–54. For a broader analysis of the national security strategy in the context of Japan's evolving national security policies, see Noboru Yamaguchi, "Evolution of Japan's National Security Policy under the Abe Administration," *Asan Forum*, April 11, 2014, http://www.theasanforum.org/evolution-of-japans-national-security -policy-under-the-abe-administration/.

18. "Difference between 'Dynamic Defense Force' and 'Dynamic Joint Defense Force,'" *Defense of Japan 2014*, 145.

19. *Defense of Japan 2014*, 148–58. The complete text of these documents is available at http://www.mod.go.jp/e/d_act/d_policy/national.html.

20. For an analysis of this shift in defense posture, see Toshi Yoshihara, "Japanese Hard Power: Rising to the Challenge," *National Security Outlook*, August 2014.

21. This document is available at http://www.mod.go.jp/e/pressrele/2014/ 140401_02.pdf.

22. "Three Principles on Transfer of Defense Equipment and Technology," 2.

23. Michael Swaine et al., *China's Military and the U.S.-Japan Alliance in 2030: A Strategic Net Assessment* (Washington, DC: Carnegie Endowment for International Peace, 2013), 143, expands on this point.

24. Saadia M. Pekkanen and Paul Kallender-Umezu, *In Defense of Japan: From the Market to the Military in Space Policy* (Stanford, Calif.: Stanford University Press, 2010), discusses changes in space policy related to national defense leading up to the more recent changes, showing the continuity of policy under Japan's security renaissance.

25. The new mission statement and vision for JICA is available on its homepage: http://www.jica.go.jp/english/about/mission/index.html; it was announced via a cabinet statement on February 10, 2015: http://www

.mofa.go.jp/files/000067701.pdf. For a critical overview of the changes and continuities from past ODA policies, see Lean Alfred Santos, "Figuring Out Japan's New Aid Charter," https://www.devex.com/news/figuring-out-japan-s-new-aid-charter-85520.

26. Dennis T. Yasutomo, *Japan's Civil-Military Diplomacy: The Banks of the Rubicon* (New York: Routledge, 2014), provides a compelling and detailed examination of the linkage between Japan's ODA policy and its security policy evolution, focusing on the cases of Afghanistan and Iraq.

27. Jeffrey W. Hornung and Mike M. Mochizuki, "Japan: Still an Exceptional Ally," *Washington Quarterly* 39, no. 1 (spring 2016): 95–116, provides a useful analysis of Japan's continued exceptionalism in its military posture and practices in comparison with other "middle power" US allies—even factoring in the recent series of changes implemented under the Abe government.

28. Brad Glosserman and Scott A. Snyder, *The Japan–South Korea Identity Clash: East Asian Security and the United States* (New York: Columbia University Press, 2015), provides timely analysis of this issue.

29. The JSDF was initially invited to join the multinational relief efforts following the Sichuan earthquake in 2008 that resulted in the deaths of about seventy thousand people, but the Chinese leadership rescinded landing permission after public criticism quickly emerged.

30. For an examination of the domestic and international politics related to Takeshima Day, see Alexander Bukh, "Shimane Prefecture, Tokyo, and the Territorial Dispute over Dokdo/Takeshima: Regional and National Identities in Japan," *Pacific Review* 28, no. 1 (March 2015): 47–70.

31. One of many such examples is Muneo Narusawa, "Abe Shinzo: Japan's New Prime Minister a Far-Right Denier of History," *Asia-Pacific Journal* 11, no. 1 (January 14, 2013), http://japanfocus.org/-Narusawa-Muneo/3879/article.html.

32. An explanation of this petition and a reprint of its contents and signatories are provided in Hiroki Manabe, "Japan Scholars in West Issue Statement Calling for 'Unbiased' Accounting of Past," *Asahi Shimbun*, Asia and Japan Watch, May 7, 2015, http://www.asahi.com/ajw/articles/AJ201505070028.htm.

33. Christopher W. Hughes, *Japan's Foreign and Security Policy under the "Abe Doctrine": New Dynamism or New Dead End?* (New York: Palgrave Macmillan, 2015), 4. "In the end," Hughes concludes, "the Doctrine may lead to a dead end and Japan's shift to 'Resentful Realism'" (91).

34. "Sugomu dake no Abe gaikō wa Kimu Jon'un, Shū Kinpei, Paku Kune, Pūchin ni kanzen ni namerareteiru" [Abe's intimidation diplomacy totally played around by Kim Jong Un, Xi Jinping, Pak Geun-hye, and Putin], *Shūkan posuto*, November 11, 2014, criticizes what is described as a "warmongering Abe."

35. Tsuneo Watanabe, "Abe shushō ni tsutaetai 'waga taikenteki Yasukuni-ron'" [Message to Prime Minister Abe: My experiential Yasukuni theory], *Bungeishunjū*, September 2014. Beyond this extended critique, each of Japan's major daily newspapers criticized the Yasukuni visit, apart from *Sankei shimbun*, but tended to focus on the reaction from abroad rather than direct criticism at Abe himself.

36. The Cabinet Office maintains transcripts of several statements by Chief Cabinet Secretary Suga to this effect, for example, at the May 8, 2013, press conference: http://www.kantei.go.jp/foreign/tyoukanpress/201305/08_a.html.

37. Abe stated, "First of all, I would like to state very clearly that the Abe cabinet upholds the position on the recognition of history of the previous administrations, in its entirety, including the Murayama Statement [apologizing in 1995 for the damage and suffering caused by Japan to its Asian neighbors] and the Koizumi Statement [of 2005, stating that Japan must never again take the path to war]. I have made this position very clearly, on many occasions, and we still uphold this position. Also we have made it very clear that the Abe cabinet is not reviewing the Kōnō Statement [of 1993, in which the government of Japan extended its sincere apologies and remorse to all those who had suffered as comfort women]. On the question of comfort women, when my thought goes to these people, who have been victimized by human trafficking and gone through immeasurable pain and suffering beyond description, my heart aches. And on this point, my thought has not changed at all from previous prime ministers" Prime Minister Shinzō Abe, interview by David Ignatius, *Washington Post*, March 26, 2015, https://www.washingtonpost.com/blogs/post-partisan/wp/2015/03/26/david-ignatiuss-full-interview-with-japanese-prime-minister-shinzo-abe/.

38. Chief Cabinet Secretary Suga described the main findings and process of the report at a press conference on June 20, 2014; available in Japanese at http://www.kantei.go.jp/jp/tyoukanpress/201406/20_p.html. The full report is available in English at http://japan.kantei.go.jp/96_abe/documents/2014/__icsFiles/afieldfile/2014/06/20/JPN_ROK_EXCHANGE.pdf.

39. "Japan PM Shinzo Abe Marks War Criminal Ceremony," *BBC News*, August 27, 2014; Jonathan Soble, "Shinzo Abe Stays Away as Japanese Lawmakers Visit Contentious Yasukuni Shrine," *New York Times*, October 20, 2015.

40. "Japan Is Back: A Conversation with Shinzo Abe," *Foreign Affairs*, July/August 2013, https://www.foreignaffairs.com/interviews/2013-05-16/japan-back.

41. "Report of the Advisory Panel on the History of the Twentieth Century and on Japan's Role and the World Order in the Twenty-First Century," August 6, 2015, http://www.kantei.go.jp/jp/singi/21c_koso/pdf/report_en.pdf.

42. See, for example, Muneo Narusawa, "Abe Shinzō to kyoku-u rekishi shūseishugisha wa sekai no teki dearu" [Shinzō Abe and ultra-right-wing history revisionists are the enemy of the world], *News for the People in Japan*, January 2, 2013, www.news-pj.net/toukou/narusawa-20130105.html.

43. The JCP newspaper *Akahata* reported that ten members of the Abe cabinet were affiliated with the Kōnō Statement Denial Caucus ("Kōnō danwa nitei no giren, Abe seiken ni shusshin kakuryō 10 shi" [Ten cabinet members of the Abe administration affiliated with the "Kōnō Statement Denial" Caucus], *Akahata shimbun*, October 13, 2014).

44. Note that Japanese media refer to the cabinet chosen in December 2012 as the "second" Abe cabinet, counting as the first members selected for his first term as prime minister in 2006; the figures noted here refer to the second Abe cabinet. Matthew Penney provides a summary of group membership of each member of this cabinet and a short description of each group: "The Abe Cabinet: An Ideological Breakdown," *Asia-Pacific Journal/Japan Focus*, January 2013, http://apjjf.org/-Matthew-Penney/4747/article.html. Group membership information for the third Abe cabinet (appointed on October 7, 2015) is provided in table format in "Dai sanji Abe Shinzō naikaku no chōtakaha (kyoku-u) no daijintachi" [Ultra-hawkish (ultra-right-wing) members of the third Abe cabinet], *Harbor Business Online*, http://hbol.jp/25122/takahagiin, accessed January 17, 2016. The Nippon Kaigi website provides a wide account of their activities (in Japanese): http://www.nipponkaigi.org/.

45. Emma Chanlett-Avery et al., *Japan-U.S. Relations: Issues for Congress*, CRS Report 7-5700, September 29, 2015 (Washington, DC: Congressional Research Service), 7.

46. Some of many newspaper articles include "Sengo 68-nen to kinrin gaikō: Uchimuki shikō o nukedasō" [Sixty-eight years from the end of the war and our neighborhood diplomacy: Need to depart from inward orientation], *Asahi shimbun*, August 15, 2013; "Kokka anpo senryaku, naze kakikomu 'aikokuhin'" [National security strategy, why is patriotism included?], *Tōkyō shimbun*, December 12, 2013; "Minshushugi to iu ki, edaha o yutaka ni shigerasō" [A tree called democracy, let it grow thick and leafy], *Mainichi shimbun*, January 1, 2014. A more extended treatment is provided in Nozomu Yamazaki, ed., *Kimyōna nashonarizumu no jidai: Haigaishugi ni kōshite* [The era of odd nationalism: Defying jingoism] (Tokyo: Iwanami shoten, 2015). One example of concern over rising militarism is seen in "Yomigaeru gunkokushugi: Sengo nanajūnen tokushū" [Resurging militarism: Special issue on seventy years since the war], *Shūkan kin'yōbi*, July 31, 2015.

47. Brad Glosserman and Scott A. Snyder, *The Japan–South Korea Identity Clash: East Asian Security and the United States* (New York: Columbia University Press, 2015), 31.

48. Ibid., citing research reported in Juan Díez-Nicolás, "Cultural Differences on Values about Conflict, War, and Peace," *World Values Research* 3, no. 1 (2010), 6.
49. Glosserman and Snyder, *Japan–South Korea Identity Clash*, citing Pew polling data, 32.
50. Cabinet Secretariat, *National Security Strategy: December 17, 2013*, 1.
51. Ibid.
52. This issue of challenges to Japan's "security identity" under Abe is analyzed in a more explicitly theoretical fashion in Andrew L. Oros, "International and Domestic Challenges to Japan's Postwar Security Identity: 'Norm Constructivism' and Japan's New 'Proactive Pacifism,'" *Pacific Review* 28, no. 1 (March 2015): 139–60.
53. Paul Midford, *Rethinking Japanese Public Opinion and Security* (Stanford, Calif.: Stanford University Press, 2011), reproduces extensive polling data that illustrate this point in the post–Cold War period through 2009; Corey J. Wallace, "The Evolution of the Japanese Strategic Imagination and Generation Change: A Generationally-Focused Analysis of Public and Elite Attitudes towards War and Peace in Japan" (PhD diss., University of Auckland, 2014), and Glosserman and Snyder, *Japan–South Korea Identity Clash*, analyze polling data through 2014 that also illustrate this point.
54. NHK polling from 2010 to 2014, cited in Wallace, "Evolution," 178.
55. NHK polling in 2013, cited ibid., 155.
56. *Asahi* polling 2013, 2014, cited ibid., 134.
57. Ibid., 186.
58. Interpreting polling on the specific issue of CSD is somewhat tricky given the broad nature of the policy. When Japanese are polled with a specific example of CSD, majorities have been found in support of the exercise of CSD in some cases—such as aiding a US ship under attack in an area near Japan. When asked the more abstract question of support for CSD, a majority did not support a policy change in numerous polls over time. For explication of this point and specific polling data, see Wallace, "Evolution," 157.
59. *Japan Times*, July 26, 2015.
60. Although for over sixty years conservatives and nationalists in Japan have consistently sought to formally revise Article Nine, until the twenty-first century, there was no time when it looked as if a vote for revision could obtain the necessary two-thirds affirmative vote in the Diet. The process by which the subsequently required national referendum would be conducted had not even been determined by legislation until 2007 (under the first Abe administration), as no national referendum of any sort has ever been conducted in Japan.
61. *Defense of Japan 2012*, 110.

62. Cabinet Secretariat, "Cabinet Decision on Development of Seamless Security Legislation to Ensure Japan's Survival and Protect Its People," July 1, 2014, http://japan.kantei.go.jp/96_abe/decisions/2014/__icsFiles/afieldfile/2014/07/03/anpohosei_eng.pdf, 8.

63. *Defense of Japan 2015*, 139–52, provides an overview of the different aspects of the new legislation as well as of issues related to its implementation.

64. *Japan Times*, July 9, 2014.

65. Ibid.

66. Yoichi Funabashi writes that the invitation in 1997 to the chairman of the US Joint Chiefs of Staff John Shalikashvili for a meal in the prime minister's office was totally unprecedented (*Alliance Adrift* [New York: Council on Foreign Relations Press, 1999], 118). He also discusses the cautious attitudes of Japanese prime ministers in the 1990s toward interacting with the military.

67. Yuki Tatsumi, "Great Expectations During Japan Military Chief's US Visit," *Diplomat*, July 24, 2015, http://thediplomat.com/2015/07/great-expectations-during-japan-military-chiefs-us-visit/, notes the significance of this public appearance. A video of Admiral Takei's speech (in English) is available at http://carnegieendowment.org/2015/07/29/from-ocean-of-war-to-ocean-of-prosperity/idt3.

68. National Institute for Defense Studies, *East Asian Strategic Review 2013*, 118.

69. For a discussion of the depth of the Japan-Australia security partnership circa 2015, see Thomas S. Wilkins, "The Japan Choice: Reconsidering the Risks and Opportunities of the 'Special Relationship' for Australia," *International Relations of the Asia-Pacific*, 2015, doi:10.1093/irap/lcv025. A more comprehensive, earlier overview can be found in William Tow and Rikki Kersten, eds., *Bilateral Perspectives on Regional Security: Australia, Japan and the Asia-Pacific Region* (Basingstoke, U.K.: Palgrave Macmillan, 2012).

70. The full restrictions beyond just that Japan's survival must be threatened are explained as follows in *Defense of Japan 2015*, 140, figure II-1-3-1, section 3: "The Government believes that not only when an armed attack against Japan occurs but also when an armed attack against a foreign country that is in a close relationship with Japan occurs and as a result threatens Japan's survival and poses a clear danger to fundamentally overturn people's right to life, liberty and pursuit of happiness, and when there is no other appropriate means available to repel the attack and ensure Japan's survival and protect its people, use of force to the minimum extent necessary should be interpreted to be permitted under the Constitution as measures for self-defense."

71. *Defense of Japan 2012*, 474.

72. Polling data of 2015 is available at http://survey.gov-online.go.jp/h26/h26
-bouei/gairyaku.pdf.

73. For example, Ichirō Ozawa had left the DPJ to form the People's Life Party,
which fared poorly in the December 2012 election; Shizuka Kamei left
the LDP to form the People's New Party but is now an independent; and
Shintarō Ishihara left the LDP to support the further-right JIP only to see
electoral support for that party also wane. An article in the *Shūkan posuto*
argues this general point: "Beitsuishō no Nihonjin wa 'kōfukuna dorei':
Media riterashī kakutoku hitsuyō" [US-following Japanese are "happy
slaves": We need media literacy], October 2, 2012.

74. Polling data of 2015 is available in Japanese at http://survey.gov-online.
go.jp/h26/h26-bouei/gairyaku.pdf. *Defense of Japan 2014* (Tokyo: Urban
Connections, 2014) provides longitudinal polling data reporting that over
70 percent of Japanese responding view the US-Japan Security Treaty as
"helpful" since the 2000 survey, rising from 63.9 percent in 1991 (465).

75. *Shūkan posuto* argues this general point in "Beitsuishō no Nihonjin wa
'kōfukuna dorei': Media riterashī kakutoku hitsuyō" [US-following Japanese are "happy slaves": We need media literacy], October 2, 2012.

76. *New York Times*, February 22, 2014.

77. Hugh White, *The China Choice: Why We Should Share Power* (Oxford:
Oxford University Press, 2013).

78. See, for example, Hiroshi Yuasa, "Great Power Relationship vs. Rebalance: The 'New Model of Great Power Relations' Trap," *Sankei News*,
March 30, 2014, http://watchingamerica.com/WA/2014/04/09/great-power
-relationship-vs-rebalance-the-new-model-of-great-power-relations-trap/.

79. Mike M. Mochizuki, *Japan: Domestic Change and Foreign Policy* (Santa
Monica, Calif.: RAND, 1995).

80. The White House, Office of the Press Secretary, "U.S.-Japan Joint Vision
Statement," April 28, 2015, https://www.whitehouse.gov/the-press-office/
2015/04/28/us-japan-joint-vision-statement.

81. The full text of "The Guidelines for US-Japan Defense Cooperation" is
available at http://www.mofa.go.jp/files/000078188.pdf.

82. "US-Japan Joint Vision Statement," 2.

83. The full text of the 1997 guidelines is reproduced in *Defense of Japan
2014*, 417–20.

84. "Guidelines for US-Japan Defense Cooperation," 3.

85. Ibid., 18.

86. Chanlett-Avery et al., *Japan-U.S. Relations*, 1.

87. Embassy of the United States, Tokyo, Japan, "Statement on Prime Minister Abe's December 26 Visit to Yasukuni Shrine," December 26, 2013,
http://japan.usembassy.gov/e/p/tp-20131226-01.html.

Conclusion: Implications and Next Steps
in Japan's Security Renaissance

1. The panel's full name is the Advisory Panel on the History of the Twentieth Century and on Japan's Role and the World Order in the Twenty-First Century. The report of this panel was issued on August 6, 2015, and is available at http://www.kantei.go.jp/jp/singi/21c_koso/pdf/report_en.pdf.

2. Brad Glosserman and Scott A. Snyder, *The Japan–South Korea Identity Clash: East Asian Security and the United States* (New York: Columbia University Press, 2015), provides an excellent contemporary overview of such opportunities lost and the multiple challenges to attaining that path.

3. Mary M. McCarthy examines this international-domestic linkage in "US Comfort Women Memorials: Vehicle for Understanding and Change," *Asia Pacific Bulletin*, no. 275 (August 12, 2014), http://www.eastwestcenter.org/sites/default/files/private/apb275.pdf.

4. James Steinberg and Michael E. O'Hanlon, *Strategic Reassurance and Resolve: U.S.-China Relations in the Twenty-First Century* (Princeton, N.J.: Princeton University Press, 2014), makes a strong case for seeing the US-China relationship in this manner.

5. Paul Midford, "The Logic of Reassurance and Japan's Grand Strategy," *Security Studies* 11, no. 3 (spring 2002): 1–43, among others, develops this point.

6. Note that Japan does not officially recognize that it has a territorial dispute with China over the Senkaku Islands, despite China's increasingly more strident claims. Japan's position is that the matter was unequivocally settled more than half a century ago, as discussed in chapter 3.

7. For a recent discussion of likely next steps in deepening Japan-Australia security cooperation, see Yuki Tatsumi, ed., *US-Japan-Australia Security Cooperation: Prospects and Challenges* (Washington, DC: Stimson Center, 2015).

8. Glosserman and Snyder, *Japan-South Korea Identity Clash*, reaches a similar conclusion, providing considerable context and support for this view.

9. Bhubhindar Singh, *Japan's Security Identity: From a Peace State to an International State* (London: Routledge, 2013); Lindsay Black, *Japan's Maritime Security Strategy: The Japan Coast Guard and Maritime Outlaws* (New York: Palgrave Macmillan, 2014).

10. The new mission statement and vision for JICA is available at http://www.jica.go.jp/english/about/mission/index.html; it was announced via a Cabinet Statement on February 10, 2015, available at: http://www.mofa.go.jp/files/000067701.pdf. For a critical overview of the changes and continuities

from past ODA policies, see Lian Alfred Santos, "Figuring Out Japan's New Aid Charter," at https://www.devex.com/news/figuring-out-japan-s-new-aid-charter-85520.

11. Dennis Yasutomo provides a compelling and detailed examination of the linkage between Japan's ODA policy and its security policy evolution, focusing on the cases of Afghanistan and Iraq, in *Japan's Civil-Military Diplomacy*.

12. This and other new institutional approaches at JICA were presented by JICA president Akihiko Tanaka at the Brookings Institution in Washington, DC: "Japan's Proactive Contribution to Peace: What It Means in Development," July 27, 2015. An audio transcript is available at http://www.brookings.edu/events/2015/07/27-japan-proactive-contribution-peace.

13. Gerald Curtis, *The Logic of Japanese Politics* (New York: Columbia University Press, 1999), explains the complicated political realignment of the 1990s and the forces that led to it; T. J. Pempel, *Regime Shift: Comparative Dynamics of the Japanese Political Economy* (Ithaca, N.Y.: Cornell University Press, 1998), links these changes to a broader socioeconomic context.

14. Toshi Yoshihara, "Japanese Hard Power: Rising to the Challenge," *National Security Outlook*, August 2014, 11.

15. Douglas McGray wrote about Japan's "gross national cool" in *Foreign Policy* magazine in 2009: http://foreignpolicy.com/2009/11/11/japans-gross-national-cool/.

16. Jeff Kingston, *Japan's Quiet Transformation: Social Change and Civil Society in the Twenty-First Century* (London: RoutledgeCurzon, 2004), and a follow-up edited volume, *Critical Issues in Contemporary Japan* (New York: Routledge, 2014), provide an excellent overview of such broader societal change.

17. R. Taggart Murphy, *Japan and the Shackles of the Past: What Everyone Needs to Know* (Oxford: Oxford University Press, 2014), 385.

18. A broad-based study organized by the global consulting giant McKinsey and Company after the triple disaster of March 2011 contains short essays by over eighty Japan experts across the political-economic-social spectrum arguing for the need to take a fresh look at Japan and its most pressing challenges: *Reimagining Japan: The Quest for a Future That Works* (San Francisco: VIZ Media, 2011).

19. Michael Swaine et al., *China's Military and the U.S.-Japan Alliance in 2030: A Strategic Net Assessment* (Washington, DC: Carnegie Endowment for International Peace, 2013), considers these two, among other, possible scenarios for China—as well as different scenarios for Japan and the United States, setting out the likely security implications of each together with the likelihood of each scenario.

20. Corey J. Wallace, "The Evolution of the Japanese Strategic Imagination and Generation Change: A Generationally-Focused Analysis of Public and Elite Attitudes towards War and Peace in Japan" (PhD diss., University of Auckland, 2014), addresses this issue through elite interviews and a survey of Diet members, contrasting his findings with public opinion polling and previous literature on the subject.

21. Gerald L. Curtis, *The Japanese Way of Politics* (New York: Columbia University Press, 1988), develops this point broadly; Andrew L. Oros, *Normalizing Japan: Politics, Identity, and the Evolution of Security Practice* (Stanford, Calif.: Stanford University Press, 2008), chapters 2, 4, and 5 illustrate this in the context of specific security policies during the Cold War period.

22. When the Ministry of Defense was upgraded in status from Japan Defense Agency in January 2007, the core mission of the ministry was expanded to not only the defense of Japan but also international contributions to peace (*Defense of Japan 2007*, 183–84).

Bibliography

Abe Shinzō. *Atarashii kuni e: Utsukushii kuni e* [Toward a new country: Toward a beautiful country]. Tokyo: Bungei shunju, 2013.

——. "Japan Is Back: A Conversation with Shinzo Abe." *Foreign Affairs*, July / August 2013. https://www.foreignaffairs.com/interviews/2013-05-16/japan-back.

"Anpo hōsei dewa heiwa ni naranai" [The security bill will not make peace]. *SPA!*, September 15, 2015.

"Anpo hōsei mada kutsugaeseru" [We can still overturn the security bill]. *Shūkan pureibōi*, August 3, 2015.

Armitage, Richard L., and Joseph S. Nye, Jr. *The US-Japan Alliance: Getting Asia Right through 2020*. CSIS Report. Washington, DC: Center for Strategic and International Studies, 2007. http://csis.org/files/media/csis/pubs/070216_asia2020.pdf.

Ashizawa, Kuniko. *Japan, the US, and Regional Institution-Building in the New Asia: When Identity Matters*. New York: Palgrave Macmillan, 2013.

Auer, James. "Japan's Military Capability in 2015." SAIS Policy Forum Series, no. 5. Baltimore: Johns Hopkins University, December 1998.

Auer, James, and Robyn Lim. "The Maritime Basis of American Security in East Asia." *Naval War College Review* 54, no. 1 (2001): 39–58.

Auslin, Michael. *Pacific Cosmopolitans: A Cultural History of U.S.-Japan Relations*. Cambridge, Mass.: Harvard University Press, 2011.

"Beitsuishō no Nihonjin wa 'kōfukuna dorei': Media riterashī kakutoku hitsuyō" [US-following Japanese are "happy slaves": We need media literacy]. *Shūkan posuto*, October 2, 2012.

Berger, Thomas U. *Cultures of Antimilitarism: National Security in Germany and Japan.* Baltimore: Johns Hopkins University Press, 1998.

——. *War, Guilt, and World Politics after World War II.* Cambridge: Cambridge University Press, 2012.

Betts, Richard K. "Wealth, Power, and Instability: East Asia and the United States after the Cold War." *International Security* 18, no. 3 (winter 1993–1994): 34–77.

Bix, Herbert. *Hirohito and the Making of Modern Japan.* New York: Harper Collins, 2000.

Black, Lindsay. *Japan's Maritime Security Strategy: The Japan Coast Guard and Maritime Outlaws.* New York: Palgrave Macmillan, 2014.

Bobrow, Davis B. "Japan in the World: Opinion from Defeat to Success." *Journal of Conflict Resolution* 33, no. 4 (December 1989): 571–604.

Boyd, J. Patrick, and Richard J. Samuels. *Nine Lives?: The Politics of Constitutional Reform in Japan.* Policy Studies 19. Washington, DC: East-West Center Washington, 2005.

Bukh, Alexander. "Shimane Prefecture, Tokyo, and the Territorial Dispute over Dokdo/Takeshima: Regional and National Identities in Japan." *Pacific Review* 28, no. 1 (March 2015): 47–70.

Bush, Richard. *The Perils of Proximity: China-Japan Security Relations.* Washington, DC: Brookings Institution, 2010.

Cabinet Secretariat. "Cabinet Decision on Development of Seamless Security Legislation to Ensure Japan's Survival and Protect Its People," July 1, 2014. http://japan.kantei.go.jp/96_abe/decisions/2014/__icsFiles/afieldfile/2014/07/03/anpohosei_eng.pdf.

——. *National Security Strategy: December 17, 2013.* http://www.cas.go.jp/jp/siryou/131217anzenhoshou/nss-e.pdf.

Calder, Kent. *The Pacific Alliance: Reviving U.S.-Japan Relations.* New Haven, Conn.: Yale University Press, 2009.

Calder, Kent, and Francis Fukuyama. *East Asian Multilateralism: Prospects for Regional Security.* Baltimore: Johns Hopkins University Press, 2008.

Calder, Kent, and Min Ye. *The Making of Northeast Asia.* Stanford, Calif.: Stanford University Press, 2010.

Catalinac, Amy. *Electoral Reform and National Security: From Pork to Foreign Policy.* Cambridge: Cambridge University Press, 2016.

Chanlett-Avery, Emma, et al. *Japan-U.S. Relations: Issues for Congress.* CRS Report 7-5700, September 29, 2015. Washington, DC: Congressional Research Service.

Christensen, Thomas J. "China, the U.S.-Japan Alliance, and the Security Dilemma in East Asia." *International Security* 23, no. 4 (spring 1999): 49–80.

Council on Security and Defense Capabilities. *Japan's Vision for Future Security and Defense Capabilities* [Araki Report]. Tokyo, October 2004.

Curtis, Gerald L. *The Japanese Way of Politics.* New York: Columbia University Press, 1988.

———. "Japan's Cautious Hawks: Why Tokyo Is Unlikely to Pursue an Aggressive Foreign Policy." *Foreign Affairs* 92, no. 2 (February 2013): 77–86.

———. *The Logic of Japanese Politics.* New York: Columbia University Press, 1999.

de Koning, Philippe, and Phillip Y. Lipscy. "The Land of the Sinking Sun: Is Japan's Military Weakness Putting America in Danger?" *Foreign Policy,* July 30, 2013. http://foreignpolicy.com/2013/07/30/the-land-of-the-sinking -sun/.

Dian, Matteo. *The Evolution of the US-Japan Alliance: The Eagle and the Chrysanthemum.* Oxford: Chandos, 2014.

Dower, John W. *Embracing Defeat: Japan in the Wake of World War II.* New York: Norton, 1999.

———. *Ways of Forgetting, Ways of Remembering: Japan in the Modern World.* New York: New Press, 2012.

Ehrhardt, George, et al., eds. *Kōmeitō: Politics and Religion in Japan.* Berkeley: Institute of East Asian Studies, University of California, 2014.

Finnegan, Michael. *Managing Unmet Expectations in the US Japan Alliance.* NBR Special Report, no. 17. Seattle: National Bureau of Asian Research, November 2009.

Fouse, David. "Japan's FY 2005 National Defense Program Outline: New Concepts, Old Compromises." *Asia-Pacific Security Studies* 4, no. 3 (March 2005): 2–8

Friedberg, Aaron L. "Ripe for Rivalry: Prospects for Peace in a Multipolar Asia." *International Security* 18, no. 3 (winter 1993–1994): 5–33.

Frost, Ellen. *Asia's New Regionalism.* Boulder, Colo.: Rienner, 2008.

Funabashi, Yoichi. *Alliance Adrift.* New York: Council on Foreign Relations Press, 1999.

Glosserman, Brad, and Scott A. Snyder. *The Japan–South Korea Identity Clash: East Asian Security and the United States.* New York: Columbia University Press, 2015.

Glosserman, Brad, and Tomoko Tsunoda. "The Guillotine: Demographics and Japan's Security Options." *PacNet,* no. 45 (June 17, 2009). http://csis. org/files/publication/pac0945.pdf.

Goh, Evelyn. *The Struggle for Order: Hegemony, Hierarchy, and Transition in Post–Cold War East Asia.* Oxford: Oxford University Press, 2013.

Green, Michael. "Japan Is Back: Unbundling Abe's Grand Strategy." *Analysis,* December 17, 2013. Canberra: Lowy Institute for International Policy. http://www.lowyinstitute.org/files/green_japan_is_back_web_0.pdf.

———. *Japan's Reluctant Realism: Foreign Policy Challenges in an Era of Uncertain Power*. New York: Palgrave, 2001.

———. "Japan's Role in Asia: Searching for Certainty." In *International Relations of Asia*, edited by David Shambaugh and Michael Yahuda, 197–223. 2nd ed. Lanham, Md.: Rowman and Littlefield, 2014.

Green, Michael, and Zack Cooper, eds. *Strategic Japan: New Approaches to Foreign Policy and the US-Japan Alliance*. Washington, DC: Center for Strategic and International Studies, 2015.

Green, Michael, and Patrick Cronin, eds. *The U.S.-Japan Alliance: Past, Present, and Future*. New York: Council on Foreign Relations Press, 1999.

Green, Michael, and Bates Gill. *Asia's New Multilateralism: Cooperation, Competition, and the Search for Community*. New York: Columbia University Press, 2009.

Grønning, Bjørn Elias Mikalsen. "Japan's Shifting Military Priorities: Counterbalancing China's Rise." *Asian Security* 10, no. 1 (2014): 1–21.

Hagström, Linus. "The 'Abnormal' State: Identity, Norm/Exception and Japan." *European Journal of International Relations* 20, no. 2 (2014): 1–24.

Hagström, Linus, and Karl Gustafsson. "Japan and Identity Change: Why It Matters in International Relations." *Pacific Review* 28, no. 1 (March 2015): 1–22.

Hashimoto, Akikazu, Mike Mochizuki, and Kurayoshi Takara, eds. *The Okinawa Question and the U.S.-Japan Alliance*. Washington, DC: George Washington University, Sigur Center for Asian Studies, 2005.

He, Yinan. *The Search for Reconciliation: Sino-Japanese and German-Polish Relations since World War II*. Cambridge: Cambridge University Press, 2009.

Hein, Laura Elizabeth, and Mark Selden, eds. *Islands of Discontent: Okinawan Responses to Japanese and American Power*. Lanham, Md.: Rowman and Littlefield, 2003.

Hook, Glenn D. "The Erosion of Anti-Militaristic Principles in Contemporary Japan." *Journal of Peace Research* 25, no. 4 (December 1988): 381–94.

———. *Language and Politics: The Security Discourse in Japan and the United States*. Tokyo: Kuroshio shuppan, 1990.

———. *Militarization and Demilitarization in Contemporary Japan*. London: Routledge, 1996.

Hornung, Jeffrey. "Japan's Growing Hard Hedge Against China." *Asian Security* 10, no. 2 (2014): 97–122.

———. "Learning How to Sweat: Explaining the Dispatch of Japan's Self-Defense Forces in the Gulf War and Iraq War." PhD diss., George Washington University, 2009.

Hornung, Jeffrey W., and Mike M. Mochizuki. "Japan: Still an Exceptional Ally." *Washington Quarterly* 39, no. 1 (spring 2016): 95–116.

Hornung, Jeffrey, and Andrew L. Oros. "Enhancing U.S.-Japan Defense Co-operation: New Strategies and the Challenges Ahead." In *Challenges Facing Japan: Perspectives from the U.S.-Japan Network for the Future*, 63–74. Washington, DC: Mansfield Foundation, 2014.

Hosokawa, Morihiro. "Are U.S. Troops in Japan Needed? Reforming the Alliance." *Foreign Affairs* 77, no. 4 (July/August 1998): 2–5.

Hughes, Christopher. "The Democratic Party of Japan's New (but Failing) Grand Security Strategy: From 'Reluctant Realism' to 'Resentful Realism'?" In *Japan under the DPJ: The Politics of Transition and Governance*, edited by Kenji E. Kushida and Phillip Y. Lipscy, 333–67. Stanford, Calif.: Walter H. Shorenstein Asia-Pacific Research Center, 2013.

——. *Japan's Foreign and Security Policy under the "Abe Doctrine": New Dynamism or New Dead End?* New York: Palgrave Macmillan, 2015.

——. "Japan's Military Modernization: In Search of a 'Normal' Security Role." In *Strategic Asia 2005–06: Military Modernization in an Era of Uncertainty*, edited by Ashley J. Tellis and Michael Wills, 105–36. Seattle: National Bureau of Asian Research, 2005.

——. *Japan's Re-emergence as a "Normal" Military Power.* New York: Oxford University Press, 2004.

——. *Japan's Remilitarisation.* London: International Institute for Strategic Studies, 2009.

——. "Japan's Response to China's Rise: Regional Engagement, Global Containment, Dangers of Collision." *International Affairs* 85, no. 4 (2009): 837–56.

——. *Japan's Security Agenda: Military, Economic, and Environmental Dimensions.* Boulder, Colo.: Rienner, 2004.

Hughes, Christopher, and Ellis Krauss. "Japan's New Security Agenda." *Survival* 49, no. 2 (summer 2007): 157–76.

Ikegami Akira. *Sekai kara sensō ga nakunaranai hontō no riyū* [True reasons why war will not disappear from the world]. Tokyo: Shōdensha, 2015.

"Ikura heiwashugi o tanaetemo, Nihon wa Isuramukoku ni nerawareru" [Chanting pacifism will not make Japan immune from the Islamic State's threats]. *Sapio*, April 2015.

Inoguchi, Takashi, and G. John Ikenberry. *The Troubled Triangle: Economic and Security Concerns for the United States, Japan, and China.* New York: Palgrave Macmillan, 2013.

Ishikawa Tatsuzō. *Nankin kōryakusen rupo* [Reportage on the Nanking invasion war]. Tokyo: Bungei shunjū, 1999.

Izumikawa, Yasuhiro. "Explaining Japanese Antimilitarism: Normative and Realist Constraints on Japan's Security Policy." *International Security* 35, no. 2 (fall 2010): 123–60.

Jervis, Robert. "Cooperation Under the Security Dilemma." *World Politics* 30, no. 2 (January 1978): 167–214.

Kahn, Herman. *The Emerging Japanese Superstate.* Englewood Cliffs, N.J.: Prentice-Hall, 1970.

Kan, Naoto. "My Vision of a New Party." *Japan Echo* 23, no. 4 (winter 1996): 14–21.

Kang, David. *China Rising: Peace, Power, and Order in East Asia.* New York: Columbia University Press, 2007.

Kaplan, Robert. *Asia's Cauldron: The South China Sea and the End of a Stable Pacific.* New York: Random House, 2014.

Katz, Richard. *Japan: The System That Soured; The Rise and Fall of the Japanese Economic Miracle.* New York: M.E. Sharpe, 1998.

Katzenstein, Peter J. *Cultural Norms and National Security: Police and Military in Postwar Japan.* Ithaca, N.Y.: Cornell University Press, 1996.

Katzenstein, Peter J., and Nobuo Okawara. *Japan's National Security: Structures, Norms, and Policy Responses in a Changing World.* Ithaca, N.Y.: Cornell University East Asia Program, 1993.

Kawasaki, Tsuyoshi. "Postclassical Realism and Japanese Security Policy." *Pacific Review* 14, no. 2 (June 2001): 221–40.

Kingston, Jeff, ed. *Critical Issues in Contemporary Japan.* New York: Routledge, 2014.

——. *Japan's Quiet Transformation: Social Change and Civil Society in the Twenty-First Century.* London: RoutledgeCurzon, 2004.

Kōda Yōji. *Sansei, hantai o iumae no shūdan jieiken nyūmon* [Introduction to collective self-defense, before deciding yes or no]. Tokyo: Gentōsha, 2014.

Konishi, Weston S. *From Rhetoric to Reality: Foreign-Policy Making under the Democratic Party of Japan.* Boston: Institute for Foreign Policy Analysis, 2012.

Krauss, Ellis S., and Robert J. Pekkanen. *The Rise and Fall of Japan's LDP: Political Party Organizations as Historical Institutions.* Ithaca, N.Y.: Cornell University Press, 2011.

Kushida, Kenji E., and Phillip Y. Lipscy, eds. *Japan under the DPJ: The Politics of Transition and Governance.* Stanford, Calif.: Walter H. Shorenstein Asia-Pacific Research Center, 2013.

LaFeber, Walter. *The Clash: U.S.-Japanese Relations throughout History.* New York: Norton, 1997.

Lieberman, Robert C. "Ideas, Institutions, and Political Order: Explaining Political Change." *American Political Science Review* 96, no. 4 (December 2002): 697–712.

Lind, Jennifer. "Pacifism or Passing the Buck? Testing Theories of Japanese Security Policy." *International Security* 29, no. 1 (summer 2004): 92–121.

———. *Sorry States: Apologies in International Politics.* Ithaca, N.Y.: Cornell University Press, 2008.

Manicom, James. *Bridging Troubled Waters: China, Japan, and Maritime Order in the East China Sea.* Washington, DC: Georgetown University Press, 2014.

Matsumoto Kenichi. "(Right Tilt?): Is 'Japan Moves to Right' True? Second Abe Administration Faces Test of Realism." Discuss Japan: Japan Foreign Policy Forum, nos. 13–15, March 5, 2013. http://www.japanpolicyforum. jp/archives/politics/pt20130305180000.html.

Matthews, Ron, and Keisuke Matsuyama, eds. *Japan's Military Renaissance?* New York: St. Martin's Press, 1993.

McCarthy, Mary M. "US Comfort Women Memorials: Vehicle for Understanding and Change." *Asia Pacific Bulletin*, no. 275 (August 12, 2014). http://www.eastwestcenter.org/sites/default/files/private/apb275.pdf.

McCormack, Gavan. *Client State: Japan in the American Embrace.* New York: Verso, 2007.

McKinsey and Company, ed. *Reimagining Japan: The Quest for a Future That Works.* San Francisco: VIZ Media, 2011.

Meyer, Claude. *China or Japan: Which Will Lead Asia?* New York: Columbia University Press, 2011.

Midford, Paul. "Japan's Response to Terror: Dispatching the SDF to the Arabian Sea." *Asian Survey* 43, no. 2 (April 2003): 329–51.

———. "The Logic of Reassurance and Japan's Grand Strategy." *Security Studies* 11, no. 3 (spring 2002): 1–43.

———. *Rethinking Japanese Public Opinion and Security.* Stanford, Calif.: Stanford University Press, 2011.

Ministry of Defense. *Defense of Japan.* Various years.

———. "National Defense Program Guidelines, FY 2005–." December 10, 2004. http://www.mod.go.jp/e/d_act/d_policy/pdf/national_guidelines.pdf.

———. "National Defense Program Guidelines for FY 2011 and Beyond." December 17, 2010. http://www.mod.go.jp/e/d_act/d_policy/pdf/guidelinesFY2011.pdf.

———. "National Defense Program Guidelines for FY 2014 and Beyond." December 17, 2013. http://www.mod.go.jp/j/approach/agenda/guideline/2014/pdf/20131217_e2.pdf.

Miyashita, Akitoshi. "Where Do Norms Come From? Foundations of Japan's Postwar Pacifism." *International Relations of the Asia-Pacific* 7, no. 1 (January 2007): 99–120.

Mochizuki, Mike M. *Japan: Domestic Change and Foreign Policy.* Santa Monica, Calif.: RAND, 1995.

———. "Japan's Search for Strategy." *International Security* 8, no. 3 (winter 1983–1984): 152–79.

———. "Strategic Thinking under Bush and Koizumi: Implications for the U.S.-Japan Alliance." *Asia-Pacific Review* 10, no. 1 (May 2003): 82–98.

———. "The Yasukuni Conundrum: Japan's Contested Identity and Memory." In *Northeast Asia's Difficult Past: Essays in Collective Memory*, edited by Mikyoung Kim and Barry Schwartz, 31–52. New York: Palgrave Macmillan, 2010.

Mochizuki, Mike M., and Samuel Parkinson Porter. "Japan under Abe: Toward Moderation or Nationalism?" *Washington Quarterly* 36, no. 4 (2013): 25–41.

Murphy, R. Taggart. *Japan and the Shackles of the Past: What Everyone Needs to Know*. Oxford: Oxford University Press, 2014.

Naím, Moisés. *The End of Power: From Boardrooms to Battlefields and Churches to States, Why Being in Charge Isn't What It Used to Be*. New York: Basic Books, 2013.

Narusawa Muneo. "Abe Shinzo: Japan's New Prime Minister a Far-Right Denier of History." *Asia-Pacific Journal* 11, no. 1 (January 14, 2013). http://japanfocus.org/-Narusawa-Muneo/3879/article.html.

National Institute for Defense Studies. *East Asian Strategic Review*. Various years.

Nishihara, Masashi. "Expanding Japan's Credible Defense Role." *International Security* 8, no. 3 (winter 1983–84): 180–205.

Nye, Joseph S., Jr. *The Future of Power*. New York: PublicAffairs, 2011.

"Okāsan koso kaiken no maeni chiken" [We mothers need to know about the constitution before the constitution changes]. *VERY*, March 2014.

Okuno Takeo. *Taiheiyō sensō: Heishi to shimin no kiroku* [The Pacific War: A record of soldiers and citizens]. Tokyo: Sōgōsha, 1995.

Oros, Andrew L. "Does Abe's Rightward Shift Threaten His Legacy?" *PacNet*, no. 2 (January 7, 2014). http://csis.org/files/publication/Pac1402.pdf.

———. "International and Domestic Challenges to Japan's Postwar Security Identity: 'Norm Constructivism' and Japan's New 'Proactive Pacifism.'" *Pacific Review* 28, no. 1 (March 2015): 139–60.

———. "Japan's Cabinet Seeks Changes to Its Peace Constitution: Issues New 'Interpretation' of Article Nine." *Asia Pacific Bulletin*, no. 270 (July 1, 2014). http://www.eastwestcenter.org/sites/default/files/private/apb270_0.pdf.

———. "Japan's Strategic Culture: Security Identity in a Fourth Modern Incarnation?" *Contemporary Security Policy* 3, no. 2 (August 2014): 227–48.

———. *Normalizing Japan: Politics, Identity, and the Evolution of Security Practice*. Stanford, Calif.: Stanford University Press, 2008.

Oros, Andrew L., and Weston S. Konishi. "Beyond Haiyan: Toward Greater U.S.-Japan Cooperation in HADR." *NBR Analysis*, February 2014. http://nbr.org/publications/analysis/pdf/brief/020614_Kinoshi-Oros_US-Japan_HADR.pdf.

Oros, Andrew L., and Yuki Tatsumi. *Global Security Watch: Japan*. Santa Barbara: Praeger, 2010.

Ōsaka Iwao. "Sōsharu media ga kaeru seiji to sono genkai" [Politics in the era of social media: Its impact and limits]. *Voters*, February 2012, 10–12.

Ozawa, Ichiro. *Blueprint for a New Japan: The Rethinking of a Nation*. Translated by Louisa Rubinfien. Tokyo: Kodansha International, 1994.

Patalano, Alessio. *Post-war Japan as a Sea Power: Imperial Legacy, Wartime Experience and the Making of a Navy*. London: Bloomsbury Academic, 2015.

Pekkanen, Saadia M., and Paul Kallender-Umezu. *In Defense of Japan: From the Market to the Military in Space Policy*. Stanford, Calif.: Stanford University Press, 2010.

Pempel, T. J. "Japan's Search for the 'Sweet Spot': International Cooperation and Regional Security in Northeast Asia." *Orbis* 55, no. 2 (spring 2011): 255–73.

——. *Regime Shift: Comparative Dynamics of the Japanese Political Economy*. Ithaca, N.Y.: Cornell University Press, 1998.

Pempel, T. J., and Chung-Min Lee, eds. *Security Cooperation in Northeast Asia: Architecture and Beyond*. New York: Routledge, 2012.

Penney, Matthew. "The Abe Cabinet: An Ideological Breakdown." *Asia-Pacific Journal/Japan Focus*. January 2013. http://apjjf.org/-Matthew-Penney/ 4747/article.html.

Pyle, Kenneth B. *Japan Rising: The Resurgence of Japanese Power and Purpose*. New York: PublicAffairs, 2007.

Reed, Steven R., Ethan Scheiner, and Michael F. Thies. "The End of LDP Dominance and the Rise of Party-Oriented Politics in Japan." *Journal of Japanese Studies* 38, no. 2 (summer 2012): 353–76.

Rose, Gideon. "Neoclassical Realism and Theories of Foreign Policy." *World Politics* 51, no. 1 (October 1998): 144–72.

Roy, Denny. *Return of the Dragon: Rising China and Regional Security*. New York: Columbia University Press, 2013.

Samuels, Richard. *Machiavelli's Children: Leaders and Their Legacies in Italy and Japan*. Ithaca, N.Y.: Cornell University Press, 2005.

——. "'New Fighting Power!' Japan's Growing Maritime Capabilities and East Asian Security." *International Security* 32, no. 3 (winter 2007/2008): 84–112.

——. *Securing Japan: Tokyo's Grand Strategy and the Future of East Asia*. Ithaca, N.Y.: Cornell University Press, 2007.

Schaller, Michael. *Altered States: The United States and Japan since the Occupation*. New York: Oxford University Press, 1997.

"Sebuntīnzu de kangaeyō sengo nanajūnen" [Let's think about the seventy years of the postwar period at the age of seventeen]. *Sebuntīn*, September 2015.

Shambaugh, David. *China Goes Global: The Partial Power*. Oxford: Oxford University Press, 2013.

———, ed. *Power Shift: China and Asia's New Dynamics.* Berkeley: University of California Press, 2005.

Shambaugh, David, and Michael Yahuda, eds. *International Relations of Asia.* 2nd ed. Lanham, Md.: Rowman and Littlefield, 2014.

Shibusawa, Naoko. *America's Geisha Ally: Reimagining the Japanese Enemy.* Cambridge, Mass.: Harvard University Press, 2010.

Shinoda, Tomohito. *Contemporary Japanese Politics: Institutional Changes and Power Shifts.* New York: Columbia University Press, 2013.

———. *Koizumi Diplomacy: Japan's Kantei Approach to Foreign and Defense Affairs.* Seattle: University of Washington Press, 2007.

Singh, Bhubhindar. *Japan's Security Identity: From a Peace State to an International State.* London: Routledge, 2013.

Smith, Sheila A. *Intimate Rivals: Japanese Domestic Politics and a Rising China.* New York: Columbia University Press, 2015.

———. *Japan's New Politics and the U.S.-Japan Alliance.* Washington, DC: Council on Foreign Relations Press, July 2014.

Sneider, Daniel. "The New Asianism: Japanese Foreign Policy under the Democratic Party of Japan." In *Japan under the DPJ: The Politics of Transition and Governance,* edited by Kenji E. Kushida and Phillip Y. Lipscy, 369–402. Stanford, Calif.: Walter H. Shorenstein Asia-Pacific Research Center, 2013.

Soeya Yoshihide. *Nihon no "midoru pawā" gaikō* [Japan's middle-power diplomacy]. Tokyo: Chikuma shobō, 2005.

Soeya Yoshihide, Masayuki Tadokoro, and David A. Welsh, eds. *Japan as a "Normal" Country? A Nation in Search of Its Place in the World.* Toronto: University of Toronto Press, 2011.

Steinberg, James, and Michael E. O'Hanlon. *Strategic Reassurance and Resolve: U.S.-China Relations in the Twenty-First Century.* Princeton, N.J.: Princeton University Press, 2014.

Stockholm International Peace Research Institute. SIPRI Military Expenditure Database 2015. http://www.sipri.org/research/armaments/milex/.

"Sugomu dake no Abe gaikō wa Kimu Jon'un, Shū Kinpei, Paku Kune, Pūchin ni kanzen ni namerareteiru" [Abe's intimidation diplomacy totally played around by Kim Jong Un, Xi Jinping, Pak Geun-hye, and Putin]. *Shūkan posuto,* November 11, 2014.

Sun, Jing. *Japan and China as Charm Rivals: Soft Power in Regional Diplomacy.* Ann Arbor: University of Michigan Press, 2012.

Sunohara Tsuyoshi. *Nihonban NSC to wa nani ka* [What is the Japan-style NSC?]. Tokyo: Shinchōsha, 2014.

Suzuki, Shogo. "The Rise of the Chinese 'Other' in Japan's Construction of Identity: Is China a Focal Point of Japanese Nationalism?" *Pacific Review* 28, no. 1 (March 2015): 95–116.

Swaine, Michael, et al. *China's Military and the U.S.-Japan Alliance in 2030: A Strategic Net Assessment.* Washington, DC: Carnegie Endowment for International Peace, 2013.

Takagi, Masayuki. "The Japanese Right Wing." *Japan Quarterly* 36, no. 3 (July–September 1989): 300–305.

Takahara Akio and Hattori Ryūji, eds. *Nitchū kankeishi, 1972–2012* [A history of Japan-China relations, 1972–2012]. Tokyo: University of Tokyo Press, 2012.

Tatsumi, Yuki. "Self-Defense Forces Today—Beyond an Exclusively Defense-Oriented Posture?" In *Japan's New Defense Establishment: Institutions, Capabilities, and Implications*, edited by Yuki Tatsumi and Andrew L. Oros, 23–46. Washington, DC: Stimson Center, 2007.

——, ed. *US-Japan-Australia Security Cooperation: Prospects and Challenges.* Washington, DC: Stimson Center, 2015.

Tellis, Ashley J., and Travis Tanner, eds. *Strategic Asia 2012–13: China's Military Challenge.* Washington, DC: National Bureau of Asian Research, 2011.

Tellis, Ashley J., Travis Tanner, and Jessica Keough, eds. *Strategic Asia 2011–12: Asia Responds to Its Rising Powers, China and India.* Washington, DC: National Bureau of Asian Research, 2011.

Togo, Kazuhiko. "The Assertive Conservative Right in Japan: Their Formation and Perspective." *SAIS Review of International Affairs* 30, no. 1 (winter–spring 2010): 77–89.

——. "Greater Self-Assertion and Nationalism in Japan." *Copenhagen Journal of Asian Studies* 21 (2005): 8–44.

——. *Japan's Foreign Policy 1945–2003: The Quest for a Proactive Policy.* Leiden: Brill, 2005.

Tow, William, ed. *Security Politics in the Asia-Pacific: A Regional-Global Nexus?* Cambridge: Cambridge University Press, 2009.

Tow, William, and Rikki Kersten, eds. *Bilateral Perspectives on Regional Security: Australia, Japan and the Asia-Pacific Region.* Basingstoke, U.K.: Palgrave Macmillan, 2012.

Toyota Aritsune. *Kokubō onchi ga kuni o horobosu* ["Defense tone deafness" will destroy our nation]. Tokyo: Shōdensha, 2015.

Tsuda Daisuke et al. *Abe seiken no netto senryaku* [The Abe government's "net" strategy]. Tokyo: Tsukuru shuppan, 2013.

Twomey, Christopher P. "Japan, a Circumscribed Balancer: Building on Defensive Realism to Make Predictions about East Asian Security." *Security Studies* 9, no. 4 (summer 2000): 167–205.

Umehara Takashi et al. *Kenpō kyūjō wa watashitachi no anzen soshō desu* [Our security rests on Article Nine]. Tokyo: Iwanami shoten, 2015.

Vosse, Wilhelm, Reinhard Drifte, and Verena Blechinger-Talcott, eds. *Governing Insecurity in Japan: The Domestic Discourse and Policy Response.* New York: Routledge, 2014.

Wallace, Corey J. "The Evolution of the Japanese Strategic Imagination and Generation Change: A Generationally-Focused Analysis of Public and Elite Attitudes towards War and Peace in Japan." PhD diss., University of Auckland, 2014.

——. "Japan's Strategic Pivot South: Diversifying the Dual Hedge." *International Relations of the Asia-Pacific*, 2013, 479–517.

Wan, Ming. *Sino-Japanese Relations: Interaction, Logic, and Transformation.* Stanford, Calif.: Stanford University Press, 2006.

Watanabe Tsuneo. "Abe shushō ni tsutaetai 'waga taikenteki Yasukuni-ron'" [Message to Prime Minister Abe: My experiential Yasukuni theory]. *Bungeishunjū*, September 2014.

Westad, Odd Arne. *Restless Empire: China and the World Since 1750.* New York: Basic Books, 2012.

White, Hugh. *The China Choice: Why We Should Share Power.* Oxford: Oxford University Press, 2013.

Wilkins, Thomas S. "The Japan Choice: Reconsidering the Risks and Opportunities of the 'Special Relationship' for Australia." *International Relations of the Asia-Pacific*, 2015. doi:10.1093/irap/lcv025.

Yahuda, Michael. *Sino-Japanese Relations after the Cold War: Two Tigers Sharing a Mountain.* New York: Routledge, 2013.

Yamada Atsutoshi. "Sensō o shiranai Abe seiken no bōsō o ureru riberaru-ha no chōrōtachi" [Liberal elders lament the runaway Abe administration ignorant of war]. *Keizaikai*, August 5, 2014.

Yamaguchi, Noboru. "Evolution of Japan's National Security Policy under the Abe Administration." *Asan Forum*, April 11, 2014. http://www.theasanforum.org/evolution-of-japans-national-security-policy-under-the-abe-administration/.

Yamazaki Nozomu, ed. *Kimyōna nashonarizumu no jidai: Haigaishugi ni kōshite* [The era of odd nationalism: Defying jingoism]. Tokyo: Iwanami shoten, 2015.

Yasutomo, Dennis T. *Japan's Civil-Military Diplomacy: The Banks of the Rubicon.* New York: Routledge, 2014.

"Yomigaeru gunkokushugi: Sengo nanajūnen tokushū" [Resurging militarism: Special issue on seventy years since the war]. *Shūkan kin'yōbi*, July 31, 2015.

Yomiuri Shimbun. *Who Was Responsible? From Marco Polo Bridge to Pearl Harbor.* Tokyo: Yomiuri Shimbun, 2006.

Yoshihara, Toshi. "Japanese Hard Power: Rising to the Challenge." *National Security Outlook*, August 2014.

Index

Abe, Shinzō (*continued*)
171, 179, 184, 216n39; and South
Korea–Japan relations, 105, 106,
126, 142, 164; statement on seventi-
eth anniversary of ending of World
War II, 26, 53, 146, 184, 199–203;
term lengths of, 102–3, 127, 167; and
US–Japan alliance, 32, 104, 105, 106,
156, 160, 162, 186; and Yasukuni
Shrine, 24, 81, 144, 145, 146, 165,
234n35
Abe Doctrine, 143–44, 233n33
acquisition and cross-servicing agreement (ACSA), 114
Advisory Panel on Japan's Role and the
World Order in the Twenty-First
Century, 207–8n18
Advisory Panel on the History of the
Twentieth Century, 52, 54, 55, 60,
146, 172, 207–8n18, 216n39, 218n51,
220n79
Advisory Panel on the Reconstruction
of the Legal Basis for Security, 140
Afghanistan, 31, 44, 45, 63, 90, 97, 178,
229n31
air-defense network, 40–41
Al Qaeda, 44
anti-submarine warfare (ASW) network, 40
Anti-Terrorism Special Measures Law
(2001), 44
APEC (Asia-Pacific Economic Cooperation), 90
arms export restrictions: and Abe's
NDPG of 2013, 100; Abe's relaxation policies of 2014, 8, 33, 57, 92,
93, 128, 151, 176, 178; and Japan's
regional security partnerships, 92,
93, 176; principles of, 139–40; public
opinion of, 8, 151; and US–Japan
alliance, 57
Article Nine of Japan's postwar constitution: Abe's interpretation of, 9,
22, 32, 104, 105, 106, 133, 153–54,
206n9, 227n12, 237n60; Diet's efforts to change, 48, 60, 106, 133,
152, 216n41, 236–37n60; and postwar antimilitarist security practices,
3–4, 28, 152–54, 236–37n60; public

opposition to changes in, 8–9, 15,
152, 182; text of, 205n2
ASEAN (Association of Southeast
Asian Nations): and Abe's meetings
with head of states, 142; defense
spending of ASEAN-8, 72, 88; GDP
of, 70, 70, 71, 72; Japan's security
partnership with, 97, 175; members
of, 206n7; and regional economic
growth, 5; and regional security
engagement, 67; US–ASEAN outreach, 91
ASEAN Defense Minister's Meeting–
Plus (ADMM+), 94
ASEAN Regional Forum (ARF), 90,
93, 94
Asia: defense spending in region, 67,
71, 72, 88–89; and implications of
Japan's security renaissance, 9, 168,
175–77; multipolar nature of, 7–8,
67, 88, 183; security environment of,
4–5, 16, 34, 66, 67; studies of nationalist sentiment in, 147–48; and US
rebalance policy, 9, 67, 69, 71, 89–92,
121, 132, 174. *See also* East Asia;
South Asia; Southeast Asia
Asia Barometer, 147–48
Asian Women's Fund, 52–53, 218n54
Asō, Tarō, 98, 99, 101, 104, 105,
109–10, 116
atomic bombings of Japan, 26, 27, 29,
48–49, 54, 216–17n43
Auer, James, 41
Australia: Abe's meeting with head of
state of, 142; and China, 161, 176;
and Japan's historical reconciliation,
51–52; Japan's security partnership
with, 9, 23, 77, 86, 92, 93, 97, 106,
109, 114, 117, 125, 156–57, 159, 176,
229n34; and regional distribution
of power, 9; and regional security
engagement, 67; and trilateral
cooperation, 164; and US–Japan
alliance, 159

Battle of Iwo Jima, 162
Berger, Thomas U., 49, 50, 54, 210–
11n45, 217n48
Bitzinger, Richard A., 224n38

Black, Lindsay, 177
Blair, Dennis, 231–32n12
Britain, 41
Bungeishunjū, 52
Bush, George W., 63, 64, 82, 90, 104, 162, 185

Cabinet Legislative Bureau (CLB), 153
Cambodia, 175
Carnegie Endowment for International Peace, 94
Chiavacci, David, 221n9
Chidorigafuchi National Cemetery, 165
China: Asian states aligned with, 175; asymmetrical warfare strategy, 85; and Cold War, 50; defense planning documents of, 85; defense spending of, 42, 67, 71, 72, 84, 86–87, 88, 88, 96, 114, 183, 224n38, 225n47; demographic challenges of, 75; economic growth of, 4, 10, 13, 16, 19, 62, 66, 80, 84, 85–86, 89, 96, 114, 161, 179, 181, 183, 208n25; GDP of, 36, 36, 70, 70, 71, 73, 89, 89, 99; Japan's peace treaty with, 27, 51, 217n49; manned space flight of, 214n20; maritime claims of, 78–79; military capabilities of, 4, 13, 16, 18, 19, 43, 67, 68, 69, 76, 77, 79, 81, 83, 84, 85, 86, 90, 91, 117, 121, 161, 170, 176, 179, 187; missile testing of, 43; nationalists of, 82; and North Korea, 77, 87; nuclear weapons of, 42, 77, 79, 86, 87; and Philippines, 93–94, 131, 175; population of, 73; postwar civil war of, 39, 77; as regional power, 19; security planning of, 9, 18; social media in, 24; soft power of, 181; as super-aged society, 75; and Taiwan, 20, 43, 77, 182; US normalization with, 80, 161; Western imperialism as threat to, 11
China–Japan relations: and Abe, 4, 81, 99, 105, 106, 107, 126, 131, 142, 145, 164; and China's military capabilities, 77, 79, 81, 84, 85, 86, 94, 124; and Chinese military and quasi-military actions, 84–85, 86, 87; and competition over influence in Southeast Asia and Oceania, 86;

and defense spending, 86–87; and domestic political environment, 113, 114; and Hatoyama, 92, 112, 114; and historical reconciliation, 81, 107, 142, 143, 174, 223–24n32; history of, 80–82, 223n27; and Japanese foreign direct investment, 4, 80, 81; and Japanese militarism, 50, 51, 53, 142, 147; Japanese perception of Chinese threat, 86, 87, 99, 100, 116, 150–51, 225n46; and Japanese public opinion, 116, 129, 149, 150–51; and Japan's regional security partnerships, 92, 94; and Japan's security policies, 129, 174, 183; and JSP, 56; and Koizumi, 81, 82, 120, 145; and mitigating factors, 87, 224–25n44; and multinational earthquake relief, 142, 233n29; and Noda, 120, 168; regional rivalry of, 67; and security dilemma, 18, 79–80, 85; and Senkaku Islands, 19, 21, 23, 27, 35, 61, 68, 82–84, 87, 97, 99, 112, 119–20, 121, 131, 132, 145, 160–61, 168, 174, 177, 209n34, 239n6; and territorial disputes, 19, 27, 49, 50, 142, 209–10n34, 222n17; and tourism, 80; and trade, 4, 80, 81, 84, 86; and US–Japan alliance, 85, 86, 87, 150, 160–61, 173–75, 177, 185, 231n6
China Security Reports, 84
Clinton, Hillary, 90, 109
Clinton-Okada joint statement, 115
Cold War: and China, 50; division of Asia, 27; emergence of, 39–40; ending of, 4, 27–28, 35, 41; Japan's balancing Soviet military threat during, 38, 40, 222n17; Japan's military policies during, 38, 41, 206n8; and Japan's security policies, 56–57, 78; and nuclear weapons, 39–40; and US–Japan relations, 32, 59, 61, 103. *See also* post–Cold War period
collective self-defense (CSD) activities: Abe's commission on, 106, 153; as antimainstream position, 22, 41; and Article Nine of Japan's postwar constitution, 153–54; Japanese public opinion on, 8, 151–52, 154,

East Asia: China's role in, 4; defense spending of states in, *88*; demographics of, 75; economic growth of states in, 10, 66, 88, 95, 182; institutional networks of, 94–95; Japanese expansion in, 12, 26, 27, 83, 141; and Japan's security renaissance, 173, 188; maritime security in, 78, 79; military growth of states in, 10, 66; multilateral approaches to security in, 94; population in, 73; and regional security concerns, 76–79, 150, 163, 188; security dilemma in, 18; territorial disputes in, 27; US involvement in, 9, 90, 164

East Asian Strategic Review 2014, 134
East Asian Summit (EAS), 94
East China Sea, 81, 82, 84–85, 109, 114, 176
Enola Gay, 217n43
Europe: coalitions of, 130; defense spending in region, 67; East Asia compared to, 78; European powers' postwar retreat from global empires, 39; and Russia, 166; shift to right in, 148
European Renaissance, changes in Japan's security policies compared to, 3–6, 7, 29, 32, 169–70
exclusive economic zone (EEZ), 11, 82

Fishing Trawler Incident of 2010, 82–83, 101, 112, 116, 120, 134
Foreign Affairs, 145–46
France, 76
Fukuda, Takeo, 52, 108
Fukuda, Yasuo, 82, 98, 99, 101, 105, 107, 108–9
Fukuda Doctrine, 52, 108
Fukushima nuclear power plant, 69
Funabashi, Yoichi, 237n66

Germany: demographics of, 74; GDP of, 36, *36*; military capabilities of, 76
global financial crisis of 2008 (Lehman shocks), 13, 90, 105, 109, 113
Global Firepower, 76, 222n14
Glosserman, Brad, 54, 86, 147–48

Google, 6
gray-zone conflicts: and NDPGs, 21, 118, 132, 138; and Senkaku Islands, 183; and US–Japan Guidelines for Defense Cooperation, 163
Great Hanshin earthquake of 1995, 226n5
Greece, 74
Green, Michael, 208n20, 211n45
Grønning, Bjørn, 85
Guam, 187
Gulf of Aden, 1, 14, 69, 78, 79, 159

Hagel, Chuck, 165
Hatoyama, Yukio: cabinet appointments of, 111; on China–Japan relations, 92, 112, 114; founding of DPJ, 108, 124; institutional reforms of, 116; Noda compared to, 119; and Obama, 90, 113; resignation of, 117; on US–Japan alliance, 32, 99, 102, 113–15, 117, 125; and US–Japan relations, 101, 113, 114, 115, 168, 229n31
Hirohito (emperor of Japan), 13, 27, 52
Hiroshima, atomic bombing of, 26, 49, 217n43
history issues: Abe on historical narrative, 14–15, 51, 53, 54, 55, 60, 105, 107, 125, 126, 141–47, 172, 207–8n18, 227n12, 234n37; and contemporary Japanese history course, 172; and domestic political environment, 37, 54, 96–97, 100–101, 143, 147, 158, 162, 165; and historical reconciliation, 27, 37, 49, 50, 51–54, 81, 120, 125, 141, 144, 172, 174, 217nn47, 48, 51, 229n34, 234n37; and historical revisionism, 5, 56, 126, 146, 148, 164; influence on Japan's security practices, 14–15, 24–32, 33, 37–38, 55, 65, 96–97, 100, 113, 126, 128, 133, 141, 146, 169–70, 172, 174, 184, 185–86, 229n34; and Japanese colonialism, 25, 26, 27, 33, 35, 37, 38, 48–55, 101, 113, 120, 126, 142, 143, 172, 183–84, 198–99; and Japanese militarism, 48–55, 101,

and postwar antimilitarist policies, 41, 56; SDP as successor to, 111; and US–Japan alliance, 59, 112

Japan's security identity: and cooperation with states other than US, 157; and cyberspace, 78; evolution of, 18, 33, 37, 67, 125, 150, 152; and outer space, 78; and post–Cold War period, 45; and postwar antimilitary policies, 18, 28–29, 35, 37, 55, 56, 57–58, 150, 155, 206n8, 218n65, 218–19n67; role of political parties in, 57–58, 67, 68

Japan's security policies: and airspace, 78; and Cold War, 56–57, 78; and cyberspace, 157, 163; and development of military capabilities, 9, 12, 23, 35, 38, 39, 40–41, 42, 43, 46–47, 55, 58, 64, 65, 68, 75, 76, 77, 79, 83, 97, 105, 123, 127, 129, 131–32, 134–35, 137, 138, 222n15, 227n12; domestic component of, 10, 13, 21–24, 29, 34, 37, 47–48, 49, 56, 68, 87, 96, 98–102, 104–10, 122–23, 125, 126, 213n8; evolution of, 33, 37, 38–48, 55, 64, 65, 77, 97, 122–23, 150, 176, 179; international component of, 19–21, 23, 67, 123; and international-domestic interactive dynamic, 13, 15–24, 17, 32–33, 68, 87, 123; and international security environment, 2, 9, 16–21, 23, 31, 33, 38, 55, 65, 67–68, 79, 112, 121, 123, 124, 125, 126, 127, 130, 132, 150, 216n39; Japanese elites' responses to, 7, 8, 152; and maritime security, 78; military security, 20–21, 36, 38, 39, 40, 41, 42, 43, 213n8; misleading narratives of, 33, 38, 41; and normalization discourse, 10, 15, 38, 46, 103, 124, 207nn14, 15, 226n2; and ODA, 139–40, 178, 181, 233n26, 240n11; and outer space, 139, 140, 163, 232n24; political discourse on, 21–24, 72; and post–Cold War period, 33, 37, 38, 46, 52, 65, 103, 134, 178; and postwar antimilitarist security, 99, 122, 125, 132, 150–58; postwar

legacies of, 12; and pragmatism, 1, 2; and proactive contributions to peace, 14, 38, 50, 137, 139, 140, 141, 149, 166, 170, 171, 178, 181, 184, 208n23; public responses to, 7, 8–9; and regional security environment, 2, 4–5, 8, 9, 13, 16, 19–21, 33, 38, 67–70, 76–79, 87, 99, 122, 124, 138–39, 143, 150–51, 157; resiliency of, 118–19; and seamless defense approach to, 134–35, 138, 139, 163–64, 173; and types of threats, 10–11; and US–Japan alliance, 12, 15, 36, 37, 39, 52, 68, 99, 106, 122, 123, 137, 138, 213n10

Japan's security renaissance: Abe's efforts to advance, 127, 167; China's leading role in, 79–87, 183; and civilian-military interaction, 155–56, 237n66; and coalition building, 111; and domestic political environment, 95, 96–97, 100, 101, 104, 111, 112, 125, 128–29, 171, 184–85; and DPJ rule, 231n3; European Renaissance compared to, 3–6, 7, 29, 32, 169–70; future of, 34, 179–85, 188; and history issues, 141–43, 146, 166, 169–70, 172, 184; implications for Asia, 9, 168, 175–77; implications for Japan, 171–72; implications for US, 173–75; implications of, 7–10, 168, 169, 170–78; institutionalization of, 123–25, 166, 169; and international security environment, 100, 166, 168, 170–71, 177–78, 179, 187, 188; and Japanese militarism, 143; JSDF officers' role in defense planning, 155–56, 169, 187–88; and JSDF training, 161; national security strategy of 2013, 7, 9, 12, 14, 19, 33–34, 55, 91, 106, 133, 137, 139, 149, 150, 155, 157, 213n11; and postwar antimilitarist security, 149–58; and regional security dynamics, 87, 92–94, 96, 156–57, 168, 170, 182–83, 187, 188; relationship to past practices, 6–7, 9, 14, 33, 126, 130, 136, 139–40, 141, 146, 171,

Japan's security renaissance (*continued*)
187–88, 232n24; steps toward, 33,
37, 47, 54, 64, 65, 101, 107, 170, 177;
and US–Japan alliance, 159–68; and
US–Japan Guidelines for Defense
Cooperation, 163; and US rebalancing policy, 9, 89–90, 91, 174
Joint Declaration on Security (1996),
44, 63
Joint Staff Office, 137–38, 156
Jordan, 178

Kallender-Umezu, Paul, 232n24
Kamei, Shizuka, 238n73
Kan, Naoto: cabinet appointments
of, 111; founding of DPJ, 108, 124;
popularity of, 116; proposal for
revision of US–Japan Guidelines for
Defense Cooperation, 163; resignation of, 118; security policies of,
102, 115–19; and Senkaku Islands,
23, 101, 112; statement on one-
hundredth anniversary of Japan-
Korea annexation treaty, 120, 198–99
Kaplan, Robert, 72, 78
Katō, Kōichi, 22
Kawano, Katsutoshi, 156
Kerry, John, 165
Kim Jong Un, 77, 120
Kimura, Hikaru, 217n47
Kishi, Nobusuke: "Basic Policy for National Defense" approved by cabinet,
40, 213n10; foreign policy agenda of,
103; and historical reconciliation,
51–52; and historical revisionism,
56; internationalist school of, 22;
political rehabilitation of, 60, 127;
political reign of, 207n14; release
from prison for war crimes, 59, 127;
in Tōjō cabinet, 227n10; and US–
Japan relations, 30, 59, 162
Kitaoka, Shin'ichi, 140
Kitazawa, Toshimi, 114
Koizumi, Juni'ichirō: and George W.
Bush, 63, 64, 82, 90, 104, 162, 185;
and China–Japan relations, 81, 82,
120, 145; internationalist school of,
22; and LDP faction system, 101;

popularity of, 13, 64, 97, 105, 123;
security policies of, 38, 48, 65, 97,
98, 103, 104, 105, 107, 109, 117, 123,
124, 141, 152; and special measures
laws, 44; statement on sixtieth anniversary of end of World War II, 53,
196–98, 234n37; term length of, 102;
and US–Japan alliance, 63, 109, 123,
141, 156; and Yasukuni Shrine visits,
53, 81, 145
Kōmei Party: LDP's alliance with, 98,
107, 110, 130–31, 154, 163, 167;
name of, 207n12; peace agenda of,
56–57; and proportional representation votes, 130; security approaches
of, 8, 21, 122, 130, 131; and single-
member district votes, 130, 131
Kongō-class destroyers, 46
Konishi, Weston, 111, 112, 228n26,
230n40
Kōno, Yōhei, statement on comfort
women, 26, 52, 105, 142, 144–45,
146, 174, 193–94, 234n37, 235n43
Kōno Statement Denial Caucus, 235n43
Korean Constitutional Court, 120
Korean Peninsula, 12, 27, 63, 120, 142,
182. *See also* North Korea; South
Korea
Korean War, 5, 39, 50–51
Kumagai, Naoko, 218n54
Kushida, Kenji E., 229nn37, 39
Kyodo News, 151

Law Concerning Special Measures on
Humanitarian and Reconstruction
Assistance (2003), 44
Lee Myung-bak, 91, 120
Lehman shocks (global financial crisis
of 2008), 13, 90, 105, 109, 113
Liberal Democratic Party (LDP): Abe
as president of, 166–67, 179; and
Abe's return to power, 128, 129;
and alternating political power with
DPJ, 7, 8, 13–14, 52, 53, 65, 95, 96,
97, 98, 99, 101, 103–4, 107, 110, 112,
119, 128–29, 130, 131; and Article
Nine changes, 9, 60, 104, 152, 153,
154; coalition with JSP, 208n22; in

Cold War period, 56; and economic issues, 129; factions of, 21–22, 24, 56, 99, 101, 108, 122; and history issues, 147, 184; Ishihara on, 23; Kōmei Party's alliance with, 98, 107, 110, 130–31, 154, 163, 167; and Kōmei Party's security approaches, 8, 21, 122, 130, 131; loss to rival coalition, 226n1; and postwar antimilitarist policies, 41, 57; and pragmatism in security policies, 2; right of center security policies of, 21, 22, 23; security policies of, 2, 21, 22, 23, 98–100, 102, 103, 108–9, 112, 115, 116, 122, 123, 129, 153, 169, 184; and shift to right, 147, 148; and South Korea, 105; study of Kōnō statement, 144–45; and US–Japan alliance, 59, 64–65, 119; and Yasukuni Shrine, 147

Liberal Party, 108

Lim, Robyn, 41

Lind, Jennifer, 54, 210n43

Lipscy, Phillip Y., 229nn37, 39

Lower House: and division of power in Japan's Diet, 98, 226n3; and DPJ loss of 2012, 23, 121, 168; and DPJ victory of 2009, 96, 98, 104, 110, 128, 229n31; elections of December 2018, 167, 179; and Japanese electoral system, 102, 128–29, 226n6; LDP loss in Okinawa, 165; LDP victory of 2012, 98, 121, 128, 130, 148; LDP victory of 2014, 98, 130, 148; percentage of party vote and seats in national elections, *191*; SMD in, 111, 128, 130–31; voter turnout for elections, 182

MacArthur, Douglas, 29

Maehara, Seiji, 117

mainstream media: and Abenomics, 129; on Abe's cabinet, 235n44; and Abe's nationalism, 130; on arms export restrictions, 139; on Article Nine interpretation, 152; and China–Japan relations, 149; on Chinese economic challenge,

85–86; on Chinese military actions, 84; effect of new media on, 24; on historical legacy of World War II, 50, 53, 141, 143, 144–45, 234n35; on Japanese nationalism, 147, 148; on military security, 43; on public demonstrations against Abe, 230n1; on regional security environment, 66; on security policies, 3–4, 99, 182; on twisted Diet, 98

Malaysia, 71, 94

Manchukuo, 12

Manchuria, 27

Mansfield, Mike, 174

March 11, 2011 triple disaster: and Japan's energy imports, 66, 68–69; logistical challenges of, 118; and US–Japan alliance, 185; and US military assistance to Japan, 31, 101, 118, 119, 124–25, 160

Matsumoto, Kenichi, 227n10

media. *See* mainstream media; new media; social media

Middle East, 43, 71, 132, 166

Mid-Term Defense Plan (MTDP), 40, 137, 138, 139, 154–55, 157, 213n11

Miki, Takeo, 103

Ministry of Defense (MOD): annual defense white papers of, 84, 115, 136, 213n11; core mission of, 186, 241n22; creation of, 1, 14, 105, 135, 241n22; and defense spending, 46, 215n32; and National Security Council, 134, 135, 155–56; and NDPG, 155; and overseas deployments, 215n30; and security cooperation, 93, 158, 187–88; and state secrets, 135–36, 231–32n12

Ministry of Economy, Trade, and Industry (METI), 134

Ministry of Foreign Affairs (MOFA), 133, 151

Ministry of Land, Infrastructure, Transport, and Tourism, 134

Mitsubishi Materials, 217n47

Mitsubishi Mining, 217n47

Miyako Strait, 84

Mochizuki, Mike M., 222n15, 233n27

Murayama, Tomiichi: on Abe's security policies, 127; foreign policy agenda of, 103; statement on fiftieth anniversary of end of World War II, 26, 53, 144, 146, 194–96, 234n37

Murphy, R. Taggart, 181, 227n12

Myanmar, 91, 94, 175

Nagasaki, atomic bombing of, 26

Nakaima, Hirokazu, 165

Nakasone, Yasuhiro: and historical reconciliation, 52; internationalist school of, 22; security policies of, 103, 134; term length of, 102; and Yasukuni Shrine visits, 53

National Defense Program Guidelines (NDPGs): and amphibious assault capabilities, 84, 118; and China–Japan relations, 99, 100, 124; comparison of changes in Japan's military forces, 45–47, 45; comparison of personnel and major equipment, 138, 138; dynamic joint defense concept in, 32, 100, 117, 138, 157; and gray-zone conflicts, 21, 118, 132, 138; and Japan's cooperation with countries other than US, 157; and Japan's development of military capabilities, 40, 97, 117, 118, 124, 138–39, 157; and Japan's security strategy, 128, 135, 137–38, 154–55, 213n11; and MOD, 155; and regional security environment, 100, 115; and repositioning of Japan's military forces, 7, 19, 23, 100, 115, 116, 117; and US–Japan alliance, 104, 124

National Defense Program Outlines (NDPOs), 40, 42, 117

National Institute for Defense Studies, 84, 156

National Police Agency, 231n7

National Security Council (NSC): creation of, 32, 106, 128, 133, 137, 155; and crisis management, 133, 231n7; and Four-Minister Meeting, 134, 135; and Ministry of Defense, 14, 134, 135, 155–56; and Nine-Minister Meeting, 134, 231n11; structure of, 1, 134–35, 138, 155–56

National Security Secretariat (NSS), 133, 134–35

NATO, 62, 106

New Frontier Party, 108

new media: and Abe's net strategy, 6, 24, 206n10; on China–Japan relations, 149; political extremes empowered by, 24, 147. See also social media

Nippon Hoso Kyokai (NHK), 149, 150, 160

Nippon Kaigi (Japan Conference), 147

Nixon, Richard, 51

Nobel Peace Prize, 103, 137

Noda, Yoshihiko: cabinet appointments of, 228n24; and China–Japan relations, 120, 168; and Ozawa, 121; security policies of, 97, 102, 119–23; and Senkaku Islands, 23, 113, 119–20, 210n40; and South Korea–Japan relations, 120; and US–Japan alliance, 119

Nodong missile tests, 20

Nonaka, Hiromu, 22

nonstate actors, 19, 44

Northern Territories, 42, 51, 166, 216n42

North Korea: abduction of Japanese citizens during Cold War, 51, 105; and China, 77, 87; defense spending of, 71; GDP of, 36; Japanese public opinion on, 149; Japan's adversarial relationship with, 27, 49, 51, 66; Japan's response to military threat of, 8, 13, 16, 17, 20, 42–43, 66–67, 68, 77, 121, 131; and JSP, 56; militarized border, 77; military capabilities of, 20, 42–43, 77, 121, 161; missile tests over Japan, 16, 17, 20, 35, 42–43, 66, 183, 214n20, 226n5; nuclear weapons of, 42, 51, 66–67, 161, 182, 214n20, 226n5; and South Korea, 20, 43, 67, 77, 120; and US–Japan alliance, 159, 161–62

nuclear weapons: of China, 42, 77, 79, 86, 87; and emergence of Cold War,

39–40; Japan's official three principles on, 111; and Japan's plutonium stockpiles, 213n9; and Japan's secret agreements with US, 110–11; of North Korea, 42, 51, 66–67, 161, 182, 214n20, 226n5; Obama's policies on, 91; of Russia, 77; of United States, 77; and US–Japan relations, 173

Obama, Barack: and Abe's domestic agenda, 164; and Hatoyama, 90, 113; and Okinawa base realignment, 109; rebalancing strategy in Asia, 9, 90–91; and Senkaku Islands, 83, 161; Sunnylands Summit of 2013, 91; and US–Japan alliance, 162, 164–65
Oceania, 69, 86
Okinawa: opposition to new US military facilities, 15, 20, 187; opposition to US–Japan alliance in, 165, 175, 185; population of, 11, 216n42; and postwar antimilitarist security, 165; relocation of Futenma Air Station to, 109, 165, 186–87; reversion of administrative control to Japan, 30, 60, 103, 165; and US–India naval exercises, 93; US military bases on, 11, 30, 60, 63, 83, 84, 113, 114, 127, 160, 165, 172, 185, 186–87, 216n42
Operation Tomodachi, 118, 124–25
Organisation for Economic Co-operation and Development, 5
Oros, Andrew L., *Normalizing Japan,* 206n8, 208n20, 214n20, 218n65
Ōsumi-class transport ships, 46, 216n35
outer space, 139, 140, 163, 164, 172, 232n24
Outer Space Treaty of 1967, 140
overseas development assistance (ODA): and defense-related aid, 8, 128; and Japan's regional security partnerships, 93; and Japan's security policies, 139–40, 178, 181, 233n26, 240n11; Japan's strategic use of, 100
Ozawa, Ichirō: and China–Japan relations, 114; and Kan, 116; marginal-

ization of, 238n73; and merger of Liberal Party with DPJ, 108, 124; and Noda, 121; on normalization, 114, 207n14; resignation as DPJ president, 113, 229n31

Pacific Review, 208n25, 225n45
Pacific War. *See* World War II
Pearl Harbor attack, 26, 49, 54
Pekkanen, Saadia M., 232n24
Pempel, T. J., 92
Penney, Matthew, 235n44
People's Life Party, 121, 238n73
People's New Party, 238n73
Perry, Matthew, 11
Persian Gulf War (1990–1991), 35, 44, 45, 214n26, 229n31
Philippines: and Asian Women's Fund, 53, 218n54; and China, 93–94, 131, 175; and comfort women issue, 142; GDP of, 73; Japan's security partnership with, 9, 86, 92, 93–94, 159, 175, 176; and JMSDF, 14, 94; JSDF providing disaster relief assistance in, 142; population growth in, 73; and regional distribution of power, 9; and US–Japan alliance, 159
piracy: and China's participation in international security regimes, 79; and Japan's participation in international security regimes, 1, 14, 31, 38, 78, 79, 92, 97, 125, 159, 176; as threat to Japan, 43, 69; and US–Japan alliance, 159
postclassical realism, 209n26
post–Cold War period: direct military threats to Japan emerging, 42–44, 45, 77, 214n20; and international security environment, 41–42, 44, 214n26, 226n5; Japan's adaptation to, 41–44; Japan's security identity in, 45; Japan's security policies during, 33, 37, 38, 46, 52, 65, 103, 134, 178; and JMSDF's cooperation with US Navy, 78, 155; and US–Japan alliance, 44, 59, 62
postwar antimilitarist security: and Abe, 149–58; and Article Nine of Japan's

postwar antimilitarist security
(*continued*)
postwar constitution, 3–4, 28,
152–54, 236–37n60; historical legacy
of, 3–4, 12, 15, 22, 25, 28–29, 32, 33,
35, 37, 38, 41, 44, 48, 53, 55–58, 64,
65, 113, 125, 126–27, 150–52, 154,
155, 156, 157, 158, 159, 161, 164,
165, 184, 185, 187; and Japan's security identity, 18, 28–29, 35, 37, 55,
56, 57–58, 150, 155, 206n8, 218n65,
218–19n67; and Japan's security
policies, 99, 122, 125, 132, 150–58;
and Japan's security renaissance,
149–58; and nostalgia for past, 5–6;
and US–Japan alliance, 156, 159, 161
proportional representation (PR),
128–29
purchasing power parity (PPP), 70, 84,
93, 225n47
Putin, Vladimir, 166
Pyle, Kenneth, 226n2

Quadrennial Defense Review, 90

Rape of Nanjing, 52
rare earths export ban, 134
Reagan, Ronald, 103
realist international relations theory,
17–18, *17*, 33, 36, 87, 121, 208–9n26
regional contingency, 63
regional security environment: and Abe,
107, 156–57; and balance of power,
9, 16, 19, 33, 67, 69, 85, 96; and
defense spending, 71, 76; and diffusion of power, 19; in early postwar
period, 39; economic growth in,
69–76; future challenges of, 34; and
Japan's relative decline, 16, 19, 66,
67, 68, 69–76, 85; and Japan's security partnerships, 9, 23, 67, 76–77,
78, 86, 92–94, 97, 106, 109, 117, 125,
156–57, 159, 174–76, 179, 229n34;
and Japan's security policies, 2, 4–5,
8, 9, 13, 16, 19–21, 33, 38, 67–70,
76–79, 87, 99, 122, 124, 138–39, 143,
150–51, 157; and Japan's security
renaissance, 87, 92–94, 96, 156–57,
168, 170, 182–83, 187, 188; and mili-

tary escalation, 43, 69; and multilateral institutions, 68, 72, 73, 77, 79,
94, 125, 164, 175; perceptions of, 68,
87, 225n45; and US–Japan alliance,
58, 63–64, 76, 174–75, 186, 187
relational constructivism, 208n25
Rice, Susan, 161
Roh Moo-hyun, 142
Roy, Denny, 81, 224–25n44
Russia: China as military threat to,
87; defense spending of, 71, 72, 88;
in early post–Cold War period,
42; GDP of, 36, *36*, 70–71, *70*; and
gray-zone conflicts, 21, 132; Japan's
lack of peace treaty with, 51, 166;
Japan's territorial disputes with, 27,
42, 49, 51, 77, 166, 222n17; military
capabilities of, 76; nuclear weapons
of, 77; and US–Japan alliance, 159,
166
Russo-Japanese War of 1904–1905, 12

Sakigake politicians, 111
Samuels, Richard, 208n20, 210n37,
226n2
San Francisco Peace Treaty, 50, 53
Satō, Eisaku, 102, 103
Sea of Japan, 174
Second Armitage-Nye report, 228n18
Security Consultative Committee (2+2
talks), 165
security dilemma, 18
Senkaku Islands: and China–Japan
relations, 19, 21, 23, 27, 35, 61, 68,
82–84, 87, 97, 99, 112, 119–20, 121,
131, 132, 145, 160–61, 168, 174, 177,
209n34, 239n6; and Fishing Trawler
Incident of 2010, 82–83, 101, 112,
116, 120, 134; and gray-zone con-
flict, 183; nationalization of, 119–20,
168; and Noda, 23, 113, 119–20,
210n40; and possibility of military
conflict, 182; protection of, 11, 19
September 11 attacks, 35, 44–48, 183
Shalikashvili, John, 237n66
Shangri-la Dialogue, 94
Shinoda, Tomohito, 226n5
Sichuan earthquake of 2008, 233n29
Singapore, 78, 86, 93

Singh, Bhubhindar, 45, 177
Singh, Manmohan, 114
single-member districts (SMD), 111,
   128, 130–31
Sino-Japanese war of 1894–1895, 4,
   11–12, 26, 27, 83
Sino-Japanese War of 1945, 80
situations in areas surrounding Japan
   (SIASJ), 63, 220n81
Smith, Sheila A., 80–81, 91–92, 208n25,
   225n46
Smithsonian Institution, 216–17n43
Sneider, Daniel, 106, 119, 121–22,
   229n31
Snyder, Scott, 54, 86, 147–48
Social Democratic Party (SDP), 110,
   111, 112, 117, 132
social media, effect on discourse over
   security issues, 6, 16, 24, 136,
   206n10
South Asia, 69
South China Sea: anti-piracy efforts
   in, 159; and China–Japan relations,
   43, 84, 92, 93–94, 114, 121, 176–77;
   China's actions in, 131; and Japan's
   energy imports, 69; and Japan's regional security partnerships, 93–94,
   176; and Japan's security policies,
   170, 175; Kaplan on, 72
Southeast Asia: and China–Japan
   relations, 86; China's security
   interests in, 79; economic growth
   in, 5; Japan's economic and security
   interests in, 23, 69, 71, 72, 78, 79,
   106, 108; Japan's economic size
   compared to, 72; and Japan's historical reconciliation, 52, 217n51;
   and Japan's role in regional security
   environment, 175; piracy in, 43, 78,
   79; population growth in, 72, 73.
   See also ASEAN (Association of
   Southeast Asian Nations)
South Korea: and Asian Women's Fund,
   53, 218n54; defense spending of, 72,
   88; economic growth of, 5, 71; GDP
   of, 36, 70, 70, 71; Japanese peace
   treaty with, 27, 51; militarized border, 77; military capabilities of, 76,
   77; and North Korea, 20, 43, 67, 77,

120; and regional security partnership, 67, 117, 125, 177; as super-aged
   society, 75; and trilateral cooperation, 164; US forces in, 87
South Korea–Japan relations: and Abe,
   105, 106, 126, 142, 164; and benefits
   of security cooperation, 9, 177; and
   comfort women issue, 120, 142, 144,
   174; and historical reconciliation,
   54, 120, 142, 172, 174, 177, 198–99,
   229n34; and Japanese militarism,
   50–51, 53, 142, 143, 147; and
   Japanese public opinion, 149; and
   politicization of history and territorial issues, 5; and territorial disputes,
   5, 19, 49, 120
Soviet Union: dissolution of, 4; and
   emergence of Cold War, 39, 59, 79;
   Japan's balancing military threat
   during Cold War, 38, 40, 41, 222n17;
   Japan's territorial dispute with, 19,
   50, 216n42; and JSP, 56; military
   planning of, 40; and regional security environment, 68
specially designated secrets (SDS), 136,
   137
state apologies, 210n43
Stockholm International Peace Research
   Institute (SIPRI): data on defense
   spending in Asia, 67, 88–89; data on
   defense spending in Japan, 215n32,
   230–31n3
Strait of Malacca, 78
Students Emergency Action for Liberal
   Democracy (SEALDs) student
   group, 136, 232n14
Suga, Yoshihide, 234n38
Supreme Commander for the Allied
   Powers (SCAP), 29–30
survivors of the atomic bombings
   (hibakusha), 48
Swaine, Michael, 215–16n35,
   240–41n19
Syrian refugee assistance, 178

Taepodong missile test, 20, 183
Taisei Yokusankai, 227n10
Taiwan: and Asian Women's Fund,
   218n54; and China, 20, 43, 77, 182;

of, 156; and international security environment, 58, 63–64, 162, 186, 187; Japanese political opposition to, 59–60, 61, 64; Japanese public support for, 31, 59, 117, 118, 159–60, 161, 186; and Japan's exceptionalism, 233n27; and Japan's international reputation, 60–61; and Japan's military capabilities, 76, 100, 183; and Japan's missile defense technology, 43, 47, 57, 153, 163, 172, 174, 183; and Japan's patrols of sea lanes, 78, 79; and Japan's security policies, 12, 15, 36, 37, 39, 52, 68, 99, 106, 122, 123, 137, 138, 213n10; and JSDF, 30–31, 61, 62, 63, 64, 118, 156, 159, 161, 163–64, 170, 177, 219n71; and military security, 39, 41, 42, 213n8; and military-to-military cooperation, 156, 163–64; in post–Cold War period, 44, 59, 62; and postwar antimilitarist security, 156, 159, 161; and regional security environment, 58, 63–64, 76, 174–75, 186, 187; and state secrets, 135–36, 231–32n12; strengthening of, 7, 9, 24, 44, 69, 79–80, 85, 88, 90, 105, 109, 114, 117, 118, 119, 123, 124–25, 162–63, 165, 185, 186; unequal relationship, 3, 15, 25, 31, 32, 35, 58, 61–62, 64, 100, 112, 113, 159, 173, 187; and US nuclear umbrella, 36, 40, 42, 43, 56, 213n9

US–Japan–China strategic triangle, 88

US–Japan Guidelines for Defense Cooperation: and Alliance Coordination Mechanism, 163–64; and expansion of security cooperation with US, 33–34, 157; and flexibility in US–Japan military cooperation, 163–64; implementation of April 2015 guidelines, 185–87; and Japan's contributions to international security, 177; negotiation of, 159, 162–64; revisions of 1997, 6, 44, 62–63, 156; revisions of April 2015, 9, 20, 31, 58, 64, 65, 68, 91, 106–7, 124, 127–28, 135, 138, 157, 160,

161, 162–64, 185; and trilateral and multilateral cooperation, 164

US–Japan Joint Vision Statement, 163

US–Japan Mutual Defense Treaty, 29, 30, 61, 68, 207n14, 220n78

US–Japan relations: and Bush-Koizumi alliance, 63, 64, 82, 90, 104, 162, 185; and China, 170, 172; and Cold War, 32, 59, 61, 103; DPJ policies on, 7; and enhanced security cooperation, 14; and Hatoyama, 101, 113, 114, 115, 168, 229n31; and Japan's fear of US economic and military decline, 13, 113; and Japan's historical reconciliation, 54; joint statement of 2015, 91; and Kishi, 30, 59, 162; Mansfield on, 174; and postwar Allied occupation of Japan, 18, 27, 29–30, 32, 49, 59, 60, 83, 127, 165, 211n48; and postwar bombings of Japan, 29; and trade, 31

US–Japan Security Treaty: fiftieth anniversary of, 31–32; Kishi's signing of, 30, 59; public protests against, 103, 127; public support for, 238n74; reliability of commitments, 129, 160; and Senkaku Islands, 83; and US protection of Japanese territory, 160–61, 209n34

US military bases, on Okinawa, 11, 30, 60, 63, 83, 84, 113, 114, 127, 160, 165, 172, 185, 186–87, 216n42

US National Security Advisor, 133

US Navy, JMSDF's cooperation with, 78, 155

US Republican Party, 23–24

US Seventh Fleet, 41

USS Missouri, 26

US–South Korea "Joint Vision for the Alliance," 91

USS Ronald Reagan, 30

US Tea Party, 23

"Unmet Expectations" report, 228n18

Upper House: and changes in security policy, 152; creation of, 226n3; and division of power in Japan's Diet, 98, 226n3; DPJ loss of 2010, 98, 116; DPJ loss of 2016, 123; DPJ victory

Upper House (*continued*)
of 2007, 229n31; DPJ victory of
2010, 112; and Japanese electoral
system, 102; LDP loss of 2007, 98,
107, 110, 133, 167; LDP victory of
2010, 116; LDP victory of 2013,
98, 130, 131; national elections of
July 2016, 167–68, 169, 179, 180;
percentage of party vote and seats in
national elections, *192*

Vietnam: and China, 131, 175; GDP
of, 73; Japan's security partnership
with, 9, 86, 92, 93, 94, 159, 175, 176;
military capabilities of, 77; population growth in, 73; and regional distribution of power, 9; and US–Japan
alliance, 159; US relations with, 91

Wallace, Corey, 93
Weiner, Tim, 219n72
Wen Jiabao, 80, 81, 82, 107, 109,
223–24n32
Western colonialism: Japan's World
War II mission of liberating Asia
from, 11, 14, 28, 227n12; postwar
retreat from, 39
White, Hugh, 161
WikiLeaks, 114
World Values Survey, 148
World War II: Abe's statement on seventieth anniversary, 26, 53, 146, 184,
199–203; atomic weapons used in,
2; contested memories of, 3, 14–15,
25–28, 32, 37, 48–50, 52, 53, 59, 107,
115, 165, 172, 216–17n43; disagreement on origins of, 59, 208n18;
fiftieth anniversary of end of, 26, 53,

144, 146, 194–96, 234n37; Japan's
school textbook descriptions of, 48,
50, 79, 120; and Japan's state secrets,
135; Koizumi's statement on, 53,
196–98, 234n37; legacies of, 72, 120;
Murayama's statement on, 26, 53,
144, 146, 194–96, 234n37; POWs of,
49, 50, 54, 201, 217n47; seventieth
anniversary of end of, 26, 53, 146,
172, 183–84, 199–203; sixtieth anniversary of end of, 37, 53, 196–98,
234n37. *See also* postwar antimilitarist security
Worshipping at Yasukuni Shrine
Together group, 147

xenophobia, 148, 149
Xi Jinping, 91, 145

Yachi, Shotarō, 133
Yalta peace accords, 27
Yamada, Atsutoshi, 210n37
Yasukuni Shrine: and Abe, 24, 81, 144,
145, 146, 165, 234n35; and China–
Japan relations, 79; and historical
revisionism, 5, 59; and Koizumi,
53, 81, 145; museum connected
to, 49–50, 59; and Nakasone, 53;
Worshipping at Yasukuni Shrine
Together group, 147
Yasutomo, Dennis T., 233n26, 240n11
Yoshida, Shigeru, 30, 102, 103, 208n20
Yoshida Doctrine, 28, 103, 208n20,
211n45
Yoshida school, 22
Yoshihara, Toshi, 180
Your Party (YP), 23, 121

GPSR Authorized Representative: Easy Access System Europe, Mustamäe tee
50, 10621 Tallinn, Estonia, gpsr.requests@easproject.com

www.ingramcontent.com/pod-product-compliance
Lightning Source LLC
Chambersburg PA
CBHW032118020426
42334CB00016B/997